The Faith Factor

Counting Every Vote: The Most Contentious Elections in American History
—Robert Dudley and Eric Shiraev

The Faith Factor

How Religion Influences American Elections

John C. Green

Potomac Books, Inc.
Washington, D.C.

This paperback edition published in the United States by Potomac Books, Inc.

The Faith Factor: How Religion Influences American Elections, by John C. Green, was originally published in hardcover by Praeger Publishers, http://www.greenwood.com/praeger, an imprint of Greenwood Publishing Group, Inc., Westport, CT. Copyright © 2007 by John C. Green. This paperback edition by arrangement with Greenwood Publishing Group, Inc. All rights reserved.

Library of Congress Cataloging-in-Publication Data

Green, John Clifford, 1953–
 The faith factor : how religion influences American elections / John C. Green.
— 1st ed.
  p. cm.
 Originally published: Westport, CT. : Praeger Publishers, 2007.
 Includes bibliographical references and index.
 ISBN 978-1-59797-430-1 (pbk. : alk. paper)
 1. Religion and politics—United States. 2. Presidents—United States—
Election—2004. 3. Church membership—Political aspects—United States. 4.
Church attendance—Political aspects—United States. 5. United States—
Religion. I. Title.
 BL2525.G74 2010
 324.973'0931—dc22

                                                          2009052399

Printed in the United States of America on acid-free paper that meets the American National Standards Institute Z39-48 Standard.

Potomac Books, Inc.
22841 Quicksilver Drive
Dulles, Virginia 20166

First Edition

10 9 8 7 6 5 4 3 2 1

Table of Contents

Figures and Tables

Figures

Tables

Series Foreword

A generation ago, there was a religious revolution in American politics. Its harbinger was Jimmy Carter, a white Southern Baptist who did not hesitate to identify himself as "born again." By the end of his presidency—and possibly because of it—his evangelical Protestant co-religionists were firmly in the sights of Republican political operatives. The "New Christian Right" that burst upon the national scene in 1980 was the result of a determined—and remarkably successful—campaign to transform white evangelicals into committed Republican voters. Today, they have become the electoral base of the Republican Party and the source of its most important body of activists. Any Republican who would be president must find a way to appeal to them. To offend them, as Senator John McCain found out in 2000, is to touch the third rail of GOP politics.

Even as the fortunes of marquee national Christian right organizations like the Moral Majority and the Christian Coalition have ebbed and flowed, at the state and local levels the mobilization of evangelical churches has gone on apace. Just as the labor movement became tied to the Democratic Party in the 1930s, gradually replacing the big city political machines as the party's engine of activism and voter mobilization in the industrial heartland, so during the past two decades the evangelical churches have become the organizational base of the Republican Party across the South and in parts of the Midwest.

In one sense there is nothing so remarkable about the emergence of this new ethno-religious voting bloc. American political history is, among other things, the story of such blocs. Once upon a time, Catholics were a solid Democratic constituency. Jews still are. Mormons vote Republican. As for white Protestants, thanks to the Civil War they tended to be Republicans in the North and Democrats (overwhelmingly) in the South. Over time, some of the blocs have shifted in their political preferences, for various social, cultural, and economic reasons.

Before the religious right was a gleam in Republican eyes, white Southerners were drifting into the Republican camp for the same reason that African American Protestants moved away from the party of Lincoln and into Democratic arms: the position of the national parties on civil rights.

But whereas civil rights, like Abolition and Temperance before it, strongly engaged religious voters both pro and con, the signature issues of the religious right—abortion and gay rights and manifestations of religion in the public square—have helped create a partisan religious divide transcending sectarian differences for the first time in American history. Beginning in the 1990s, if you were someone who attended religious services of any kind once a week or more, you were significantly more likely to vote Republican than Democratic. The reverse was also true: You were significantly more likely to vote Democratic if your attendance was less than once a week.

By 2000, this new religion gap, which professional pollsters had been aware of for some years, was considerably larger than the better known gender gap. It caught the news media's attention during George W. Bush's first term not only because of its size but because the Bush presidency supplied such good evidence for it. Personally, the president conveyed the impression that, as the nation's leader, he was powerfully motivated by his religious convictions. Meanwhile, his political operatives made appealing to all "people of faith"—if especially to the evangelical base—central to their electoral strategy. And so, during the first decade of the twenty-first century, a religious-versus-secular party politics took hold that was more reminiscent of Western European history than American. It seemed like something new under the sun. No subject in American public life is so in need of clarification and explanation.

Over the past two decades, no one has done more to meet that need than John C. Green, Professor of Political Science at the University of Akron. For nearly 20 years he has directed the Ray C. Bliss Institute of Applied Politics, and has analyzed and illuminated America's religious politics in scores of articles and book chapters, both scholarly and popular, as a single author and in collaboration with others. He is frequently quoted in newspapers from coast to coast, and his distinctive voice and full-bearded visage are staples of radio and TV when the subject turns to religion and politics.

In an age of forensic social science, academic experts all too often wear their partisanship on their sleeves. Green is an exception—a source of dispassion scrutiny, evenhanded appraisal, and good will. He gives all sides the benefit of the doubt, even as the sides often fail to give it to each other. With the advantage of many years in the field, he has seen all that the new religious politics has to offer, and tells it like it is without fear or favor.

But until now, Green has told the story piecemeal—group by group, episode by episode—as it has evolved. In this book, for the first time, he puts the pieces together. This is nothing less than the authoritative account by the nation's leading authority. It is required reading for anyone who wants to know how American politics works in the era of the religious right.

Mark Silk
Director
The Leonard E. Greenberg Center for
the Study of Religion in Public Life
Trinity College
Hartford

Preface to the Paperback Edition

The Faith Factor was originally published in 2007 with an eye toward helping political observers understand faith-based voting in the upcoming 2008 presidential campaign. The goal was to simultaneously offer a good description of the 2004 campaign, and also provide useful background on the links between religion and the vote. The primary audience intended for the book was journalists, but scholars and other students of American politics were kept in mind as well. For this reason, the book was designed to be helpful beyond 2008.

Then two things happened: Potomac Books decided to bring out a paperback edition of *The Faith Factor* in 2009 and the 2008 election took place as scheduled. The editors of Potomac Books have graciously allowed me to add a postscript on the faith-based vote in 2008. There, readers will find a brief update of the book's themes, including the Old and New Religious Gaps and the fate of the "values voters." The election of Barack Obama was a momentous event, but one that involved more continuity than change in faith-based voting. More changes may well occur in the future, of course, and I hope that this edition of *The Faith Factor* will help its readers better understand such eventualities.

I have always depended on the patience of editors, and in this case, I am deeply grateful to Elizabeth Demers and Claire Noble of Potomac Books. And I owe a special thanks to my most important editor, Lynn R. Green, whose patience with me knows no bounds.

John C. Green
Akron, Ohio

Preface

The genesis of this book is found in a long and rewarding relationship with Mark Silk of the Leonard E. Greenberg Center for the Study of Religion and Public Life at Trinity College in Hartford, Connecticut. Since the Center's founding, I have participated in a number of its projects, conferences, and seminars, and collaborated with Mark on several articles for *Religion in the News*, the Center's regular publication.

Mark is one of the most perceptive observers of the role of religion in American public life, and he is particularly interested in how the news media cover this important subject. Indeed, one of his principal goals is to help improve journalists' understanding of religion and politics, so that the broader American public would be better informed on these matters. As luck would have it, I have spent much of my career engaged in this same task, though perhaps more by accident than design.

The Faith Factor resulted from this common goal of providing basic information on American religion and its relationship to American elections. I am indebted to Mark for the opportunity to write such a book, and also for his advice, assistance, and encouragement.

This book was designed to be rich in survey data, and the following sources of these data are acknowledged with gratitude. In terms of contemporary data sets, the Pew Charitable Trusts and the Pew Forum on Religion & Public Life have provided support for my research for more than a decade, often in the company of my colleagues James Guth, Lyman Kellstedt, and Corwin Smidt. The Pew Research Center, with which I have collaborated since 1996, was an additional source of contemporary survey data.

As for past data sets, the Roper Center for Public Opinion Research was the source of the Gallup and Roper polls in the 1940s and 1950s, and the Interuniversity Consortium for Political and Social Research was the source of the American

National Election Studies 1944-2004 as well as other data. It goes without saying that the interpretation and use of these surveys in this book are my responsibility alone.

A very special thanks goes to Suzanne Staszak-Silva, Senior Editor at Praeger Press, who shepherded this project from start to finish with extraordinary patience. Janet Bolois prepared the final manuscript with her usual dedication and skill. Last, but certainly not least, the gracious support of my wife and children made the completion of this project possible.

John C. Green
Akron, Ohio

— 1 —

Consternation and Surprise: Religion and the 2004 Presidential Election

The impact of religion on the 2004 presidential election provoked widespread consternation and surprise. Given the closeness of the results, the consternation was hardly surprising. For one thing, the full spectrum of religious (and non-religious) opinion was engaged by the issues at stake, including same-sex marriage, the Iraq war, and economic inequality. Many voters found themselves on either the winning or losing side of this heated contest—and realized their places might easily have been reversed. To many Americans of many walks of life, the country appeared deeply divided.

But the surprise over the political influence of religion is a cause for consternation in its own right. After all, religion has long mattered in American elections, and well-publicized evidence forecast its importance in 2004. Furthermore, the presidential candidates and their allies used extensive religious appeals to mobilize voters. In fact, much of the commentary and coverage of the campaign recognized the crucial links between religion and politics.[1] Here, three common accounts of religion's influence in the campaign are instructive.

The "Fundamentalists" Did It

If there was any doubt about the controversy occasioned by religion in the election, one need only turn to the op-ed page of the *New York Times* two days after the balloting. Three well-respected columnists offered the same explanation for President Bush's re-election: the "fundamentalists" did it. For example, Maureen Dowd asserted:

> The president got re-elected by dividing the country along fault lines of fear, intolerance, ignorance and religious rule...W. ran a jihad in America so he can fight one in

Iraq—drawing a devoted flock...to the polls by opposing abortion, suffocating stem cell research and supporting a constitutional amendment against gay marriage.[2]

Nearby, Thomas Friedman was more specific in his critique of the "fundamentalists":

> My problem with the Christian fundamentalists supporting Mr. Bush is not their spiritual energy or the fact that I am of a different faith. It is the way in which he and they have used that religious energy to promote divisions and intolerance at home and abroad.[3]

In this same vein, historian Garry Wills waxed eloquent on the character of this group:

> Where else do we find fundamentalist zeal, a rage at secularity, religious intolerance, fear of and hatred for modernity?...We find it in the Muslim world, in Al Qaeda...[4]

Here the term "fundamentalist" carried the negative connotations of intolerance, ignorance, and even violence. Such negative perceptions among many Americans are well-documented.[5]

Such comments were exaggerations, of course, expressing the natural frustration of election losers. But it is worth noting that this commentary resembled Reverend Jerry Falwell's blaming of the September 11 terrorist attacks on:

> the pagans, and the abortionists, and the feminists, and the gays and the lesbians who are actively trying to make that an alternative lifestyle, the ACLU, People For the American Way—all of them who have tried to secularize America...[6]

A self-identified fundamentalist, Falwell was also expressing his frustration with being on the losing side of politics, albeit over a longer time period. It is hardly an accident that Falwell's list of suspects ends with secularists, a group that, like "fundamentalists," are viewed unfavorably by many Americans.[7]

However, beneath such exaggerations there was a valuable insight: *affiliation with a religious community matters in politics.* In fact, Bush did receive strong support from members of conservative religious groups—a few of which actually were "fundamentalists," properly so called. And members of liberal religious groups backed Senator Kerry, including some who favored "alternative lifestyles" or wanted to "secularize America." Of course, this dichotomy hardly exhausts the wide variety of religious groups in the United States, most of which participated in the 2004 election in one way or another. Nevertheless, this commentary recognized a crucial link between religion and electoral politics that has long been important in presidential elections. It might be called the "politics of belonging," or in short, the "Old Religion Gap."

The "God Gap" Dominates

Perhaps one reason for *New York Times* columnists' focus on "fundamentalists" was the widespread discussion of another aspect of religion in the run up to the election. A typical description of this phenomenon was the following:

> Want to know how Americans will vote next Election Day? Watch what they do the weekend before—If they attend religious services regularly, they probably will vote Republican by a 2-1 margin. If they never go, they likely will vote Democratic by a 2-1 margin.[8]

Although most evidence for this voting gap was based on worship attendance, it was quickly christened the "God gap" on the assumption that religious practice implied religious belief. One headline proclaimed "Religious Voters Go Own Way: Many Christians Vote by Ideology, Not Denomination"—although "theology" might have been a more accurate term.[9] Republicans were thus portrayed as the party of the "believers" and Democrats the party of "non-believers."

Another *New York Times* columnist, Nicholas Kristof, described this new religious division this way:

> America is riven today by a "God gulf" of distrust, dividing churchgoing Republicans from relatively secular Democrats. A new Great Awakening is sweeping the country, with Americans increasingly telling pollsters that they believe in prayer and miracles, while only 28 percent say they believe in evolution. All this is good news for Bush Republicans, who are in tune with heartland religious values, and bad news for Dean Democrats who don't know John from Job.[10]

But not all commentators accepted the "God gap" as an accurate view of reality, taking Kristof and others to task:

> Fortunately for liberals, conservatives, and all those in between, it isn't so simple. Kristof—neglect[s] the large number of Americans who subscribe to conservative evangelical beliefs and liberal politics; the growing social justice movement within conservative Christianity, which defies easy categorization; and, of course, all the libertarian pagans.[11]

Although these views were overstated, they also carried a valuable insight: *religious behavior and belief matter in politics.* In fact, many people who held traditional beliefs and engaged in traditional practices did vote for Bush, while many people with less traditional religiosity or none at all backed Senator Kerry. Of course, religious beliefs and behavior include far more than just worship attendance, as important as that may be. Nonetheless, this reporting recognized another crucial link between religion and electoral politics that has become increasingly important in recent presidential elections. It might be called the "politics of behaving and believing," or for short, the "New Religion Gap."

The "Values Voters" Triumph

Surely the best-known election controversy began on Election Night, when the exit polls revealed that the single largest group of voters chose "moral values" from a list of seven issue priorities that most influenced their vote. This finding prompted a snap judgment that President Bush had won because of his conservative stands on abortion and same-sex marriage. One typical report described the "values voters" this way, also with reference to Islamist terrorists:

> Aspiring jihadists condemn the United States for being full of moral decay. Last week, Americans seemed to agree...Moral values emerged as the top concern among voters in the presidential election, unexpectedly edging out terrorism and the economy.[12]

Another story described the role of such conservative values at the ballot box with a colorful set of everyday symbols:

> A maroon Ford Explorer making its way down I-85 Wednesday morning provided a rolling summary of the previous day's presidential election: A Christian fish symbol on the bumper, an American flag on the fender and, in the back window, an oval W '04 sticker...Wednesday-morning quarterbacks poring over exit polls seemed surprised to find that "moral values" drove many people to vote for Bush, even if they were concerned about the economy and worried about the war in Iraq.[13]

And columnist Ellen Goodman summed up the initial perception of the new importance of "values voters":

> Take an afternoon off for recriminations, a morning for whining, then race through the Kubler-Ross stages of grief and get back to work. Job No. 1: moral values.[14]

Such judgments certainly fit with the importance of "fundamentalists" and the "God gap," but they were quickly challenged on evidentiary and political grounds. First, critics pointed out that "moral values" was chosen by just over one-fifth of the electorate, only slightly ahead of "economy/jobs" and "terrorism." So, "moral values" were hardly the dominant priority of voters.[15]

Other commentators went further and asserted that the "values voters" were a myth: "[T]he official story is that throngs of homophobic, Red America values-voters surged to the polls to put George Bush over the top. This theory...is certainly wrong."[16] And still others minimized the significance of such voters to the election outcome: "John Kerry was not defeated by the religious right. He was beaten by moderates who went—reluctantly in many cases—for President Bush."[17]

Taken as a whole, these exchanges were less inaccurate than incomplete and they pointed to a valuable insight as well: *religion matters in politics because of issues and priorities.* In fact, Bush would have lost the close election without the support of conservative "values voters," especially in the battleground states. But by the same token, he also needed the support of many other kinds of voters. And Senator Kerry certainly benefited from ballots cast on the basis of various kinds of liberal "values." Of course, Americans hold many different kinds of values and not all values matter to every voter. Nonetheless, this post-election debate recognized yet another crucial link between religion and politics, the role of issues in electoral coalitions. Thus, the "Old" and "New" Religion Gaps were in large part about differences in issues and priorities.

Religion Out of Context

The discussion of the "fundamentalists," the "God gap," and the "values voters" reflected genuine puzzlement over the role of religion in the campaign. Many observers were accustomed to the idea that voters' social characteristics affected their votes, so much was naturally made over the "gender gap," the "generation gap," and the "income gap," not to mention the celebrated regional gap between the "red" and "blue" states.[18] However, religion did not fit comfortably into these standard demographic categories. More than a few analysts suspected that religion was either a proxy for other kinds of social status, or if not, some form of false consciousness that masked these real influences. In fact, religion was both a potent independent force in the election as well as closely related to both demography and geography.

The "fundamentalists," the "God gap," and the "values voters" were seen in large measure as the product of campaign politics, much of it intentionally divisive and more than faintly illegitimate. The fact that some religious leaders and activists were deeply involved in political organizations and the waging of the campaign only compounded these suspicions. And there was a tendency to focus narrowly on conservative Christians instead of the full range of religious groups involved in the campaign. The truth is that the presidential candidates and their allies engaged in an extraordinary effort to bring religious voters to the polls, reaching a wide range of religious communities. And most of this activity was simply the normal electoral process at work.[19]

Religion and the 2004 Presidential Vote by the Numbers

This book is a primer on religion and American elections, written with the goal of illuminating this complicated subject. To accomplish this goal, the book provides basic information about religion and elections in the United States, some of it conceptual and historical, and some of it statistical, presented in the form of simple tables and figures. It begins by describing the Old and New Religion Gaps, and then explores the relationship of the religion gaps to issues and coalitions, other demographic traits, region, and campaign politics.

The 2004 presidential election is used as a principle illustration throughout the book. Hence a good place to begin is by reviewing the actual impact of religion on the 2004 vote "by the numbers."

On the Exit Polls

What impact did religion actually have in the 2004 presidential vote? The National Election Pool (NEP, the formal name for the exit polls in 2004) reveals the strong connections between religious affiliation and worship attendance and the vote, and sheds some light on voter priorities, coalitions, and campaigns. Thus a brief digression on the NEP is in order.

For illustrative purposes, the NEP has a number of virtues. Because the survey was administered to respondents as they exited polling places, it is certain that they actually voted. This fact avoids a common problem in telephone surveys, namely the tendency of respondents to "over report" their vote. In addition, the NEP involved a large number of respondents (more than 13,000), many times more than the typical survey (with 1,000 or less), which allows for an analysis of many differences among voters. Finally, the NEP had simple but serviceable measures of religion, a feature that many surveys lack.

Of course, the NEP has limitations, some peculiar to its administration and others shared with surveys in general. On the first count, questions were raised about the validity of its sample of voters, especially given its inaccuracy in predicting the election results on Election Night. These problems have been investigated and the data weighted to more accurately reflect known population characteristics, a common practice in survey research.[20]

On the second count, all surveys are statistical phenomena, providing estimates of characteristics in the public rather than hard, immutable facts. Thus there is always a degree of uncertainty in survey results and considerable variability among surveys. For this reason, we will also use a variety of other surveys when warranted. However, all survey data must be viewed with some caution, and not just the NEP.

The Old Religion Gap in 2004

As the commentators recognized, religious affiliation was indeed important at the ballot box in 2004. Table 1.1 presents 10 religious groups and the two-party presidential vote, with the relative size of these communities listed in the right hand column.[21] Patterns such as these have long been common in American elections.

Protestants. The first four categories in table 1.1 are varieties of Protestants, together accounting for just over one-half of the electorate. The largest group is white Evangelical Protestants, at a little more than one-fifth of the total. Evangelicals were at the center of much of the consternation and surprise in the 2004 election—containing in their ranks, for instance, most "fundamentalists," properly so called. Evangelical Protestants were President Bush's strongest supporters, casting almost four-fifths of their ballots for him.

White Mainline Protestants are slightly less numerous than Evangelicals in this survey, at a little less than one-fifth of the total. In these data, they divided their votes fairly evenly, with a slim advantage for Bush. The remaining two groups were racial and ethnic minorities. Substantially representing the historic African-American churches, Black Protestants made up a bit less than one-twelfth of the electorate, and gave Senator Kerry more than four-fifths of their ballots. Latino Protestants, a much smaller but rapidly growing group, showed a different pattern: a solid majority voted for Bush.

Table 1.1   Religious Belonging and the 2004 Two-Party Vote

	Bush	*Kerry*	*Total*	*% of Electorate*
White Evangelical Protestants	78.8	21.2	100	21.8
White Mainline Protestants	53.3	46.7	100	19.7
Black Protestants	13.5	86.5	100	7.6
Latino Protestants	56.6	43.4	100	2.5
Non-Latino Catholics	55.3	44.7	100	22.7
Latino Catholics	31.9	63.1	100	4.3
Other Christians	74.0	26.0	100	3.8
Other Faiths	17.6	82.4	100	2.5
Jews	23.4	76.6	100	2.4
Unaffiliated	27.1	72.9	100	12.7
ALL	**51.0**	**49.0**	**100**	**100**

Source: 2004 National Election Pool (NEP)

Catholics. The next two groups were Roman Catholics, the largest single religious denomination in the United States. Non-Latino Catholics (mostly of European ancestry) made up a bit more than one-fifth of the electorate and gave Bush a solid majority of their ballots. Latino Catholics accounted for about one-twentieth of the voters and backed Kerry with nearly two-thirds of their votes.

Other Religious Groups. The next three religious groups are much smaller (each less than one-twentieth of the electorate) and the first two are composites of even smaller groups: Other Christians (such as Latter Day Saints, Eastern Orthodox, and Christian Scientists) and Other Faiths (such as Muslims, Hindus, and Buddhists). The Other Christians gave Bush nearly three-quarters of their ballots, while four-fifths of the Other Faiths voted for Kerry. The third group, Jews, also voted strongly Democratic, with more than three-quarters backing Kerry.

The final category is the respondents without a religious affiliation of any kind, which made up one-eighth of the electorate. The Unaffiliated also voted heavily for Kerry, providing him with nearly three-quarters of their ballots.

The Affiliation Gap. These patterns are quite impressive, especially given the simple religion measures in the NEP. The difference between the vote of the most Republican of these categories (Evangelical Protestants) and the most Democratic (Black Protestants) was 65.3 percentage points (78.8 minus 13.5 percent). The possible conflating effects of race can be avoided if this "affiliation gap" is calculated between Evangelicals and the Unaffiliated, which produces a gap of 51.7 percentage points (78.8 minus 27.1 percent).

Such affiliation gaps represent massive differences in an election that was won with 51 percent of the two-party vote. However, it is important to note that there were large religious groups that divided their votes more evenly between the major candidates, such as white Mainline Protestants and non-Latino Catholics. Thus, the Old Religion Gap was quite important in 2004.

The New Religion Gap in 2004

As journalists recognized, worship attendance (a common form of traditional religious behavior) was also important in the 2004 election. Table 1.2 lists the frequency of worship attendance and the two-party vote, with the size of the various categories in the right hand column. This pattern in elections is a relatively recent phenomenon. (The NEP did not have any questions on religious belief, so the "God gap" cannot be investigated directly.)

Worship Attendance and the Vote. In this survey, there was a nearly symmetrical pattern between the most and least frequent worship attenders. On the one hand, some 64 percent of voters who reported attending worship more than once a week voted for Bush, while almost exactly the same percentage of those who claimed to never attend worship voted for Kerry. In this survey, both the first and last categories were about the same size, roughly one-sixth of the electorate.

Bush received almost three-fifths backing from respondents who claimed to attend worship once a week. In a similar fashion, Kerry obtained a solid majority of those who reported attending worship just a few times a year. Both groups made up more than one-quarter of the electorate, but with the "yearly attenders" slightly more numerous (27.7 to 26.0 percent).

Finally, the middle category (those who said they attended worship a few times a month) was almost perfectly divided between Bush and Kerry, and accounted for about one-seventh of the electorate.

The Attendance Gap. The "attendance gap" between the most observant (attend more than once a week) and the least religiously observant (never attend) was some 28.0 percentage points. This voter gap was also large in the context of the very close 2004 election. However, it is important to note that this attendance gap was far smaller than the affiliation gaps measure in table 1.1: it was roughly

Table 1.2   Worship Attendance and the 2004 Two-Party Vote

	Bush	*Kerry*	*Total*	*% of Electorate*
More than once a week	64.7	35.3	100	15.8
Once a week	58.9	41.1	100	26.0
A few times a month	50.7	49.3	100	13.6
A few times a year	45.2	54.8	100	27.7
Never	36.7	63.3	100	16.9
ALL	**51.0**	**49.0**	**100**	**100**

Source: 2004 National Election Pool (NEP)

one-half of the size of the gap in the two-party vote between Evangelicals and Black Protestants (28 to 65.3 percentage points) and a bit less when compared to the gap between Evangelicals and the Unaffiliated (28 to 51.7 percentage points). Thus, this New Religion Gap mattered in 2004 as well.

Combining the Old and New Religion Gaps

Since both religious affiliation and attendance were associated with the 2004 presidential vote, what happens if they are combined? Table 1.3 reports such a combination, dividing up the largest four affiliation categories into those who reported attending worship weekly or more often, and those who claimed to be less observant.

The Impact of Attendance. Weekly worship attendance clearly makes a difference in the presidential vote within each of the relevant religious affiliations in

Table 1.3   Religious Affiliation and Attendance, and the 2004 Two-Party Vote

	Bush	*Kerry*	*Total*	*% Electorate*
Weekly Attending Evangelical Protestants	82.5	17.5	**100**	14.3
Less Observant Evangelical Protestants	71.9	28.1	**100**	7.5
Latino Protestants	56.6	43.4	**100**	2.5
Weekly Attending Mainline Protestants	57.3	42.7	**100**	4.5
Less Observant Mainline Protestants	52.1	47.9	**100**	15.2
Weekly Attending Black Protestants	16.9	83.1	**100**	4.4
Less Observant Black Protestants	8.5	91.5	**100**	3.2
Weekly Attending Catholics	59.9	40.1	**100**	10.3
Less Observant Catholics	51.4	48.6	**100**	12.4
Latino Catholics	36.9	63.1	**100**	4.3
Other Christians	74.0	26.0	**100**	3.8
Other Faiths	17.6	82.4	**100**	2.5
Jews	23.4	76.6	**100**	2.4
Unaffiliated	27.1	72.9	**100**	12.7
ALL	**51.0**	**49.0**	**100**	**100.0**

Source: 2004 National Election Pool (NEP)

the table. For example, weekly attending Evangelical Protestants voted 82.5 percent for Bush, but their less observant co-religionists voted just 71.9 percent for the President, a difference of about 11 percentage points. Slightly smaller divisions appear among Mainline Protestants (57.3 versus 52.1 percent for Bush) and Catholics (59.9 versus 51.4), and also among Black Protestants, with Kerry obtaining 83.1 percent of the weekly attenders and 91.5 percent of the less observant.

Thus the New Religion Gap occurred within the context of the Old Religion Gap. This makes sense intuitively: worship tends to occur at a particular place and time, and most such locales have some kind of religious affiliation.

No Religious Majority. One thing is worth noting in table 1.3: there was no "religious majority" in the 2004 electorate (see the right-hand column of the table). In these data, the two largest groups (Less Observant Mainline Protestants and Weekly Attending Evangelical Protestants) each accounted for less than one-sixth of the entire electorate. The next two largest groups, Less Observant Catholics and the Unaffiliated each made up about one-eighth of the electorate, while Weekly Attending Catholics made up just one-in-ten of all 2004 voters. Overall, eight of the groups made up less than five percent of the total electorate, including such politically important groups as Weekly Attending Black Protestants, Latino Catholics, and Jews.

Religion and 2004 Voter Coalitions

Both the large number of religious communities in the 2004 electorate and their relatively small size highlight the importance of coalition building in winning presidential elections. The contribution of each group to the Republican and Democratic coalitions is presented in table 1.4. This table reorganizes the religious groups in order of the two-party vote, starting with the strongest Bush supporters at the top and ending with the strongest Kerry supporters at the bottom. The first two rows of the table list the two-party vote for each of the religious communities (summing to 100 percent), and the last two columns report each group as a percentage of the entire Bush and Kerry vote.

Looked at from this perspective, the religious categories fall neatly into three groupings: six "Republican" religious constituencies (that voted strongly for Bush); two "swing" constituencies (that divided their votes fairly evenly); and six "Democratic" constituencies (that voted strongly for Kerry).

Republican Constituencies. In these data, Weekly Attending Evangelical Protestants were the strongest supporters of President Bush, giving him more than four-fifths of their votes, and providing more than one-fifth of all Bush's ballots. This group comes closest to the "fundamentalists" the *New York Times* columnists stressed right after the election. There is no doubt that these voters were crucial to Bush's re-election.

However, there were other religious groups that also strongly backed the President. The composite category of Other Christians gave nearly three-quarters of its votes to Bush and Less Observant Evangelicals were almost as

Table 1.4   Religion and 2004 Presidential Voter Coalitions

| | Two-Party Vote | | | % of Total Vote | |
Religious Communities	*Bush*	*Kerry*	Total	*Bush*	*Kerry*
Weekly Attending Evangelical Protestants	82.5	17.5	**100.0**	*22.9*	*5.2*
Other Christians	74.0	26.0	**100.0**	*5.5*	*2.0*
Less Observant Evangelical Protestants	71.9	28.1	**100.0**	*10.5*	*4.4*
Weekly Attending Catholic	59.9	40.1	**100.0**	*12.0*	*8.5*
Weekly Attending Mainline Protestants	57.3	42.7	**100.0**	*5.0*	*4.0*
Latino Protestant	56.6	43.4	**100.0**	*2.7*	*2.2*
Less Observant Mainline	52.1	47.9	**100.0**	*15.4*	*15.1*
All	*51.0*	*49.0*	*100.0*	*100.0*	*100.0*
Less Observant Catholic	51.4	48.6	**100.0**	*12.4*	*12.5*
Latino Catholic	36.9	63.1	**100.0**	*3.0*	*5.4*
Unaffiliated	27.1	72.9	**100.0**	*6.6*	*18.9*
Jews	23.4	76.6	**100.0**	*1.1*	*3.9*
Other Faiths	17.6	82.4	**100.0**	*0.9*	*4.3*
Weekly Attending Black Protestants	16.9	83.1	**100.0**	*1.5*	*7.6*
Less Observant Black Protestants	8.5	91.5	**100.0**	*0.5*	*6.0*

Source: 2004 National Election Pool (NEP)

supportive. Together, these groups contributed another one-sixth of all Bush's ballots. The Republicans also did well with Weekly Attending Catholics and Mainline Protestants, who voted a bit less than three-fifths for Bush, and provided yet another one-sixth of all the Republican ballots. Latino Protestants completed the picture with a solid majority for Bush (but just a few percent of his ballots).

All together, these six Republican constituencies provided almost three-fifths of all Bush's ballots, and 30 of the 51 percentage points of the two-party vote President Bush obtained on Election Day. Clearly, both affiliation and attendance were crucial to the GOP coalition in 2004. However, these Republican groups were hardly monolithic: Senator Kerry obtained more than one-quarter of all his ballots from these constituencies (or 13 of the 49 percentage points of the two-party vote he obtained on Election Day).

Democratic Constituencies. On the other end of the political spectrum, six religious constituencies gave Kerry strong majorities. The Democratic nominee did best with both groups of Black Protestants, which combined for a little less than one-seventh of all Kerry's ballots. Other religious minorities also backed Kerry, including Jews, Other Faiths, and Latino Catholics. Together, these groups also contributed a bit less than one-seventh of Kerry's votes. Such patterns highlight the well-known importance of minorities to the Democratic Party—and the religious aspect of these minority groups.

In these data, the single largest source of Democratic votes was the Unaffiliated. They gave more than seven in ten of their votes to Kerry and contributed almost one-fifth of all the Democratic ballots—nearly as large a proportion of the Kerry vote as Weekly Attending Evangelicals provided to Bush. This evidence reveals the importance of the Unaffiliated to the Democratic Party—most of whom were the "secularists" who filled Jerry Falwell with consternation. But like "fundamentalists" in the GOP, these "secularists" were just one part of the Democratic coalition.

All told, these six Democratic groups accounted for more than two-fifths of all Kerry's ballots, and 23 of the 49 percentage points Kerry obtained in the election. But these groups were not monolithic either, and Bush obtained a little less than one-seventh of all his ballots from these Democratic constituencies (and 7 of the 51 percent of the two-party vote he obtained on Election Day). On the one hand, these ballots were more than Bush's overall margin of victory. But on the other hand, the votes were about one-half of the number of the ballots Kerry obtained from the six Republican constituencies.

Swing Constituencies. The final two groups, Less Observant Mainline Protestants and Catholics, divided their ballots fairly evenly. In these data, Bush won both groups with slim majorities. Surveys with better measures of religion showed Kerry winning these religious communities,[22] but even here, the Democrats did markedly better with these less observant white Christians than with their weekly worship attending co-religionists.

Interestingly, the swing groups made up about the same proportion of both the Republican and Democratic coalitions in 2004, accounting for a little more than one-quarter of all Bush's and Kerry's ballots. Put another way, these less observant white Mainliners and Catholics supplied Bush with 14 of the 51 percentage points of the two-party vote he obtained on Election Day and more than 13 of Kerry's 49 percentage points.

This evidence supports the notion that the election was "won in the middle" of the political landscape, with Bush edging Kerry among these key swing constituencies. But it also is consistent with the contest as one of "base mobilization" by each party. And these data show why some Democrats urged greater attention to religion and "moral values" after the 2004 campaign: even slight gains among these "swing" constituencies—or among the six religious groups that voted Republican—could well have put John Kerry in the White House. But they also reveal why some Republicans are nervous about the religious aspects of George W. Bush's coalition.

Religion and "Moral Values"

Thus, religious constituencies were clearly important elements of both the Republican and Democratic voter coalitions in 2004. But what role did "moral

Table 1.5   Religious Groups and Issue Priorities, 2004

	moral values	foreign policy	economic policy	Total
Weekly Attending Evangelical Protestants	52.9	25.3	21.9	100
Other Christians	33.2	35.4	31.4	100
Less Observant Evangelical Protestants	27.2	36.1	36.7	100
Weekly Attending Catholics	25.8	39.4	34.8	100
Weekly Attending Mainline Protestants	26.2	41.7	32.1	100
Latino Protestants	34.2	28.6	36.2	100
Less Observant Mainline Protestants	16.7	41.7	41.6	100
All	**23.6**	**36.2**	**40.2**	*100*
Less Observant Catholics	13.1	45.0	41.9	100
Latino Catholics	12.9	30.1	57.0	100
Unaffiliated	13.2	41.1	45.8	100
Jewish	12.3	47.3	40.4	100
Other Faiths	14.7	31.4	54.4	100
Weekly Attending Black Protestants	17.7	20.8	61.5	100
Less Observant Black Protestants	9.7	19.0	71.3	100

Source: 2004 National Election Pool (NEP)

values" play in these coalitions? As noted earlier, the NEP question on voter priorities was the source of the "moral values" controversy in 2004, so it is worth a brief review.

Table 1.5 lists the 14 religious groups in order of the presidential vote along with their issue priorities, including the "moral values" response and comparing it to a combination of the foreign policy and economic policy priorities.[23] Overall, the "moral values" voters (23.6 percent) were less numerous than the "foreign policy" voters (36.2 percent) or the "economic policy" voters (40.2 percent) (see the "all" row in the table). In aggregate then, the critics who claimed that impact of "moral values" was overstated appear to have a point.

However, moral values priorities are clearly linked to the religious elements of the Bush and Kerry voter coalitions. First, note that the six Republican constituencies mentioned "moral values" at rates higher than the electorate as a whole. More than one-half of the Weekly Attending Evangelical Protestants chose "moral values," the largest of any category. Of course, this figure means that about one-half of Bush's strongest religious constituency reported that they voted on the basis of foreign policy or economic policy priorities. About one-third of the Other Christians and Latino Protestants also chose "moral values," while the remaining Republican constituencies had lower figures.

In contrast, note that all six of the Democratic constituencies plus the two swing groups mentioned "moral values" less than the sample as a whole, and often by at least 10 percentage points.

Just the opposite pattern occurred for economic issue priorities. All but one of the six Democratic constituencies scored at or above the figure for the entire electorate—and most of these groups scored substantially higher. For example, seven of ten Less Observant Black Protestants chose economic priorities. Meanwhile, Jews and the two swing constituencies closely resembled the overall figure. In contrast, all of the six Republican religious groups chose economic issue priorities at a lower rate than the electorate as a whole.

Foreign policy priorities showed a more complex pattern. Just three of the Republican constituencies (Weekly Attending Mainliners and Catholics plus Less Observant Evangelicals) and two Democratic constituencies (Jews and the Unaffiliated) reported foreign policy priorities at a higher rate than the entire electorate. However, both of the swing constituencies, Less Observant Mainliners and Catholics, also scored above the electorate as a whole on foreign policy priorities.

Issue Priorities and the Presidential Vote. This information on issue priorities does not tell us how these individuals voted. Table 1.6 does that by adding to the previous table the two-party presidential vote for voters with moral values, foreign policy, and economic policy priorities (for each kind of issue priority, the Bush and Kerry vote adds up to 100 percent).

Overall, more than four-fifths of voters with "moral values" priorities voted for Bush and three-fifths of those reporting foreign policy priorities backed the president (see the "all" row in the middle of the table). In contrast, only about one-quarter of voters with economic issue priorities supported Bush—and nearly three-quarters voted for Kerry.

There was, however, considerable variation in the level of support these priorities generated by religious group. For example, the moral values voters produced very strong backing for Bush in the six Republican constituencies. Indeed, Weekly Attending Evangelicals in this column voted nearly unanimously for the President. And the group with the lowest support for Bush, Weekly Attending Mainline Protestants, still gave him four-fifths of their ballots. In addition, the moral values voters among the swing constituencies, and two Democratic constituencies, Latino Catholics and Weekly Attending Mainline Protestants, also gave Bush large majorities of their votes. The remaining Democratic groups strongly backed Kerry despite their "moral values" priorities.

A mixed pattern held for foreign policy priorities. Voters with such priorities gave Bush large majorities among the Republican religious constituencies, and the President did nearly as well among the swing constituencies. However, Bush

Table 1.6   Religious Priorities, Issue Priorities, and the Presidential Vote

Issue Priorities:	Moral Values		Foreign Policy		Economic Policy	
	Bush	Kerry	Bush	Kerry	Bush	Kerry
Republican Constituencies						
Weekly Attending Evangelical Protestants	97.2	2.8	82.9	17.1	45.6	54.4
Other Christians	95.9	4.1	73.8	26.3	51.5	48.5
Less Observant Evangelical Protestants	95.2	4.8	85.5	14.5	42.8	57.2
Weekly Attending Catholics	96.3	3.7	66.3	33.7	30.9	69.1
Weekly Attending Mainline Protestants	81.3	18.7	69.7	30.3	31.2	68.8
Latino Protestants	92.0	8.0	63.6	36.4	20.0	80.0
Swing Constituencies						
Less Observant Mainline Protestants	75.3	24.7	64.1	35.9	30.1	69.9
ALL	**81.9**	**18.1**	**60.1**	**39.9**	**26.0**	**74.0**
Less Observant Catholics	64.6	35.4	67.6	32.4	31.1	68.9
Democratic Constituencies						
Latino Catholics	70.0	30.0	46.1	53.9	25.4	74.6
Unaffiliated	26.0	74.0	37.2	62.8	15.1	84.9
Jewish	11.1	88.9	30.4	69.6	20.3	79.7
Other Faiths	25.0	75.0	15.4	84.6	9.0	91.0
Weekly Attending Black Protestants	71.7	28.3	11.3	88.7	2.5	97.5
Less Observant Black Protestants	31.6	68.4	7.5	92.5	3.9	96.1

Source: 2004 National Election Pool (NEP)

lost every one of the six Democratic religious constituencies among members who stressed foreign policy at the ballot box.

A very different picture appears for economic policy priorities. Here, Bush lost all but one of the six Republican groups to Kerry when economics was salient (and his one victory was by a scant 51 percent). Kerry dominated the swing constituencies on economic matters and won lopsided majorities among such voters in the six Democratic constituencies. In fact, he garnered nearly all of the Black Protestants who were focused on the economy.

How did these patterns add up on Election Day? All told, 37.5 percent of all Bush voters reported moral values priorities, 43 percent foreign policy priorities, and 20 percent economic policy priorities. In contrast, just 8.9 percent of Kerry voters claimed moral values priorities, 30 percent cared most about foreign policy, and 61 percent stressed economic policy. So, moral values voters were four times more important to Bush than to Kerry, while economic issue voters were three times more important for Kerry than for Bush. And foreign policy voters were somewhat more important to the President than to his challenger. Taken together, these patterns graphically illustrate the coalitional nature of American presidential elections.

Religion and the Other Voter Gaps in 2004

How did the electoral impact of religion compare to other demographic factors in 2004? Put another way, how did the "affiliation" and "attendance" gaps compare other voter "gaps" in 2004? Table 1.7 compares these religion gaps to other, better-known voting gaps based on demographic characteristics. For ease of presentation, each gap is presented as a dichotomy—a crude but effective means of displaying their relative importance to the two-party presidential vote.

Not surprisingly, the largest voter gap in 2004 was the "racial gap," with a 31.1 percentage point difference between the Bush vote among whites and non-whites. After all, racial divisions are among the sharpest and most enduring in American politics.

However, the "affiliation" gap was the second largest, with a 22.8 percentage point difference between white Protestants and all other religious groups. And the "attendance" gap was nearly as large, with a 17.0 percentage point difference between weekly and less-than-weekly attenders. These religion gaps were, respectively, 73 and 55 percent of the size of the "race" gap.

In 2004, these religion gaps were larger than the "income gap," where voters of annual family incomes of $50,000 or more were 12.3 percentage points more likely to vote for Bush than voters who earned less than $50,000 a year. So, these measures of religion were more important among voters than the best-known measure of social class.

In addition, these religion gaps were larger than the "region" gap of 8.6 percentage points and the "place" gap of 7.6 percentage points. Thus, this simple measure of religiosity was relatively more important than the fabled "red state/blue state" or city/suburb divisions in terms of individual votes.

Interestingly, the religion gaps were also larger than the much celebrated "gender gap." In 2004, men were 7.3 percentage points more likely to vote for Bush than women. This finding is especially interesting since women are typically more involved in religious life than men. Finally, the religion gaps were much bigger than the "generation" or "education" gaps in 2004 as well.

In sum, this crude analysis of voter gaps reveals that religion rivaled the influence of other demographic factors. Indeed, statistical analysis shows that religion had a strong independent impact on the vote in 2004, once other demography has been taken into account.[24] However, such voter gaps are often related to one another. For example, the race gap is associated with religious affiliation (see

Table 1.7   Voter Gaps in 2004

	Bush	*Kerry*	Gap in Bush Vote
Race Gap			
White	58.7	41.3	**31.1**
Non-white	27.6	72.4	
Affiliation Gap			
White Protestants	63.3	36.7	**22.8**
Other Groups	40.5	59.5	
Attendance Gap			
Weekly attender	61.1	38.9	**17.0**
Less than weekly attender	44.1	55.9	
Income Gap			
$50,000 a year or more	57.0	43.0	**12.3**
Less than $50,000	44.7	55.3	
Region Gap			
Red states	55.2	44.8	**8.6**
Blue states	46.6	53.4	
Place Gap			
Suburbs, rural	54.5	45.5	**7.6**
Large and small cities	46.9	53.1	
Gender Gap			
Male	55.5	44.5	**7.3**
Female	48.2	51.8	
Generation Gap			
40 years or older	53.3	46.7	**4.4**
Less than 40	48.9	51.1	
Education Gap			
Some college or less	53.1	46.9	**3.2**
College degree or more	49.9	50.1	
ALL	**51.0**	**49.0**	**2.0**

Source: 2004 National Election Pool (NEP)

table 1.1) and religious communities are concentrated by geography. Indeed, geography is particularly important to the link between religion and politics in the United States because presidential ballots are cast and counted at the state level.

Religion and the Presidential Campaign

Not surprisingly, religion was one of the characteristics the political campaigns used to target voters and encourage them to turnout and cast a particular ballot. The NEP asked the respondents whether they had been contacted on behalf of the Bush or Kerry campaigns—or both. Table 1.8 reports these reported contacts by religious constituency; the table presents these data for the entire electorate and also for the competitive battleground states, where the 2004 presidential campaigning was concentrated.

These simple NEP questions may well understate the level of political contacting in 2004, but the patterns are instructive. Overall, a little more than one-third of the entire electorate reported such ontacts, with a slight edge to the Kerry campaign, but with the greatest number of respondents reporting contacts from both sides. As one might expect, the level of contact was much greater in the battleground states—with nearly three-fifths reporting a contact. In those states, the Bush and Kerry contacts were equal, and the number of respondents contacted by both campaigns was almost twice as large.

The Bush campaign enjoyed an advantage in contacting among the Republican religious constituencies, and the Kerry campaign had a similar

Table 1.8   Religious Groups and Presidential Campaign Contact, 2004

	All States			Battleground States		
	Bush	**Both**	**Kerry**	**Bush**	**Both**	**Kerry**
Republican Constituencies						
Weekly Attending Evangelicals	20.6	12.4	*4.3*	32.8	28.0	*7.2*
Other Christians	13.1	14.8	*9.0*	25.0	28.1	*3.1*
Less Observant Evangelicals	14.0	11.5	*8.9*	17.0	18.0	*14.0*
Weekly Attending Catholics	11.3	16.8	*11.6*	17.1	30.9	*19.5*
Weekly Attending Mainline Protestants	16.1	20.2	*12.1*	18.6	41.9	*7.0*
Latino Protestants	14.8	9.9	*8.6*	41.2	11.8	*0.0*
Swing Constituencies						
Less Observant Mainline Protestants	9.4	14.4	*12.4*	14.5	31.3	*18.1*
All	*10.5*	*13.6*	*11.9*	*16.2*	*26.9*	*16.2*
Less Observant Catholics	8.8	16.5	*7.6*	11.3	29.6	*8.2*
Democratic Constituencies						
Latino Catholics	3.6	10.1	*9.4*	5.1	23.1	*20.5*
Unaffiliated	3.7	11.4	*17.8*	8.2	23.1	*26.9*
Jewish	4.2	8.5	*22.5*	8.3	20.8	*33.3*
Other Faiths	5.8	15.9	*24.6*	9.1	31.8	*36.4*
Weekly Attending Black Protestants	2.1	12.8	*24.1*	7.4	18.5	*25.9*
Less Observant Black Protestants	7.6	7.6	*21.5*	17.9	14.3	*25.0*

Source: 2004 National Election Pool (NEP)

advantage among the Democratic constituencies. For example, in the battle-ground states, nearly one-third of Weekly Attending Evangelical Protestants reported only Bush contacts. And more than one-quarter of Weekly Attending Black Protestants claim to have received contact from only the Kerry campaign.

Indeed, with the exception of Weekly Attending Catholics (Kerry's own faith), Bush enjoyed a net advantage in contacts among the Republican constituencies, while Kerry enjoyed such an advantage in all the Democratic constituencies. These patterns suggest that each campaign carefully targeted congenial religious constituencies, closely contended for swing voters, and tried to reduce the other side's margin among its key constituencies.

Conclusions and Plan of the Book

Religion had a major impact on the 2004 presidential vote, provoking wide-spread consternation and surprise. The sharp political divisions between Republican and Democratic religious constituencies were the primary source of this consternation. However, this impact of religion should not have come as a surprise. Indeed, the crucial links between religion and politics, such as affilia-tion and attendance, were often recognized in the election commentary and cov-erage. The chapters that follow seek to clarify these connections.

Chapter 2 describes the "politics of belonging," or the Old Religion Gap. The chapter begins with an explanation of the political relevance of religious affilia-tion in the United States, and then introduces the useful concept of "religious tra-dition." The text then describes the major contemporary religious traditions with the "ABCs of Religious Affiliation." It turns next to a comparison of the 2004 vote to past presidential elections, using as a point of reference the 1944 presi-dential election. Conducted during the "New Deal" era sixty years before, the 1944 campaign provides a dramatic contrast to the 2004 campaign. This material illustrates the link between religious traditions and elections, and how the politics of particular religious traditions have evolved over time.

Chapter 3 describes the "politics of behaving and believing" and the New Religion Gap. It begins with a discussion of the new political relevance of reli-gious practice and doctrine, and introduces the useful concept of "religious tradi-tionalism." The text then describes some important examples of religious behavior and belief in the United States with a "Checklist of Religious Practice and Doctrine," and discusses their relationship to traditionalism. Next, the chap-ter reviews the politics of one measure of traditionalism, worship attendance, in the 2004 presidential election and past presidential elections, using the 1944 election as a point of reference. This material documents a new connection between religion and politics in recent times.

Chapter 4 seeks to clarify the political meaning of the religion gaps by review-ing the issue positions and priorities of religious communities, and how they fit into electoral coalitions. It begins by exploring the 2004 "moral values" contro-versy in more detail, and then reviews the role of issue priorities in the 2004

Republican and Democratic electoral coalitions. Next, it traces changes in issue priorities between 1944 and 2004. The chapter then reviews the issue positions of religious voters in 2004, and finally, it turns to broader political identifications, ideology, and partisanship, with a look back to the past and how religious communities have changed. This material describes the issue content of the Old and New Religion gaps.

Chapter 5 explores the role that the key demographic factors of gender, age and income play in the links between religion and politics. The text first describes the distribution of each factor among religious communities, then discusses its direct link to the vote, now and in the past, and finally reviews the joint impact of the factor and religion on the 2004 vote. While taking these other demographic factors into account does not eliminate the influence of religion on the vote, it does reveal much about the social context in which religion is connected to politics.

Chapter 6 puts the Old and New Religion gaps in regional context. It begins with a brief discussion of major regions within the United States, their role in the 2004 election, and how these patterns differ from 1944. Then, the text reviews the religious communities and the 2004 presidential vote region by region. Finally, it looks at the regional distribution of issue priorities, with a special focus on the much debated "moral values" in 2004. The Old Religion Gap matters in all the regions, but the New Religion Gap is most evident in the most politically competitive regions.

Chapter 7 describes the role of religion in presidential campaign activity in 2004, both as an object and source of mobilization efforts. It begins with an overview of religion in the campaign, followed by evidence on the incidence and partisan bias of campaign and congregational contacts in religious communities. Next, it considers the impact of such contacts on turnout and the presidential vote. Finally, it describes the religious characteristics of the political activists who waged the 2004 presidential campaigns. A look back over time suggests that congregational contacts are more common now than in the past and that the religious character of political activists has changed as well. This material highlights the impact of the Old and New Religion Gaps on campaign politics.

Chapter 8 provides a detailed summary of the book's conclusions and then speculates about the future of religion gaps in elections. In this regard, there is good reason to expect that the patterns of 2004 will persist in the immediate future. However, in the more distant future, the role of religion in elections could change, and three scenarios are explored: the New Religion Gap Becomes Dominant; the Old Religion Gap Returns to Dominance; and an Alternative Religion Gap Appears. Whatever the future brings, religion will continue to matter in American elections, remaining a source of consternation, with a great capacity to surprise.

2

The Old Religion Gap: The Politics of Belonging

The religious community to which a person belongs is a critical aspect of his or her religion. Described variously as religious "affiliation," "identification," "membership," "adherence," or in a peculiarly American way, religious "preference," belonging is central to the social aspects of faith. Religious belonging routinely creates groups of people with distinctive politics, in much the same way as demographic traits, such as race or ethnicity. A good example is the Old Religion Gap shown in table 1.1: the strong link between religious affiliation and the 2004 presidential vote. And as table 1.7 revealed, this affiliation gap in the vote was larger than most other voter gaps, such as the gender and income gaps.

The importance of religious belonging makes intuitive sense: religious communities are self-consciously organized to create and maintain a particular social identity. Indeed, one can hardly think about religion without its organizational components coming to mind: local congregations with their often imposing buildings; religious holidays, charities, and schools; and religious leaders and agencies. All these features can generate strong bonds between members, including distinct values and political attitudes. The discussion of "fundamentalists" in the 2004 election commentary recognized this tendency. However, the political importance of belonging has been unappreciated by many observers. This problem stems in part from the difficulties of measuring religious affiliation in surveys; but it also reflects confusion about the relationship between religious affiliation and other aspects of religion.

The goal of this chapter is to describe the "politics of belonging," or the Old Religion Gap. The chapter begins with an explanation of the political relevance of religious affiliation in the United States, and then introduces a useful concept, "religious tradition." The text then describes the major contemporary religious traditions with the "ABCs of Religious Affiliation." It turns next to a comparison of the 2004 vote to past presidential elections, using the 1944 election as a point of reference. This material illustrates the link between religious traditions and elections, and how the politics of particular religious traditions have evolved over time.

The Politics of Belonging and Religion Traditions

Throughout most of American history, religious belonging was the primary means by which an individual's faith was connected to the vote. Indeed, some of the best-known types of voters were members of distinctive "ethno-religious" communities. Irish Catholics, a group whose affinity for politics put them in charge of the big city politics from days of Tammany Hall to the Chicago Machine, are a good example. In many places, such as New England, the arch-enemies of the Irish Catholics were the "white Anglo-Saxon Protestants" or WASPs, the high-status and high-minded Congregationalists and Episcopalians who controlled the formal levers of power. The WASPs were nearly as hostile to the lower status Methodists and Baptists, whose emotional piety and popular appeal made them natural organizers of religion—and politics—across the South and Midwest.[1]

The list of significant ethno-religious communities is extensive, including Dutch Calvinists, Swedish Lutherans, German Jews, English Quakers, and Polish Catholics. In addition, there were indigenous American faiths, known for their religious innovations and crossing of ethnic lines, such as the Latter Day Saints, Seventh Day Adventists, Christian Scientists, and Pentecostals. Like ethnicity, race generated distinctive religious communities, such as the black Protestant churches. Although ethnic assimilation has reduced the distinctiveness of some such groups, new ones have taken their place. Good contemporary examples include Mexican Catholics, Korean Methodists, Pakistani Muslims and Japanese Buddhists.[2]

Even the assimilation of ethnic groups has left a mark on American society in the form of a vast number of religious denominations—so many, in fact, that the United States has been dubbed the "denominational society."[3] For many Americans, denominational affiliation has replaced ethnicity as a source of personal identity. Indeed, many of the most successful denominations explicitly ignored the ethnicity of prospective members. Like ethnicity, denominational affiliation is about culture and values, but in a more flexible, varied, and circumscribed fashion. Some denominational identities are forged by beliefs, others by practices, and still others by religious experiences. Denominations connect members with transcendent purposes, but also set limits on the scope of members' obligations to the denomination; they allow a religious community to make special truth claims, but require a general toleration of (most) other such claims. But perhaps most importantly, denominational affiliation is a largely voluntary source of identity, a feature that fits well with the individualistic nature of American society.

For all these reasons, American religion has always been extraordinarily diverse—and it shows no signs of becoming less so. But it is worth noting that most of the numerous denominations and other religious communities were—and still are—quite small. While a few larger denominations, such as the Roman Catholic Church, stand out in the religious landscape, they are the exception, and even so, account for only a minority of the population. Indeed, this great religious variety is one of the reasons that the United States has more "religious" people than other advanced industrial democracies.[4]

This complicated mix of mostly small religious groups (as well as the rest of the diversity of American life) was—and continues to be—funneled into politics through a two-party system. Thus, the two major political parties quickly became complex coalitions, in which ethnic and religious communities played a central role. By the early nineteenth century, some such religious communities strongly identified with the Democratic Party, and others first with the Whig Party and then the Republican Party. Still others were largely unaligned, among the original "swing" voters, and as time passed, some changed their party alignment or dropped out of politics altogether.[5]

Such "ethno-religious" alliances extended into the twentieth century, with Franklin D. Roosevelt's "New Deal" coalition being a prime example. After all, the New Deal Democrats were an alliance of northern Catholic and Jewish "ethnics," black Protestants and secular cosmopolitans, and southern white Protestants, especially Evangelicals. In contrast, the Republican coalition of that era was dominated by Mainline Protestant churches.[6] As table 1.1 (in Chapter 1) showed, religious communities were still quite important to the vote at the beginning of the twenty-first century.

Religious Traditions

One useful way to reduce the complexity of religious communities is with the concept of a "religious tradition." A religious tradition is a set of religious denominations, movements, and congregations with similar doctrines, practices, and origins.[7] This definition allows observers to aggregate the many small religious communities into categories that are both meaningful and useful. Indeed, the powerful patterns in table 1.1 are the product of a simple measure of religious tradition.

Thus, a religious tradition is defined in part by the religious behaviors and beliefs that are regarded as normative by the communities in question, either in the form of formal statements or an informal consensus. In shorthand, these norms amount to a particular kind of "traditional" behavior and belief. Such practices and doctrines provide the rationale for religious institutions, which in turn seek to make their tradition real and relevant in the lives of individual "belongers." Much of this work is accomplished by the clergy and other religious leaders, but it also occurs in the regular interaction among the laity. Of course, individual adherents may differ in the degree of "traditionalism," that is, holding to the normative practices and beliefs of the religious tradition to which they belong—a matter that will be discussed at length in the next chapter.

A religious tradition is also defined in part by history: all religious communities had specific beginnings, such as an expansion or consolidation of an existing religious body, schisms or mergers due to religious innovations, or the invention of a new faith. Such changes can come from the internal dynamics of religious life as well as from external factors, ranging from economic development to cultural conflict. Indeed, the definition of a religious tradition recognizes that religious belonging is a complicated phenomenon, including well-established denominations, fluid religious movements, and independent congregations.

There is also a practical element to the definition of religious traditions: it stresses "similar" doctrines, practices, and origins. The relevant degree of similarity is inevitably a judgment call. It depends in part on the historical era. For example, some beliefs and practices that defined religious traditions in the nineteenth century did not matter as much a century later, while differences hardly noticed in 1900 had become significant by 2000. Geographic context matters as well. In the United States, treating Jews as a single religious tradition in national politics makes practical sense because of their small numbers. However, in Brooklyn, New York, the various religious differences within the Jewish community may matter a great deal politically. These definitional questions are not just academic exercises: the members of religious communities respond to these factors as well, sorting themselves into more congenial groupings based in part on their circumstances. The great public debates of the time have often been an important element of such circumstances.[8]

But exactly how do religious traditions matter in elections? The answer is straightforward: religious belonging provides a social context in which individuals can connect their faith to political choices.[9] This context operates in at least three important and related ways. First, religious traditions are a source of *core values,* which can influence a member's vote on substantive grounds. Second, religious traditions can be a potent source of *internal cues* from denominational leaders, the clergy, and the laity that can all influence a member's vote by demonstrating the relevance of core values to the choices at the ballot box. And finally, religious communities can be the targets of *external appeals.* Candidates, political parties, and interest groups can appeal to religious communities for support, and such appeals can influence members' votes by providing actionable information. Subsequent chapters will cover these matters. The task at hand, however, is to define the major religious traditions in some detail.

The ABCs of Religious Affiliation

Scholars commonly recognize five large religious traditions in the United States at the beginning of the twenty-first century: Evangelical, Mainline and

Black Protestants, Roman Catholics, and Jews. Some analysts also separate large ethnic sub-traditions, such as Latino Protestants and Catholics, on the grounds that ethnic identity has a special association with religious affiliation (much as European ethnicities did in the past). Scholars also recognize a variety of smaller religious traditions among Christians, such as the Latter Day Saints and Eastern Orthodox, as well as non-Christian traditions, including Muslims, Hindus, and Buddhists. However, these small traditions are often aggregated into composite categories because of their small numbers in surveys. Finally, many analysts also recognize the unaffiliated population as a special case of a "religious" tradition from this perspective.[10]

Table 2.1 offers a summary of these major religious traditions and composite groups, using a special collection of surveys with a highly detailed measure of religious affiliation.[11] (See Appendix A for a list of denominational codes.) In essence, table 2.1 presents a more precise version of the categories in table 1.1, and it will serve as a guide for the subsequent discussion. The first column gives the relative size of the categories as a percentage of the adult population. The next four columns present basic religious measures: the percent of each category that reported a "strong" or "very strong" preference for their religious affiliation (that is, the affiliation that defines their religious tradition in the table), that said religion is important or very important in their lives, that believed Scripture is the literal or inerrant Word of God, and that reported attending worship weekly or more often. This information provides a general sense of the religious distinctiveness of each religious tradition. The final column contains a political measure: the percent of each category that reported that religion was relevant to their political decisions. This information assesses the extent to which the religious tradition has been politicized.[12]

Evangelical Protestants

As noted in chapter 1, Evangelical Protestants attracted a great deal of attention because of their influence in the 2004 presidential election, but they also fascinate observers due to their religious vitality and internal diversity. In fact, Evangelical Protestants have been defined in a number of ways and a variety of terms are used to describe them, including "fundamentalists."[13] While all such approaches have some virtue, a strict affiliation measure is especially useful because it makes it possible to isolate the impact of *belonging* to the Evangelical Protestant tradition from the impact of religious behavior or belief.

From this perspective, Evangelical Protestants are members of historically white Protestant denominations, religious movements, and independent congregations that share a special set of doctrines and practices. Four doctrines are generally regarded as the "Evangelical distinctives": 1) faith in Jesus Christ is the only way to salvation; 2) individuals must accept salvation for themselves (i.e. must be "born again"); 3) it is imperative to proclaim this message of salvation and make converts among non-believers; and 4) the Bible is the inerrant Word

Table 2.1 Religious Traditions in the U.S.

	Size	% Strong Preference	% Religion Salient	% Scripture Authoritative	% Weekly Worship	% Religion Politically Relevant
White Evangelical Protestants	24.8	76.2	76.6	76.0	57.6	58.3
White Mainline Protestants	17.1	59.5	53.9	45.1	34.1	32.0
Latino Protestants	2.7	74.0	74.4	67.1	60.2	51.3
Black Protestants	9.1	84.4	85.0	62.1	59.1	60.3
Non-Latino Catholics	19.0	64.1	54.4	40.1	46.7	28.8
Latino Catholics	4.2	71.1	63.3	44.8	43.3	37.2
Other Christians	3.6	82.0	65.9	44.9	55.1	46.6
Jews	2.1	54.9	28.1	18.9	19.5	28.1
Other Faiths	1.5	62.5	51.7	18.2	34.2	40.5
Unaffiliated	16.1	50.3	18.1	15.8	11.1	19.5
ALL	100.0	67.8	57.5	48.3	42.5	39.8

Source: National Surveys of Religion and Politics, 1992-2004

of God, providing the authority for the previous doctrines and other matters. These doctrines are associated with distinctive religious practices as well: high levels of religious devotion, with an emphasis on a personal, unmediated relationship with Christ; extensive personal involvement in local congregations of like-minded believers; an intense focus on "evangelizing," that is, proselytizing to make converts; and a strong emphasis on preaching and reading the Bible.[14]

One consequence of these doctrines and practices is that the Evangelical Protestant tradition is highly decentralized in organizational terms, with many denominations, nondenominational congregations, and independent agencies. It is thus hardly surprising that there is considerable variation on the form and application of these distinctive doctrines and practices, the finer points of which are a constant source of debate. Indeed, the more surprising thing is the high degree of unity on the basic doctrines and practices among Evangelical Protestants.

The Evangelical Protestant tradition is largely a product of the twentieth century. By 1900, modern intellectual and social developments were beginning to fragment American Protestantism.[15] Many of these fragments had in common a strenuous defense of traditional Protestant doctrine and practice against challenges from the modern world. In some cases, sectarian movements sought to take control of major denominations, eventually splitting off into their own separate organizations. Fundamentalism, properly so called, is the best known example of such movements (which will be discussed more fully below). Other sectarian movements sparked intense revivals, eventually producing new religious organizations as well; here, Pentecostalism is a good example. Still other fragments simply expanded their own separate institutions, including a number of ethnic and regional denominations that had remained largely aloof from the major Protestant denominations on doctrinal grounds. By the 1920s, this fragmentation was well underway.

Slowly, these traditional fragments began to coalesce. In 1942, a number of these churches founded the National Association of Evangelicals (NAE) to coordinate their common religious efforts.[16] Although not all these groups joined NAE (and many still do not belong), it provided a center and a public face for this diverse and growing set of related religious communities. As a consequence, the term "evangelical" has been increasingly used to describe all such groups, even though many individual adherents identify primarily with their own churches rather than the broader religious tradition. Overall, these religious communities and their institutions prospered during the second half of the twentieth century, steadily adding adherents and exerting influence among other religious traditions.[17]

Evangelical Protestants have had an ambivalent relationship with politics.[18] Many of their nineteenth century forbearers were deeply engaged in public affairs, including, for example, the abolition of slavery, women's suffrage, and Prohibition. In fact, one reason for the fragmentation of American Protestantism was disputes concerning the most appropriate goals and methods for public engagement. In the 1920s, the newly christened "fundamentalists" spawned a movement to ban the teaching of evolution in public schools. The limited success of this movement (including the Scopes trial in 1925) led many to withdraw from political life and focus instead on saving souls. Other political movements eventually brought Evangelicals back into politics, including opposition to communism (in the 1950s and 1960s) and declining traditional morality (in the 1980s and 1990s). By the end of the twentieth century, Evangelicals were again deeply engaged in political life.

In table 2.1, Evangelical Protestants make up 24.8 percent of the adult population, a figure consistent with other surveys. And they are religiously distinctive: three-quarters identify strongly with their religious affiliation, regard religion as salient in their lives, and hold a high view of Scriptural authority. In addition, almost three-fifths report attending worship weekly or more often. Evangelical Protestants are also highly politicized, with nearly three-fifths reporting that their faith is relevant to their politics. In these regards, only Black and Latino Protestants, and Other Christians, match or exceed the figures for Evangelicals.

The Evangelical Protestant tradition is quite diverse in denominational terms. The major groupings of Evangelicals are as follows (list by size):

Baptists. White Baptist denominations make up about 39 percent of adult Evangelicals (and one-tenth of the entire adult population). Deriving from the most radical wing of the Protestant Reformation, this group includes the giant Southern Baptist Convention (SBC), the largest Protestant denomination in the United States, which accounts for 60 percent of all Evangelical Baptists. As its name implies, the SBC had its origins in the South during the Civil War era, but is now a national denomination. However, the SBC does not belong to the NAE, reflecting the tendency of Baptists to be organizationally independent. The SBC leadership has been quite active in public affairs since the 1980s.

In fact, the second largest group of Evangelical Baptists is members of local independent churches (28 percent of adult Evangelicals), many of whom identify with religious movements, such as fundamentalism. In addition, there are numerous smaller Baptist denominations (12 percent of adult Evangelicals). Some of these denominations were the product of the twentieth century fragmentation (such as the Conservative Baptist Association and the General Association of Regular Baptists) and others products of previous religious foment (such as the Baptist General Conference and the Free Will Baptists). Some of these Baptist churches are members of the NAE and some have become quite active politically. For example, the Baptist Bible Fellowship provided the backbone of Reverend Jerry Falwell's Moral Majority.

Non-denominational Churches. In keeping with the decentralized nature of the Evangelical tradition, non-denominational churches are the second largest grouping, accounting for 23 percent of adult Evangelicals. These churches are quite diverse, including many of the best known suburban "mega-churches," but also a variety of smaller congregations. About three-fifths of these individuals simply claim to be "born again" Christians and the remaining two-fifths identify with sectarian religious movements. For instance, about 7 percent say they belong to fundamentalist churches and another 13 percent identify with the charismatic movement (closely associated with Pentecostalism), and still another 20 percent claim to be part of the "evangelical" movement. Some of these churches belong to the NAE. Non-denominational Evangelicals contain some political diversity, but they have also been the core supporters of Christian conservative and "pro-family" organizations.

Pentecostals. The third largest group of Evangelicals is Pentecostals, churches that emphasize the gifts of the Holy Spirit, such as praying in tongues and divine healing. Pentecostalism began with a series of revivals at the turn of the twentieth century. Accounting for 10 percent of adult Evangelicals, the largest denomination is the Assemblies of God (which makes up about one-half of all Pentecostals). Pentecostalism includes a number of other denominations such as the Church of God (Cleveland, Tennessee), the International Church of the Four Square Gospel, and the Pentecostal Church of God. Pentecostalism is linked to other "spirit-filled" movements, such as charismatics and neo-charismatics. And it is linked historically with the Holiness movement that produced denominations such as the Church of the Nazarene, the Free Methodist Church, and the Christian and Missionary Alliance. In these data, the Holiness churches account for about 5 percent of adult Evangelicals. Many of the Pentecostal and Holiness denominations belong to the NAE; many were also active in the Christian Right. For example, Reverend Pat Robertson is a charismatic, and the "spirit-filled" movements helped staff the Christian Coalition.

Other Evangelical Denominations. The Evangelical Protestant tradition includes a variety of other denominations. Together these diverse churches account for 23 percent of adult Evangelicals. For example, 7 percent of adult Evangelicals were in Restorationist churches, of which the largest denomination is the Church of Christ. Another 7 percent are Lutherans, including the Lutheran Church Missouri Synod, and four percent are from the Reformed tradition, including the Presbyterian Church in America and the Christian Reformed Church. Still other such denominations include the Reformed Episcopal Church, the Conservative Congregational Christian Conference, the Evangelical Covenant Church, the Evangelical Free Church, and the Seventh Day Adventists, plus most Brethren, Mennonite, and Amish churches. Many of these churches also belong to the NAE, but others do not; some are quite active in public affairs, but others remain aloof.

On "Fundamentalists." Because of the importance of the term "fundamentalist" in discussions of Evangelical Protestantism and their politics—as well as the 2004 election—a brief clarification is in order. This term is used in two ways, generating a great deal of confusion. First, the term refers to a sectarian religious movement among Anglo-American Protestants that seeks to preserve traditional doctrines and practices. Here, we refer to this usage as "fundamentalist, properly so called." Because this movement is the origin of the second usage of the term, we will discuss it first.[19]

The fundamentalist movement gets its name from *The Fundamentals,* a series of pamphlets published between 1910 and 1915, in which Protestant theologians defended what they saw as the "fundamental" Protestant doctrines against modern theology. By the 1920s, a "fundamentalist-modernist" dispute had broken out within most of the major Protestant denominations. An increasingly self-conscious movement sought to take control of denominational machinery to maintain a traditional religious perspective. They largely lost these battles and their defeat spurred the development of the Evangelical Protestant tradition (see above).

Fundamentalism is characterized by highly traditional Protestant beliefs and practices, but it has some special doctrines of its own. For example, it has a very high view of the authority of Scripture (a literal interpretation of the Bible); a special view of the Second Coming of Christ and sacred time (dispensational premillenialism); and the conviction that believers should separate themselves from apostates and non-believers (ecclesiastical separatism). In part, these doctrines embody opposition to the modern world, but ironically, they also represent an adaptation to modernity, albeit a hostile one. In fact, fundamentalists are best known for their aggressive style of operation: angry, zealous, and uncompromising, given to bitter attacks and intolerance. (However, for all their anger, American fundamentalists have never been prone to violence.) Because of this style of operation, the term carries with it negative connotations, especially among self-consciously modern people, including many scholars and journalists, who feel threatened by fundamentalists (and who often display their own brand of anger, zealotry, and intolerance in return).

By this definition, how many fundamentalists are there in the United States? A 2004 survey offers a good estimate: 10.8 percent of the adult population identified themselves as Protestant fundamentalists.[20] However, most of these people did not exhibit the minimal characteristics of fundamentalism, such as biblical literalism and hostility to religious modernization. If these factors are taken into account, 4.5 percent of adult Americans are fundamentalists. Though small, this group is hardly trivial: it is about the size of all Latino Catholics and more than twice the size of all Jews. About 70 percent of the fundamentalists are found in the Evangelical Protestant tradition (the rest evenly divided between Mainline and minority Protestants); 90 percent claim to be "born again," and almost three-fifths also identify as "evangelical." Fundamentalists are concentrated in Baptist and nondenominational churches, and make up just one-eighth of all Evangelical Protestants. It is worth noting that as a whole, Evangelicals have a positive view of "Christian fundamentalists," even though only a minority belongs to the group.

In 2004, fundamentalists voted for George W. Bush at about the same rate as Evangelical Protestants as a whole (80 percent), and provided the President with nine percent of all his ballots—a significant figure in an election won by one percent of the two-party vote. So the *New York Times* columnists were making reference to a real phenomenon in their explanation of the 2004 election, but in an exaggerated fashion: just as roughly nine of ten Evangelicals are not fundamentalists, about nine-tenths of Bush's vote came from non-fundamentalists.

The second usage of the term "fundamentalist" is more common and more problematic.[21] From the outset of the fundamentalist movement, observers applied the term to traditionalist religious groups writ large, most of whom had little in common with fundamentalists properly so called—except a critical posture toward aspects of the modernity. In recent times, the term has been applied to many faiths, as in "fundamentalist Islam," "fundamentalist Judaism," or "fundamentalist Catholicism." At its core, this usage recognizes a real phenomenon, the recent importance of religious traditionalism around the world. As we will see in the next chapter, religious traditionalism was quite important in the 2004 election.

But if used incautiously, this version of the term "fundamentalist" obscures more than it reveals. For one thing, it names the whole of a phenomenon by one of its parts. Describing all religious traditionalists as "fundamentalists" would be like labeling all Christians as "Catholics"—rather than the other way around. Furthermore, the negative connotations associated with fundamentalism can be inadvertently—or intentionally—smuggled into the discussion. Such guilt by "definitional association" is often pernicious. Finally, this usage carries with it a modernist or secularist bias against traditional religion (much like the term "secularist" carries a traditionalist religious bias). The *New York Times* columnists fell victim to these kinds of problems in their commentary on the 2004 election.

Mainline Protestants

Mainline Protestant tradition is also largely a product of the twentieth century fragmentation of American Protestantism. Indeed, these churches represented the biggest fragment: the largest, most successful, and visible of the Protestant denominations. Indeed, the term "mainline" reflects their strategic place in American culture and politics throughout most of the century. The term came originally from the railroads, referring to the most traveled tracks—the "main line." Similar usage includes "mainstream" and "brand name." All these terms share the assumption that these large Protestant bodies played a critical role in determining the dominant social and religious values in American society. But as with Evangelicals, most individual Mainline Protestants identify primarily with their own denominations instead of the broader tradition to which they belong.[22]

The mainline churches were deeply influenced by modernist theology and have slowly drifted away from a strict adherence to traditional Protestant doctrine and practice. In fact, it was just such drift, particularly modern approaches to interpreting the Bible, which was the prime catalyst for the sectarian revolts that helped create the Evangelical tradition. The net result was a more heterodox doctrine, a latitudinarian approach to religious practice and ecumenical and interfaith perspectives—developments that fit with the relatively large size and internal diversity of these denominations. Such trends continue to provoke disagreement within these churches, some of which have a significant number of more traditional members.

Mainline Protestants adopted a strong emphasis on solving social problems, seeing themselves as among the public institutions tasked with addressing them.[23] Partly in response, they favored extensive denominational and interdenominational organizations. On the first count, many of these denominations grew by merging related churches from the same Protestant sub-tradition. On the second count, the Mainline churches organized the Federal Council of Churches in 1908, which later became the National Council of Churches in 1950 (NCC). And many of these bodies supported the World Council of Churches when it was founded in 1948 and other ecumenical groups, such as the Consultation on Church Union. Not surprisingly, Mainliners have long played a prominent role in public affairs, being strong proponents of the "social gospel" of reform and a staging ground for a succession of progressive movements loosely dubbed the "religious left."

The twentieth century was not kind to Mainline Protestants.[24] Although their cultural dominance was established in the early part of the century, their numbers and prestige then steadily declined. Table 2.1 shows that white Mainline Protestants made up 17.1 percent of the adult population at the end of the twentieth century. Note the lower level of "strong preference" for their affiliation (less than three-fifths) compared to other Protestants. (It is worth noting, however, that Mainliners do have quite a positive affect toward "Protestants" in general.) Mainliners also showed lower levels of religious salience (about one-half), traditional view of Scriptural authority (less than one-half), and weekly worship attendance (roughly one-third) than the American public has a whole. And they were also less likely to say that their religion was relevant to their politics (one-third).

Mainline Protestantism is also diverse in organizational terms, and it includes the following denominations, all members of the NCC (list by size):[25]

United Methodist Church (UMC). The largest of the Mainline Protestant churches and the third largest denomination in the United States, the UMC was the product of mergers among Methodist churches deriving from John Wesley and Methodist revivals of the eighteenth and nineteenth centuries, the most recent merger occurring in 1968. Known for its "connectional" polity, it is the most socially diverse and geographically dispersed of Mainline churches. The UMC and related Methodists accounted for almost 32 percent of adult Mainline Protestants (and about five percent of the adult population).

Non-denominational Mainline Protestants. The second largest group of Mainline Protestants is outside denominations, some members of non-denominational, interdenominational, and interfaith congregations, but many who simply identify with "Protestantism" in general and with Mainline sensibilities. This diverse group accounts for 16 percent of adult Mainline Protestants.

Evangelical Lutheran Church in America (ELCA). Despite its name, the ELCA is not an Evangelical denomination, but rather the mainline variant of the Lutheran churches, deriving from Martin Luther and the Protestant Reformation. The ELCA is also the product of mergers, the most recent being in 1988. The ELCA and related Lutherans account for 15 percent of adult Mainline Protestants.

Presbyterian Church in the U.S.A (PCUSA). PCUSA is the largest denomination among the Presbyterian churches, and indeed of all the Reformed churches. Its theology and polity derive from John Calvin and the Protestant Reformation, especially by way of Scotland. It was also the product of mergers, most recently in 1983. PCUSA and related Presbyterians account for 10 percent of adult Mainline Protestants.

Episcopal Church in the U.S.A (ECUSA). ECUSA is the American national church in the Anglican Community in the United States, deriving from the Church of England. It was one of the original "established churches" in the colonial period and took its present form in 1873. The most hierarchical of the Mainline churches, ECUSA and related Anglicans account for about 8 percent of all Mainline Protestants.

American Baptist Churches in the U.S.A (ABC). The ABC is the second largest denomination in the Baptist family and the largest one outside of the Evangelical or Black Protestant traditions. A product of the congregational polity of Baptists, it reached its current organizational form in 1972. Keeping with the Baptist independence, it is the most decentralized of the major Mainline churches. The ABC and related Baptists account for about 8 percent of adult Mainline Protestants.

United Church of Christ (UCC). The UCC is the product of a series of mergers among Reformed churches, including Congregationalists, deriving from the New England Puritans (one of the "established churches" of the colonial period), and German Reformed denominations, the product of subsequent immigration. The most recent merger was in 1957, preserving a congregational polity. The most self-consciously "liberal" of the Mainline churches in theological terms, the UCC and related Congregationalists account for about 5 percent of adult Mainline Protestants.

Christian Church (Disciples of Christ). The Disciplines of Christ is the Mainline variant of the Restorationist family, which began with the efforts of Barton Stone, Thomas and Alexander Campbell in the early 19th century to restore Christian unity. The Disciples of Christ took its present form in 1968 and has a congregational polity. The Disciples and related churches account for 3 percent of Mainline Protestants.

Other Mainline Denominations. Other Mainline denominations include the Reformed Church in America; the Church of the Brethren, and the Society of Friends (Quakers). Taken together, these smaller bodies account for about 3 percent of adult Mainline Protestants.

Black and Hispanic Protestants

As noted above, ethnicity and race have been important factors in religious affiliation in the United States. Although cultural assimilation has reduced the importance of many ethno-religious communities, analysts find it useful to distinguish the Black Protestants as a separate religious tradition and to separate out Latino Protestants as well. The Black Protestant churches were created by the confluence of Protestant missionary work on the one hand, and on the other hand, slavery and racial segregation; Latino Protestantism resulted from missionary work and recent immigration.[26]

Minority Protestant affiliations are not well understood in survey research and so many analysts simply separate out Black and Latino Protestants based on race and ethnicity (the approach used here). While quite powerful empirically, such a choice may become less and less useful as minorities gain acceptance in historically white Protestant denominations. However, even in this context, African-Americans and Latinos tend to be concentrated in congregations that are racially and ethnically homogeneous.

Table 2.1 shows that at the end of the twentieth century, Black Protestants made up about 9 percent of the adult population and Latino Protestants 2 to 3 percent. Note the strong preference for their affiliations (better than seven in ten), and high levels of religious salience (three-quarters or better), acceptance of Scriptural authority (better than three-fifths), and high levels of weekly worship attendance (about three-fifths). These figures often exceed the figures of Evangelical Protestants; and like Evangelicals, they have a highly favorable view of "Christian fundamentalists." These groups also are highly politicized, with Black Protestants the mostly likely of all the religious traditions to report that religion was relevant to their politics (three-fifths).

The largest group of Black Protestants is Baptists, and they account for 58 percent of adult Black Protestants. The largest denominations are the National Baptist Convention and the Progressive National Baptist Convention. Both of these bodies belong to the NCC, but some Black Baptists associate with the NAE.

Members of Pentecostal and Holiness churches account for another 13 percent of adult Black Protestants, with the Church of God in Christ the largest denomination. Members of non-denominational churches make up another 13 percent, many of whom are associated with Pentecostalism.

Another large group of Black Protestants is Methodists, accounting for about 8 percent of adult Black Protestants. Important denominations here are the African Methodist Episcopal Church, the African Methodist Episcopal Church Zion, and the Christian Methodist Episcopal Church; all three are members of the NCC. The remaining 8 percent of Black Protestants belonged to other denominations.

Latino Protestants are nearly as diverse as Black Protestants in terms of denominational affiliation. The largest number, 31 percent, belong to non-denominational churches or have generic Protestant identifications, many linked to Pentecostalism, and another 20 percent belong to Pentecostal or Holiness churches. The second largest group of Latino Protestants is Baptists, accounting for 27 percent overall. Another 22 percent are associated with other denominations.

Catholics

The Roman Catholic Church is the single largest denomination in the United States, exceeding the size of Mainline Protestants and rivaling that of Evangelicals.[27] It is part of a global church that embodies the Catholic tradition, with its special doctrines, practices, and hierarchical organization. For much of American history, Catholics were a distinctive community within a largely Protestant nation. But by the second half of the twentieth century, the Catholics achieved broad social acceptance and moved into the mainstream of American life. An important feature of this transition was the Second Vatican Council in 1962-1964, which liberalized some Catholic doctrine and practice. A religious body this large and well-integrated into society is certain to be quite diverse internally, exhibiting most of the political tensions that characterize American society as a whole. The Catholic hierarchy and laity have long been involved in public affairs, reflecting long-standing concerns for social justice and personal morality. In recent times, lay Catholics have become organized for political purposes on both the right and the left.

Table 2.1 shows that all Catholics accounted for some 23 percent of the adult population at the end of the twentieth century (some surveys show a higher figure).[28] Non-Latino Catholics made up 19 percent of the adult population and white Catholics about 17 percent. In addition, Latino Catholics account for about 4 percent of the adult population. Put another way, white Catholics make up about 74 percent of adult Catholics, Latinos about 18 percent, and other races and ethnicities the final 8 percent.

Note that Non-Latino Catholic groups reported a middle-level of strength of preference for their affiliation (more than three-fifths), close to the figure for Americans as a whole. (They do, however, have a highly favorable view toward Catholics as a group.) Non-Latino Catholics have relatively low levels of religious salience and weekly worship attendance (roughly one-half each). Adherence to Scriptural authority was also lower (40.1 percent), but this belief is not an important Catholic doctrine. But it is worth noting that just 44 percent of this group agree or strongly agree with the Papal infallibility, which is a Catholic doctrine. Latino Catholics score lower or about the same on worship attendance and Scriptural authority, but markedly higher on religious salience and much higher on papal infallibility (61 percent). Non-Latino Catholics report a very low level of politicization (just 28.8 percent), and here too, Latino Catholics scored higher (37.2 percent).

Other Christian Traditions

The great diversity of American Christianity includes a number of smaller religious traditions.[29] As table 2.1 shows, these groups account for between 3 and 4 percent of the adult population. The largest of these groups are the Mormons, at 1.3 percent of the adult population, with the Church of Jesus Christ of the Latter Day Saints the largest component. The Jehovah's Witnesses are another important group at .6 percent of the adult population, and so are the Eastern Orthodox churches, at .4 percent. Various liberal faiths rooted in Christianity combine for about .5 percent, including Christian Scientists and the Unitarian-Universalists. Other liberal faiths outside of Christianity are included here, such as Humanists and New Age adherents, combined for another .6 percent.

Many of these denominations are active in public affairs, some on the conservative side (Mormons) and some on the liberal side (Unitarians). But others, like the Jehovah's Witnesses, are largely apolitical. Because of the composite character of the Other Christian category, the religious measures in table 2.1 are difficult to interpret, but the category scored high on strength of preference and religious salience. It also had a middle-level score on the relevance of religion to politics.

Jews, Other Faith Traditions, and the Unaffiliated

The American religious landscape has always contained a variety of non-Christian traditions.[30] At the end of the twentieth century, Judaism was by far the largest of these groups, accounting for about 2 percent of the adult population (table 2.1). Reform and Conservative Jews were the most common denominations, making up some three-quarters of the Jewish tradition. There is some controversy over the size of the Jewish population, with some analysts arguing that people of Jewish backgrounds should be counted as part of the Jewish community, even if they do not identify themselves as such. Jews have a long history of involvement in public affairs.

The second largest group of non-Christians is Islam.[31] Most analysts agree that the Muslim population is growing rapidly in the United States, but there is less agreement of the size of the Muslim population. The most sophisticated surveys find Muslims to be about .5 percent of the adult population. Of course, it is quite possible that surveys under-represent this new and controversial community. It is worth noting that Muslims are quite diverse, coming from many parts of the Islamic world and including an indigenous denomination, the Nation of Islam, that is largely African-American. All the other non-Christian religions, including Buddhism and Hinduism, also combine for about 1 percent of the adult population (table 2.1). Many of these groups have been growing rapidly, and so has their involvement in public affairs.

Another important group of "non-Christians" are the Unaffiliated.[32] Table 2.1 shows that this group made up 16 percent of the adult population at the end of the twentieth century. This category is internally diverse in ways other than affiliation. It is worth noting, however, that self-identified atheists and agnostics have become quite numerous, at roughly 3 percent of the adult population. Jerry Falwell and other critics of "secularists" typically fail to recognize this diversity.

The religious measures in table 2.1 have to be interpreted cautiously for these last several groups. After all, some of these measures have something of a Christian bias. However, note the low levels of religious salience, a measure that applies equally well to all religious traditions. The strength of strong preference for their affiliation is also relatively low. (Although some groups, like Jews, report a very high level of affect toward their own group.) These categories have relatively low levels of politicization, with only the Other Faiths scoring at the level of the population as a whole in terms of the relevance of religion to politics.

Religious Traditions and Electoral Politics: 2004 and 1944

Students of religion and politics are fond of pointing out that religion has long been a part of American electoral politics.[33] What follows is an illustration of this claim, first using survey data first from 2004 and 1944, and then surveying the years in between.

Comparing survey data over a 60 year period is problematic. Not only have the times changed dramatically, so has survey research. Fortunately, there are surveys from 1944 that allow for a cautious comparison with a special survey from 2004. In both these data sets, the denominational data were coded as comparably as possible—but as a consequence, the 2004 figures here may differ a little from the exit poll data in chapter 1 and table 2.1. Although these estimates are crude, they are quite useful.[34]

It is worth noting in passing that the more precise the measure of denominational affiliation, the more likely one is to observe significant political differences among religious traditions. A good example occurred in 2004: the best measure of affiliation showed John Kerry receiving exactly 50 percent of the Mainline vote, which marks a dramatic change from the past and even from the 2000 election. Cruder measures of affiliation, such as in tables 1.1 and 2.2, show a stronger vote for Bush, largely because some Evangelical Protestants are inadvertently counted as Mainliners. However, the "politics of belonging" is so robust that even crude measures of affiliation are strongly associated with the vote.[35]

Changes in the Religious Landscape

A good place to begin this over-time comparison is with the relative size of the major religious traditions as estimated in the 2004 and 1944 surveys, reported in table 2.2. Because the overall population is much larger in 2004, nearly all religious groups have more actual members. But there have been some important changes in their relative numbers. One thing is immediately clear: three of the religious categories used in 2004—Latino Protestants and Catholics, and Other Faiths—were too small for valid analysis in 1944. By itself, this fact reveals an

Table 2.2   Size of Religious Traditions, 2004 and 1944

	2004	*1944*	*Change*
White Evangelical Protestants	24.6	17.5	**7.1**
White Mainline Protestants	18.7	44.4	**-25.7**
Latino Protestants	2.9	*	**2.9**
Black Protestants	9.6	8.3	**1.3**
Non-Latino Catholics	17.5	17.5	**0.0**
Latino Catholics	4.5	*	**4.5**
Other Christians	3.9	3.2	**0.7**
Jews	1.9	4.0	**-2.1**
Other Faiths	1.4	*	**1.4**
Unaffiliated	15.0	5.1	**9.9**
ALL	**100.0**	**100.0**	

* Too few cases for analysis.
Source: See Note 34.

important change in the post-war era, when American religion continued to diversify with the inclusion of new ethnic and religious groups. In total, these new categories accounted for 8.8 percent of adult population in 2004, more than eight times larger than in 1944.

These estimates show that in 2004 Evangelical Protestants made up almost one-quarter of the adult population, up from a little more than one-sixth in 1944, for a 7 percentage point gain over 60 years. A much more dramatic change occurred for Mainline Protestants, who declined from more than two-fifths of the adult population in 1944 to less than one-fifth in 2004. This decline of more than 25 percentage points is *the* major religious change of this time period, being about three times larger than the size of the three new religious groups that appeared since 1944. Nevertheless, Mainline Protestants were still numerous in 2004, accounting for a little more than one-sixth of the adult population. Thus, in terms of relative size, Evangelical and Mainline Protestants have switched places.

During this same period, Black Protestants and the composite group of Other Christians grew slightly in relative terms. In both years, the former was a little less than one-tenth of the adult population and the latter was substantially less than one-twentieth. However, Black Protestants grew dramatically at the ballot box after their right to vote was secured in the 1960s.

Meanwhile, white Catholics stayed at about the same relative size over the period, at a bit more than one-sixth of the adult population. Indeed, it is the growth of Latino Catholics that has accounted for much of the relative growth of Catholics since the 1940s. Jews also declined in relative terms over the period, falling from four percentage points in 1944 to about two percentage points in 2004.

Finally, the Unaffiliated population expanded by almost 10 percentage points, from 5 to 15 percent of the adult population. The growth of the Unaffiliated, and with it the secular or non-religious population, was another important change in the American religious landscape since the 1940s.

The Presidential Vote, 2004-1944

Table 2.3 reports the two-party presidential vote for the major religious traditions in 2004 and 1944. The two elections had some things in common: in both cases, incumbent presidents were re-elected while the nation was at war. But there were some important differences as well. In 2004, Republican George W. Bush secured a second term with 51 percent of the two-party popular vote; in 1944, Democrat Franklin D. Roosevelt won an unprecedented fourth term in the White House with 53 percent of the two-party popular vote. The 2004 election came in an era of highly divided politics, while the 1944 election occurred in the midst of the partisan consolidation of the New Deal era.

Evangelical Protestants. As chapter 1 showed, Evangelical Protestants were the strongest supporters of President Bush in 2004, giving him three-quarters of their votes in these data. But in 1944, Evangelical Protestants gave President Roosevelt a solid majority of their ballots. This change represents a shift of 31

Table 2.3   Presidential Vote, 2004 and 1944

| | 2004 | | 1944 | | Change |
	Rep	Dem	Rep	Dem	Rep
White Evangelical Protestants	75.3	24.7	44.1	55.9	**31.2**
White Mainline Protestants	52.4	47.6	57.9	42.1	**-5.5**
Latino Protestants	62.9	37.1	*	*	
Black Protestants	16.9	83.1	30.2	69.8	**-13.3**
Non-Latino Catholics	52.7	47.3	31.6	68.4	**21.1**
Latino Catholics	31.4	68.6	*	*	
Other Christians	60.0	40.0	48.5	51.5	**11.5**
Jews	26.7	73.3	7.3	92.7	**19.4**
Other Faiths	17.6	82.4	*	*	
Unaffiliated	27.8	72.2	41.7	58.3	**-13.9**
ALL	**51.1**	**48.9**	**46.2**	**53.8**	**4.9**

Source: See Note 34

percentage points in the Republican direction. So, Evangelicals became both larger in relative terms as well as more Republican over this 60-year period.

Mainline Protestants. In these data, Mainline Protestants gave a slight majority to Bush in 2004. However, their Republican ballots were down sharply from the solid majority they provided the Republican presidential nominee in 1944, New York Governor Thomas Dewey. This change represents a loss of more than 5 percentage points for the GOP over the period, a timeframe when Mainline Protestants also declined in relative size.

Catholics and Other Christians. In 2004, Bush won a slim majority of the Catholic vote. But back in 1944, Roosevelt received more than two-thirds of Catholic ballots. This change represents a 21 percentage point shift toward the Republicans. The GOP also made gains among the Other Christians, receiving three-fifths of their votes in 2004, up from a little less than one-half in 1944. Thus, Christians outside of the Protestant communities remained essentially stable in size, but became more Republican in the post-war era.

Black Protestants and the Unaffiliated. Meanwhile, Democrats improved their support among Black Protestants and the Unaffiliated over the period. Both of these groups voted strongly for Roosevelt in 1944 and even more strongly for John Kerry in 2004. The Democratic vote among Black Protestants expanded from more than two-thirds to more than four-fifths; for the Unaffiliated it rose from just under three-fifths to almost three-quarters. These shifts amount to double-digit losses in these two groups for the Republicans (about 13 percentage points). So, these categories became more Democratic as each grew in relative size, and as Black Protestants became more active at the ballot box.

Jews and Other Minorities. Jews were a solidly Democratic constituency in both 2004 and 1944, but the level of Republican support increased from less than one-tenth in 1944 to better than one-quarter in 2004, a gain of about 19 percentage points. John Kerry also did quite well among some of the new religious groups in 2004, winning more than four-fifths of the Other Faiths and almost two-thirds of Latino Catholics. These gains offset some of their losses among other groups of votes. But there was a bright spot for Bush in the new diversity: he received a majority of the votes of Latino Protestants in 2004, a significant short-term gain.

The Affiliation Gap Over Time. Thus, most of the major religious traditions had clear partisan biases in both the 1944 and 2004 presidential elections, with just a few groups more evenly divided. These patterns are revealed in the size of the affiliation gap. In 1944, the difference between the most Republican group, Mainline Protestants, and the most Democratic group, Jews, was 50 percentage points. The difference between Mainline Protestants and Catholics was 26 percentage points. In 2004, the difference between Evangelical Protestants (the most Republican group) and Jews was 49 percentage points. And the difference between Evangelicals and Catholics was 23 percentage points. These are large differences by any standard, and especially given the closeness of the 1944 and 2004 contests. It is also important to note that some religious traditions became more divided politically over this period, especially Mainline Protestants and Catholics.

Voter Coalitions 2004-1944

The relative importance of the major religious traditions in presidential vote coalitions can be seen in table 2.4. (These figures differ from table 1.4 because worship attendance are not included—a point that will be covered in the next chapter.)

The Republican Coalitions. As was shown in chapter 1, Evangelical Protestants were the single largest part of President Bush's vote coalition in 2004, accounting for nearly two-fifths of all his ballots. Mainline Protestants and Catholics each provided roughly another one-fifth of the total Bush vote. If one includes the Other Christian category, white Christians accounted for 84 percent of the GOP presidential voter coalition. But in the very close 2004 contest, Bush needed the sixteen percent of his support that came from religious minorities and the Unaffiliated.

However, Bush's 2004 coalition stands in stark contrast to Governor Dewey's coalition in 1944. Then, Mainline Protestants made up three-fifths of the Republican vote. Evangelicals, Catholics, and the Other Christians combined for another one-third of Dewey's ballots, while religious minorities and the Unaffiliated together provided less than one-tenth. So, the Republican voter coalition has become much more diverse over the last 60 years.

Table 2.4   Presidential Voter Coalitions, 2004 to 1944

	2004		1944		Change	
	Rep	*Dem*	*Rep*	*Dem*	*Rep*	*Dem*
White Evangelical Protestants	37.3	*12.8*	17.1	*18.7*	**20.2**	**-5.9**
White Mainline Protestants	22.0	*21.0*	60.0	*37.5*	**-38.0**	**-16.5**
Latino Protestants	2.6	*1.6*	*	*	**2.6**	**1.6**
Black Protestants	2.6	*13.4*	2.1	*4.1*	**0.5**	**9.3**
Non-Latino Catholics	19.8	*18.6*	12.6	*23.5*	**7.2**	**-4.9**
Latino Catholics	1.9	*4.3*	*	*	**1.9**	**4.3**
Other Christians	5.0	*3.5*	3.6	*3.3*	**1.4**	**0.2**
Jews	1.4	*4.1*	0.8	*8.3*	**0.6**	**-4.2**
Other Faiths	0.4	*1.7*	*	*	**0.4**	**1.7**
Unaffiliated	7.0	*19.0*	3.8	*4.6*	**3.2**	**14.4**
ALL	**100.0**	**100.0**	**100.0**	**100.0**		

Source: See Note 34

The Democratic Coalitions. The Democrats also had a more complex voter co-alition in 2004. In these data, Mainline Protestants were the largest source of Democratic votes, making up about one-fifth of all of Senator John Kerry's bal-lots, closely followed by the Unaffiliated and Catholics, each a bit under one-fifth. Summed together, these three groups accounted for almost three-fifths of the Democratic vote. All the religious minorities combined provided another one-quarter of the Kerry vote. And if these two aggregations are put together, they account for about 84 percent of all of Kerry's ballots—about the same pro-portion as white Christians in the Bush vote coalition. Kerry made the 2004 elec-tion very close with the one-sixth of his ballots that came from Evangelical Protestants and Other Christians.

Kerry's coalition also stands in contrast to President Roosevelt's last campaign in 1944, during the consolidation of the New Deal coalition. Then, the single largest source of Roosevelt's votes was also Mainline Protestants, accounting for almost two-fifths of all his ballots. Catholics provided a little under one-quarter of the Democratic vote, and Evangelicals a little less than one-fifth, so that these two pillars of the New Deal coalition summed to a bit more than two-fifths of the Democratic vote. If the Other Christians are included, then white Christians accounted for a little more than four-fifths of Roosevelt's votes, with the remaining one-fifth coming from religious minorities and the Unaffiliated.

The Paths of Change: The Major Religious Traditions

These political changes raise a question about the path of change between 1944 and 2004. While a full discussion of 60 years of electoral politics is far beyond the scope of this chapter, the general patterns for the largest religious tra-ditions are worth briefly reviewing. Figures 2.1 and 2.2 plot the net Republican vote for the major religious groups every four years over this period (the Democratic vote percentage is subtracted from the Republican vote percentage, so that a Republican advantage is a positive number and a Democratic advantage a negative number). These patterns must be viewed with some caution since they do not include the significant independent presidential candidates over this period. But the shifts in the net two-party vote are nevertheless instructive.

Mainline Protestants and Catholics. Figure 2.1 shows the path of Mainline Protestants and Catholics, among the pillars of the Republican and Democratic coalitions in 1944 that have become divided since then. In this sense, these two large religious traditions have shifted to the middle of the partisan spectrum.

Mainliners remained solidly Republican through the 1960 election, when in reaction to John F. Kennedy, a Catholic Democratic nominee, they voted more heavily Republican. Meanwhile, Catholics drifted toward the GOP in the support of President Dwight Eisenhower, but rallied in mass to support their co-religionist, JFK.

Mainline Protestants then largely abandoned the Republican ticket in 1964 and the Goldwater candidacy, but returned to the GOP fold to support Nixon, Ford,

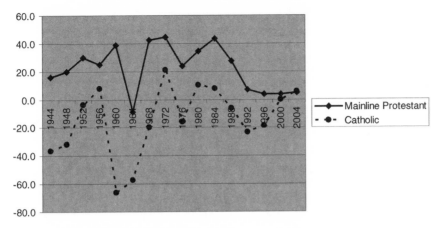

Figure 2.1   The Net Republican Vote of Mainline Protestants and Catholics, 1944-2004

Source: National Election Studies, 1944–2004

and Reagan—with a modest dip in favor of Jimmy Carter in 1976. In the same timeframe, Catholics became less Democratic, especially in 1972 and 1984. After 1984, Mainliners voted steadily less Republican, reaching a nearly even partisan division in 2004. Catholics were something of a mirror image to the Mainliners for most of the post-1984 period, but converged in 2000 and 2004, when they too evenly divided their vote.

Evangelicals, Unaffiliated, and Black Protestants. Figure 2.2 offers a similar picture for Evangelicals, Unaffiliated, and Black Protestants, Democratic constituencies in 1944 that diverged since then. Evangelicals have become the new pillar of the Republican coalition, while the Unaffiliated and Black Protestants are the new pillars in the Democratic coalition.

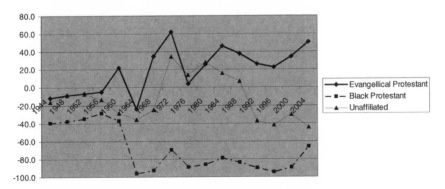

Figure 2.2   The Net Republican Vote of Evangelical Protestants, Black Protestants, and the Unaffiliated, 1944-2004

Source: National Election Studies, 1944–2004

Black Protestants had the clearest pattern: they began in the Democratic camp, and in response to the Civil Rights movement became even more Democratic, remaining so until 2004, with only modest fluctuations.

Evangelicals showed something of an opposite pattern and a bit more variation. Starting out in the Democratic column in 1944, they moved slowly into a Republican direction, voting Republican in 1960 largely in response to the Kennedy candidacy. They then returned to the Democrats in 1964, when southerner Lyndon Johnson was the Democratic nominee, before shifting into the GOP column for good in 1968. Other southern Democratic candidates with some religious credentials, Carter and Clinton, lowered the Republican vote of Evangelicals after 1968. In 2000 and 2004, they strongly supported Bush, a southerner, Republican, and openly religious candidate.

Interestingly, the pattern for the Unaffiliated resembled that of Evangelicals for most of the period. They were on balance Democratic in the 1940s, 1950s and 1960s (but did not shift Republican in response to Catholic Kennedy in 1960). However, in 1972, the Unaffiliated moved into the Republican camp, where they stayed until 1980, at which point they began a steady march away from the GOP. By 1992, they were back on the Democratic side of the ledger.

Conclusions

In conclusion, the "politics of religious belonging" and the Old Religion Gap matter greatly at the ballot box, much as they have in the past. The concept of a religious tradition is a useful way to reduce the great complexity of American religious communities and assess their political impact. The major religious traditions were important elements of presidential voter coalitions in both 1944 and 2004. In between, the politics of particular religious traditions has evolved, reflecting both religious and political developments.

On a practical note, these findings reveal that even simple measures of religious affiliation, such as used in the exit polls, are very useful in explaining the vote. Of course, more accurate measures of religious affiliation produce more accurate political assessments. However, failure to routinely include simple affiliation questions in surveys is a major mistake.[36] Nevertheless, as was shown in chapter 1 (tables 1.2 and 1.3), religious affiliation is not the only aspect of religion that matters at the ballot box. We now turn to the "politics of religious behaving and believing," and the New Religion Gap.

3

The New Religion Gap: The Politics of Behaving and Believing

Religious behavior and belief are also critical aspects of a person's religion: behavior reflects the practice of faith and belief reflects its doctrinal content. Religious behavior and belief most often occur in the context of religious affiliation, although they can occur apart from it as well. Religious behavior and belief can generate political distinctiveness in much the same way as secular activities and attitudes, such as participating in a labor union or valuing personal freedom. The distinctiveness derived from religious practice and doctrine helps create the political differences between religious traditions, but it can also create such differences within religious traditions. A good example is the political differences associated with the New Religion Gap shown in table 1.2 (in chapter 1): the strong relationship between the frequency of worship attendance and the 2004 presidential vote. And as table 1.7 revealed, the attendance gap in the vote was larger than most other voter gaps, such as the gender and income gaps.

The political impact of religious behavior and belief makes intuitive sense. One regularly speaks of individuals who "practice their faith" and have "the courage of their convictions," so it is hardly surprising that such individuals could differ politically from other co-religionists. Many observers have recently developed an appreciation of the impact of such differences, as illustrated by the news coverage of the "God gap" in the 2004 campaign. This appreciation stems in part from the ease with which worship attendance is measured in surveys, but also from the clear and recent connection between attendance and vote. But because religious beliefs are poorly measured in most surveys, there is some confusion about the relationships among behavior, belief, and politics.

The goal of this chapter is to describe the "politics of behaving and believing" and the New Religion Gap. It begins with a discussion of the new political relevance of religious practice and doctrine, and introduces the useful concept of "religious traditionalism." The text then describes some important examples of religious behavior and belief in the United States with a "Checklist of Religious Practice and Doctrine," and discusses their relationship to traditionalism. Next, the chapter reviews the politics of one measure of traditionalism, worship attendance, in the 2004 and past presidential elections, using the 1944 election as a point of reference. This material documents a new connection between religion and politics in recent times.

The Politics of Behaving and Believing, and Religious Traditionalism

As noted in the previous chapter, religious belonging has been the primary means by which an individual's faith was connected to the vote throughout most of American history. Although religious practice and doctrine helped define religious traditions, they apparently had little independent impact on voting behavior. Instead, religious behavior and belief reinforced the effects of religious affiliation and the characteristic politics associated with it.[1]

This pattern suddenly changed toward the end of the twentieth century with the appearance of political differences based on religious behavior and belief. This shift was dramatic enough that scholars spoke of a "restructuring" of American religion, particularly within the major denominations. A good recent example of such "restructuring" is within the Episcopal Church, which became internally divided over the ordination of a gay bishop in 2004, threatening the creation of a new conservative denomination. Many churches experienced similar divisions, though not all were as public.

These dramatic changes led other scholars to speak darkly of the advent of faith-based "culture wars." Here a good recent example is the proposal to teach "intelligent design" alongside evolution in public school science classes, a new version of an ongoing dispute. Similar conflicts erupted over abortion, homosexuality, and the public expression of religion. All these disputes created sharp divisions within religious communities.[2]

The net result of these disputes was the appearance of a novel kind of political alliance developed among religious groups *within* and *across* religious traditions, and not just *between* and *among* traditions. In concrete terms this means, for example, that Catholics who attended mass regularly developed different political views than Catholics who were less observant. And such differences led regular mass attenders to increasingly vote Republican, while the less observant increasingly voted Democratic. Eventually, regular mass attending Catholics began to find more in common politically with regular worship attenders in other religious traditions than with less observant Catholics—who, in turn, found common interests with the less observant elsewhere.

Although the cleavages created by such "restructuring" and "culture wars" were ostensibly about public policy, they had deep religious roots. Some scholars saw all these disagreements as revolving around the question of moral authority: are there absolute and fixed standards of right and wrong, or are moral questions inherently relative, changing with the circumstances and the boundaries of human knowledge? In this regard, the disputes invoked such foundational questions as the nature of God, religious authority, and efficacy of religious observance.

Analysts spoke of the "orthodox," "conservative," or "traditional" in various religious traditions coalescing against a union of the "progressive," "liberal," or "modernist," also drawn from many religious backgrounds. Some scholars went a step farther, adding the growing ranks of the unaffiliated population to the "modernist" coalition, understanding secularization as part of this religious "restructuring."

To some observers, these religious differences translated directly into new political divisions.[3] But other analysts saw the political process as largely the cause of this change, inflaming long-standing religious differences.[4] Observers also disagreed about the scope of these new disputes, both in terms of the issues covered and the number of religious communities involved. Certainly, these new religious divisions were especially clear on social issues, such as abortion, marriage, and gay rights, but some analysts argued that only a small number of people on each side were really engaged in these conflicts.[5] However, other observers saw such conflicts as spreading to a wider range of issues, including foreign and economic policy, and eventually to all religious traditions, producing a general political cleavage.[6]

Although the order of causality is interesting, the net results are the same whether "religious disputes invaded politics" or "political disputes invaded religion." At the minimum, this new kind of religious politics adds complexity to the party coalitions based on religious belonging, and at the maximum, new coalitions based on practice and doctrine will completely replace the old coalitions based on affiliation. In either case, religious behavior and belief exercise a new and independent impact on politics.

But how do religious behavior and belief influence an individual's vote? The last chapter noted three important ways that religious belonging can influence the political choices of individuals: *core values* of religious communities, *internal cues* about politics in religious communities, and *external appeals* from political organizations. Religious behavior can be relevant to all three.[7] First, frequent religious practice can bring adherents into fuller contact with their faith, increasing the likelihood that they will accept the core values of their religious communities. Even private religious activities, such as prayer, can have such an effect by bringing core values to mind. Second, frequent religious practice increases the likelihood that the individual will hear an internal cue, such as a sermon on a political issue, and/or receive an external appeal, such as a telephone call from a political campaign.

In partial contrast, religious beliefs influence the vote primarily by affecting the acceptance of the community's core values by individual adherents. After all, beliefs are frequently the original source of the core values espoused by a religious community and taught to its members. However, certain kinds of community beliefs, such as views on the appropriate role of religion in public affairs, can increase the believers' receptivity to internal cues and external appeals. Although conceptually distinct, religious behavior and belief often operate together: beliefs typically provide the warrant for religious practice, and practice is an important way that individuals learn about religious beliefs.

Table 1.2 (in Chapter 1) showed some strong evidence of this new pattern, the close association between frequency of worship attendance and the vote. Of course, religious behavior and belief includes far more than just worship attendance.

Religious Traditionalism

In fact, American religious behavior and belief are nearly as diverse as religious belonging (see the "ABCs of Religious Affiliation" in chapter 2). One useful way to simplify the complexity of religious practice and doctrine is through the concept of "religious traditionalism." Religious traditionalism is the extent to which individuals partake of the practices and doctrines that help define the religious tradition to which they belong. Hence, some adherents of a religious tradition may be more "traditional" (that is, more accepting of the normative behaviors and beliefs of the community) and others may be less "traditional" (less accepting of such things). Just as members of different traditions tend to vote different ways, more and less traditional members of a single religious tradition may vote differently as well.

Because there are many religious traditions in the United States, there are potentially many forms of religious traditionalism. This fact presents analysts with the challenge of measuring appropriate normative behaviors and beliefs tradition by tradition—a daunting practical problem. In this regard, two considerations are quite helpful.[8] First, scholars have identified basic features of religious practice and doctrine that occur in most religious traditions, and certainly the major traditions in the United States. Such concepts are of necessity abstract, but they allow for a comparative assessment of the degree of individual traditionalism across religious traditions.

Second, these basic features of religion can be thought of as having a common reference point, namely, the *absence* of the behavior and belief in question, the fullest expression of which would be a fully "secular" or non-religious person. Put another way, each of the basic features of practice and belief can be thought of as departures from the *absence* of such practice or belief. In this regard, the normative expectations of each religious tradition would be that individual adherents should have higher levels of these basic types of religious practice and belief rather than lower levels—and ultimately, no practice or belief at all.

These two considerations make it possible to assess the degree of an individual's traditionalism across religious traditions: by measuring the extent to which they engage in basic religious practices and hold basic religious beliefs. What follows is a checklist of the basic features of religious practice and doctrine that are important in the United States. This checklist illustrates the major elements of religious traditionalism, their relationship to each other, and the extent to which they have become politicized.

A Checklist of Religious Behavior and Belief

Scholars have identified three major features of religious behavior that are common in the major religious traditions in the United States.[9] The first is participation in *public rituals*, the best known example of which is worship attendance. The second kind of practice is *support for religious organizations*. Good examples include financial contributions to local congregations and participation in small groups for religious purposes (such as prayer, Scripture study, or support groups). The third kind of practice is *private devotion*. Here, prayer and Scripture reading outside of worship are good examples.

Scholars have also identified two kinds of religious belief that occur in most religious traditions in the United States.[10] The first might be called *theistic beliefs*, beliefs about the nature of the divine and its relationship to human kind; good examples are beliefs about God and an afterlife. The second type of belief concerns the source of *religious authority*. Here, views on the authority of the Scripture are a good example.

Tables 3.1 through 3.5 review specific examples of these five basic types of religious behavior and belief, using a 2004 survey with an extensive set of questions about religion.[11] Although this particular collection of questions is by no means comprehensive nor universal, it does fit the major religious traditions in the United States reasonably well. Limitations of the individual measures will be noted where appropriate.

In each case, the tables first describe the frequency of a behavior or belief in the adult population, listing the responses in order of what is arguably the most to the least "traditional" responses. Next, the measures are put in religious context by showing the percentage of each response category that reported that religion is salient in their lives, that supported preserving tradition within their denomination, and that claimed their religion was relevant to their political views. Salience and political relevance are measured in the same way as in table 2.1 (in chapter 2).[12] Support for preserving tradition is the percentage of respondents who agreed with the statement, "My denomination should strive to preserve traditional beliefs and practices."[13]

This information provides a common baseline for comparing the specific measures of practice and doctrine to one another. In this regard, religious salience reveals how strongly the behavior or belief is linked to the subjective importance of religion to the individual respondents. Support for preserving tradition provides a direct warrant for judgments about which response categories are more and less "traditional." And political relevance reveals the degree to which

Table 3.1   Worship Attendance

	Size	Religion Salient	Preserve Tradition	Religion Politically Relevant
More than once a week	17.4	94.9	57.6	72.6
Once a week	25.9	84.7	49.8	51.7
1-2 a month	15.9	55.8	32.0	31.8
A few times a year	16.1	36.5	23.4	23.5
Seldom	13.8	23.7	17.7	17.2
Never	10.9	18.4	11.6	15.5
ALL	100.0	58.4	35.7	38.6
"Traditionalism Gap"		76.5	46.0	57.1

Source: 2004 National Survey of Religion and Politics.

individual practice and doctrines are politicized. (The "traditionalism gap" between the more and less "traditional" responses for salience, preserving tradition, and political relevance are listed in the bottom row of each table.)

Public Ritual Behavior. Most religious traditions have strong expectations regarding participation in public rituals by their adherents. Worship attendance is the most common example in the United States, and one of the most commonly asked religion questions in surveys. Partly for this reason, journalists and other observers quickly noticed the appearance of a strong connection to the presidential vote. Indeed, this relationship was the basis for the much discussed "God gap" in the 2004 campaign. This connection made intuitive sense, given the widely reported politicking in congregations, from "voter guides" distributed in evangelical churches to get-out-the-vote drives in black churches.[14]

Table 3.1 looks at a typical measure of worship attendance. In this survey, a little more than two-fifths of the respondents reported attending worship once a week or more (more "traditional" responses), about one-third claimed to attend at least a few times a year, and the remaining one-quarter said they attend rarely or never (less "traditional" responses). So the number of reported weekly worship attenders is about the same size as all Evangelical and Mainline Protestants combined; and the number of non-attenders is about the size of all Evangelical Protestants (see table 2.1 in chapter 2 on the relative size of religious traditions).

There is considerable scholarly controversy surrounding the accuracy of worship attendance figures reported in surveys. Some scholars have argued that such responses consistently over-report the actual level of attendance.[15] After all, strong social desirability effects may lead many people to inflate their frequency of attendance, much as they do for other socially approved behaviors, like voting. In fact, question wording that seeks to correct for social desirability effects often produces lower levels of reported attendance.[16]

While these considerations raise doubts about the number of people who actually attend worship, they do not change the underlying relationship between reported attendance and the vote. Indeed, whatever is actually being measured in surveys regarding worship attendance, it has been measured with a great deal of consistency in numerous surveys for many years.[17]

In this regard, it is worth noting that in table 3.1 the frequency of attendance is strongly associated with religious salience, with nearly all of the weekly attenders reporting high religious salience compared to about just one-seventh of those who never attend (a "traditionalism gap" of 76.5 percentage points). Also note a strong positive relationship with preserving tradition: more than three-fifths of the greater-than-weekly attenders agreed with preserving tradition compared to just one-tenth of respondents who claim to never attend worship (a gap of some 46.0 percentage points). Note also that frequent attenders reported higher political relevance of their religions than the non-attenders (a gap of almost 57.1 percentage points).

In sum, the level of reported worship attendance is fairly evenly distributed across the adult population and is strongly related to religious salience, preserving tradition, and religious relevance to politics. Because of its centrality in news coverage, we will more fully explore the politics of worship attendance shortly.

Support for Religious Organizations. Nearly all religious traditions have firm expectations that adherents will donate money and time to support religious organizations. This expectation is especially true in the United States where congregations are voluntary organizations. Table 3.2 looks at two measures of support for religious organizations: financial contributions to a congregation and participation in small groups for a religious propose. These are just two examples of the rich organizational life of congregations.[18]

Both of these kinds of organizational support can have political implications. The financial resources of congregations can have a direct impact on politics, and there is considerable controversy over the rules imposed on such activities by the tax-exempt status of congregations—both in the breach and in the observance. In any event, individuals who give to congregations can also donate to political organizations. Likewise, participants in small groups are a potential recruit for political activity, whether it is Bible study groups, such as the one George W. Bush participated in as a young man in Texas, or prayer groups that engage in anti-war protests.[19]

In this survey, high levels of reported financial giving and small group participation were both less common than reported weekly worship attendance. For example, a little more than one-quarter of the adult Americans reported contributing ten percent or more of their annual income to their congregation (the most "traditional" response); almost one-half claimed to give less than ten percent of their income to a congregation; and one-quarter reported no contribution at all (the least "traditional" response).[20]

Small group participation had a similar distribution in the population: more than one-quarter reported attending a small group once a week or more often (the most "traditional" response); another one-third reported participating at least

Table 3.2   Support for Religious Organizations

	Size	Religion Salient	Preserve Tradition	Religion Politically Relevant
Financial Support				
More than 10% of income	9.5	94.8	56.8	73.8
10% income	18.4	84.4	52.0	58.4
6 to 9%	10.1	80.6	47.1	52.8
1 to 5%	36.4	55.9	33.4	31.7
None	25.4	20.0	15.2	16.5
ALL	**100.0**	**58.4**	**35.7**	**38.8**
"Traditionalism Gap"		*74.8*	*41.6*	*57.3*
Small Group Participation				
Once a week or more	27.4	89.5	52.8	64.7
Once a month or more	14.1	75.2	40.9	47.1
Occasionally	19.4	58.5	36.2	37.0
Never	39.1	30.8	21.8	18.6
ALL	**100.0**	**58.4**	**35.7**	**38.8**
"Traditionalism Gap"		*58.7*	*31.0*	*46.1*

Source: 2004 National Survey of Religion and Politics

occasionally; and the remaining two-fifths claimed to not participate in small groups at all (the least "traditional" response).[21]

Like worship attendance, financial support was also positively associated with religious salience, with more than 90 percent of those reporting a contribution of 10 percent or more reporting a high level of salience. In contrast, only about one-eighth of those who made no contributions reported religion to be highly salient (a gap of 74.8 percentage points). Similar patterns obtained for preserving tradition and political relevance (gaps of 41.6 and 57.3 percentage points, respectively).

However, small group participation showed weaker patterns with those variables, including religious salience (a gap of nearly 58.7 percentage points), preserving tradition (31.0 percentage points), and political relevance (46.1 percentage points).

Although the frequency of financial contributions was less common than worship attendance, its relationship to religious and political variables was very similar. Also, less common than worship attendance, small group participation was less strongly linked to other religious and political variables. This difference may reflect, on the one hand, the stronger connection of giving to congregational life, and on the other hand, the fact that some small groups occur outside of congregations.

Private Devotion. Most religious traditions have strong expectations concerning the private devotional life of adherents. In this regard, personal prayer is a nearly universal norm. Another common devotional practice in the United States is reading Scripture, a practice especially common among Protestants, but which has spread to non-Protestants in recent times.[22]

Private prayer and Scripture reading can have direct political implications as well. After all, religious people are frequently asked to pray for political leaders and the nation as a whole, and when scriptural passages are cited to support political arguments on issues, individuals are often urged to "look up the reference for themselves." These activities have parallels in the public prayers offered during campaigns and the use of biblical references by politicians. These kinds of activities were especially evident in 2004.[23]

The first entry in table 3.3 reports the frequency of prayer outside of worship among adult Americans. Overall, three-fifths reported praying at least once a day (a more "traditional" response), another one-sixth claimed to pray once a month or more often, and the remaining one-fifth reported praying only occasionally or never (less "traditional" responses).

The second entry in table 3.3 reports the frequency of reading Scripture outside of worship. Overall, it was less common than private prayer: one-fifth of the respondents reported reading Scripture every day (the most "traditional" response); another one-fifth doing so at least once a week; and nearly one-half

Table 3.3   Private Devotion

	Size	Religion Salient	Preserve Tradition	Religion Politically Relevant
Pray Outside of Worship				
Once a day or more	61.4	80.1	46.7	52.1
Once a week or more	13.2	44.2	31.5	29.8
Once a month or more	3.7	28.9	15.9	14.3
Occasionally	9.7	21.5	16.3	13.8
Never	12.1	4.4	7.1	9.3
ALL	**100.0**	**58.4**	**35.7**	**38.8**
"Traditionalism Gap"		*75.7*	*39.6*	*42.8*
Read Scripture Outside of Worship				
Once a day or more	21.2	93.8	57.0	71.8
Once a week or more	21.8	83.3	48.6	51.9
Once a month or more	10.4	57.3	33.6	34.5
Occasionally	20.3	48.9	28.2	24.9
Never	26.4	17.9	15.0	14.4
ALL	**100.0**	**58.4**	**35.7**	**38.8**
"Traditionalism Gap"		*75.9*	*42.8*	*57.4*

Source: 2004 National Survey of Religion and Politics

claimed to read Scripture only occasionally or never (less "traditional" responses).

Thus, daily prayer is 50 percent more common than weekly worship attendance in this survey (61 to 43 percent), but daily Scripture reading is only one-half as common as weekly attendance (21 to 43 percent).

The frequency of prayer was less strongly associated with religious salience than was worship attendance, with less than three-fifths of those who pray most frequently reporting a high level of religious salience. But there is still a sharp gradient with regard to salience (a gap of 75.7 percentage points). Likewise, frequency of prayer was less associated with preserving tradition and political relevance: only about one-half of the most frequent prayers held either view. However, there was still a large disparity between frequent prayers and non-prayers on these matters (and gaps of about 40 percentage points in each case).

In contrast, the frequency of private Scripture reading more closely resembled the patterns for worship attendance. More than 90 percent of those who read Scripture daily reported high religious salience, almost three-fifths agreed with preserving tradition, and seven of ten reported high religious relevance. In contrast, those who never read Scripture reported much lower levels in all these respects (with gaps of roughly 75.9, 42.8, and 57.4 percentage points, respectively).

These differences may reflect, on the one hand, the extensiveness of private prayer as well as the many varieties of prayer,[24] and on the other hand, the likely association of Scripture reading with the authority of Scripture (an issue to be discussed shortly.)

Theistic Beliefs. Belief in the divine is part of all religious traditions—in fact, it is often used as a defining characteristic of religion. Beliefs about the divine are quite often connected to beliefs about the afterlife. Of course, there are many views of the divine and the afterlife, but all of these conceptions are challenged by modern secular worldviews, which cast doubt on the nature, if not the very existence of the divine. Many scholars see this debate at the center of modern religious life, with important implications for politics.

Sometimes a particular vision of the divine—including its non-existence—is used in political arguments. And certainly American "civil religion" involves the general invocation of God on a regular basis. However, views of God more typically serve as the foundation for the logic of political perspectives, thus influencing issue positions indirectly. Such theistic logic is widely recognized in the United States, which is one reason journalists jumped readily from the attendance gap to the "God gap."[25]

The first entry in table 3.4 presents a composite measure of belief in God and the type of God believed in, with a focus on views common among Americans. Here, two-fifths of the adult population believed in a personal God (a more "traditional" response in the Abrahamic faiths); nearly as many believed in a more abstract deity, either a spirit inherent in the world or an impersonal force; and

Table 3.4   Belief in God and the Afterlife

	Size	Religion Salient	Preserve Tradition	Religion Politically Relevant
Believe in God				
Believe in a Personal God	*40.0*	83.0	55.1	61.3
Believe in a Spiritual God	*28.4*	60.5	30.1	32.0
Believe in an Impersonal God	*12.8*	44.5	26.9	25.3
Unsure if God Exists	*10.6*	14.6	11.3	11.5
God Does Not exit	*8.2*	9.2	5.5	8.5
ALL	**100.0**	**58.4**	**35.7**	**38.8**
"Traditionalism Gap"		*73.8*	*49.3*	*52.8*
Life After Death				
Life After Death Obtained by Right Belief	*28.6*	84.6	55.3	63.9
Life After Death Obtained by Right Behavior	*28.5*	66.8	40.0	39.8
Unsure about Life After Death	*25.9*	41.2	22.9	22.8
There is no Life After Death	*16.9*	27.4	16.3	19.4
ALL	**100.0**	**58.4**	**35.7**	**38.8**
"Traditionalism Gap"		*57.2*	*39.0*	*44.5*

Source: 2004 National Survey of Religion and Politics

one-tenth of the respondents were unsure about God and less than one-tenth claimed to not believe in God at all (the least "traditional" responses).

The second entry in table 3.4 is also a composite measure about life after death, including belief in an afterlife and views of how the afterlife is obtained. The latter is focused on views common in the United States, such as obtaining life after death by having the right beliefs (a more "traditional" Protestant view) or by engaging in the right behavior (a more "traditional" view outside of Protestantism). A little more than one-quarter of the adult population said "right belief" was the way to obtain life after death, while the same proportion chose "right behavior." Another one-quarter were unsure about life after death and the remaining one-sixth did not believe in an afterlife (the least "traditional" responses).

Both of these belief measures were strongly associated with religious salience and at about the same level: more than four-fifths of respondents who believed in a personal God and that life after death is obtained by "right belief" reported high religious salience. The salience figures for respondents who did not believe in God or an afterlife were much lower (a gap of 73.8 and 57.2 percentage points, respectively). A similar pattern held for preserving tradition and religious relevance (with gaps of around 50 and 40 percentage points, respectively).

In this survey, belief in a personal God was roughly as common as weekly worship attendance, while the first two responses on obtaining life after death were together about 14 percentage points larger. The patterns with salience, preserving tradition, and religious relevance closely resemble the patterns for worship attendance.

Source of Religious Authority. One common form of religious authority is the authority of Scripture and other sacred writings. This belief is of special importance to Protestants, but in the United States, Scripture has high status outside of Protestantism as well.[26] Of course, "biblical worldviews" face stiff challenges in the modern world, and in the United States one of the strongest challenges comes from the authority of science. A good example of this challenge is the theory of biological evolution and its account of the origins of life on earth.[27]

Unlike views of the divine, the Bible plays a direct and controversial role in contemporary politics. Indeed, much of the opposition to abortion and same-sex marriage is founded directly on interpretations of the moral standards in the Old and New Testaments. Likewise, biblical passages on justice and help for the poor are a regular staple of arguments for social welfare programs. In these and other areas, the authority of science is often contraposed with biblical mandates. Arguments over stem cell research, end of life issues, and environmental regulation are good examples, but surely the most persistent of these controversies is the debate over science curriculum in public schools. Many of these conflicts were on display in the 2004 campaign.[28]

Table 3.5 reports a composite item on the authority of the Bible. More than one-third of adult Americans believed the Bible was the Word of God to be taken literally, and roughly another one-quarter believed the Bible was the Word of God, but not to be taken literally (more "traditional" responses); another two-fifths held that the Bible was the Word of God but contained human errors in the text or that the Bible was simply a great book of wisdom and history; and about one-tenth said it was a book of myths and legends (a less "traditional" response).

The second entry in table 3.5 reports the degree of disagreement with the statement, "Evolution is the best explanation for life on earth." Almost one-half of the adult population disagreed or strongly disagreed with this statement (more "traditional" responses); another one-sixth had no opinion; and a little less than two-fifths agreed or strongly agreed (less "traditional" responses).

Views of biblical authority were strongly associated with religious salience, with more than four-fifths of biblical literalists reporting religion as important in their life. In contrast, of those who view the Bible as a book of myths and legends, less than one-sixth reported religion as salient (for a gap of 68.4 percentage points). Very similar patterns held for preserving tradition and the political relevance of religion. Better than three-fifths of biblical literalists reported high figures on both measures, while individuals with the opposite views reportedly score the lowest levels (for gaps of around 50 percentage points).

Table 3.5   Views of the Bible and Evolution

	Size	Religion Salient	Preserve Tradition	Religion Politically Relevant
The Bible is...				
Word of God, To Be Taken Literally	*35.4*	84.0	58.8	62.7
Word of God, Not to be Taken Literally	*13.2*	64.7	36.1	41.0
Word of God, but with some human errors	*14.4*	67.0	34.1	36.1
A Great Book of Wisdom and History	*27.5*	32.9	16.0	18.1
A Book of Myths and Legends	*9.5*	15.6	9.5	11.6
ALL	**100**	**58.4**	**35.9**	**38.8**
"Traditionalism Gap"		*68.4*	*49.3*	*51.1*
Evolution is the Best Explanation for Life on Earth				
Strongly Disagree	*20.6*	85.1	61.5	68.4
Disagree	*27.3*	67.1	44.5	40.8
No Opinion	*14.4*	60.1	37.4	37.4
Agree	*25.8*	39.3	21.3	21.3
Strongly Agree	*11.8*	30.5	20.0	20.0
ALL	**100.0**	**58.4**	**35.7**	**38.8**
"Traditionalism Gap"		*54.6*	*41.5*	*48.4*

Source: 2004 National Survey of Religion and Politics

A modestly different pattern appears for evolution, with more than four-fifths of the strongest anti-evolutionists reporting salient religion—but so did about one-third of the strongest backers of evolution (for a gap of 54.6 percentage points). And there were also weaker patterns for preserving tradition and political relevance. Better than three-fifths of the strongest anti-evolutionists reported high figures on both measures, while pro-evolutionists reported the lowest levels (the gap was 41.5 and 48.4 percentage points, respectively). The followers of Charles Darwin appear to include a few more traditionally religious people than common stereotypes suggest.

In this survey, individuals with the two highest views of Scriptural authority and the anti-evolutionists were a little more numerous than weekly worship attenders. The patterns for salience, preserving tradition, and relevance to politics resemble such patterns for worship attendance as well as for the measures of belief in God and life after death.

A Single Measure of Traditionalism

This checklist of religious behaviors and beliefs suggests that these matters are closely related to each other. Indeed, the consistent association of the more

Table 3.6   Elements of Religious Traditionalism, 2004

Frequency of Bible Reading	0.82
Frequency of Church attendance	0.79
View of God	0.78
Frequency of Prayer	0.74
View of the Bible	0.74
Small group participation	0.73
Contribution to Congregation	0.69
View of Life After Death	0.67
View of Evolution	0.64

Source: 2004 National Survey of Religion and Politics

traditional responses with religious salience, preservation of tradition, and political relevance points toward an overall measure of traditionalism, of which each of these items is a part. In fact, a statistical analysis of all these survey items reveals a single underlying dimension of traditionalism.[29]

Table 3.6 reports the association of all these measures with the underlying measure of traditionalism (the larger the figure, the stronger the association). Scripture reading and worship attendance scored highest in this regard (about .8), followed by views of God, frequency of prayer, views of Scriptural authority, and small group participation. Financial contributions, views of life after death, and evolution are the least strongly associated with the underlying dimension of traditionalism, but the relationship is nevertheless robust. Thus, while these particular measures of religious practice and doctrine may not cover all aspects of religiosity, they do contain elements of traditional religiosity.

What is the association of this measure of traditionalism to the vote? Table 3.7 considers this question by dividing the traditionalism dimension into deciles and reporting the 2004 two-party presidential vote for each decile, ranging from the most to least traditional categories. The results are striking, resembling the patterns in tables 1.2 and 1.3 (in chapter 1) using the simpler NEP data.

The respondents in the most traditional decile voted 82 percent for Bush and 18 percent for Kerry. Meanwhile, individuals in the least traditional decile voted just 25 percent for Bush and 75 percent for Kerry. And voters in the fifth and sixth decile—those in the middle of this traditionalism scale—divided their ballots almost evenly between the presidential candidates. Indeed, there is a smooth and steady relationship between traditionalism and the two-party vote, with just one exception: Bush does slightly worse than might have been expected in the seventh decile. This anomaly reflects the influence of religious belonging (in the form of religious traditions) on the vote, where some Mainline Protestants and Catholics voted less Republican than their level of traditionalism would suggest.

Table 3.7   Traditionalism Scale and the 2004 Two-party Presidential Vote

Traditionalism Scale Deciles	Bush	Kerry
Most Traditional 1	82.1	17.9
2	67.6	32.4
3	64.5	35.5
4	54.1	45.9
Mid-point 5	52.9	47.1
Mid-point 6	48.4	51.6
7	31.7	68.3
8	38.8	61.2
9	34.2	65.8
Least Traditional 10	25.1	74.9
ALL	51.2	48.8

Source: 2004 National Survey of Religion and Politics

Indeed, the powerful findings in table 3.7 reflect in part the degree of traditionalism that characterizes the major religious traditions—as in table 2.1 (in chapter 2). For example, the strongest Republican constituency, Evangelical Protestants, scored higher on worship attendance and Scriptural authority, two important elements of the traditionalism scale, than Mainline Protestants and Catholics, who split their votes between the parties. But similarly, Black Protestants also scored high on these religious measures and voted heavily Democratic. Thus, a full picture of the impact of traditionalism requires taking membership in a religious tradition into account.

Table 3.8 addresses the combined effects of religious belonging, behaving, and believing on the 2004 two-party presidential vote for each religious tradition (or composite category) as a whole, and then for divisions within the major traditions based on traditionalism. Evangelical Protestants, Mainline Protestants, and Catholics are divided into "traditionalists," "centrists," and "modernists" according to their score on the traditionalism measure. Using a slightly different method, the Unaffiliated are divided into "unaffiliated believers," "seculars," and self-identified atheists and agnostics.[30]

Table 3.8 shows some interesting results. For one thing, within in the three largest religious traditions, traditionalists voted more heavily for Bush and the modernists more heavily for Kerry. These differences are striking. For Evangelicals, the traditionalist-modernist "gap" is 40 percentage points, and among Mainline Protestants it was 46 percent. And note that the "centrists" always fall in between the traditionalists and modernists in terms of the vote. Similar divisions appear among the Unaffiliated, with the "unaffiliated believers" voting more for Bush than the atheists and agnostics. But also notice that the religious traditions still matter: traditionalist Evangelicals were more supportive of Bush than traditionalists among Mainline Protestants and Catholics. A similar pattern holds for the modernists, and to a lesser extent, the centrists.

Table 3.8   Religious Traditions, Traditionalism, and the 2004 Two-Party Presidential
Vote

	Presidential Vote		
	Bush	Kerry	Percent of Population
ALL EVANGELICAL PROTESTANT	*78*	*22*	*26.3*
Traditionalist Evangelical Protestant	**88**	**12**	**12.6**
Centrist Evangelical Protestant	**64**	**36**	**10.8**
Modernist Evangelical Protestant	**48**	**52**	**2.9**
ALL MAINLINE PROTESTANT	*50*	*50*	*16.0*
Traditionalist Mainline Protestant	**68**	**32**	**4.3**
Centrist Mainline Protestant	**58**	**42**	**7.0**
Modernist Mainline Protestant	**22**	**78**	**4.7**
Latino Protestant	**63**	**37**	**2.8**
Black Protestant	**17**	**83**	**9.6**
ALL NON-LATINO CATHOLIC	*53*	*47*	*17.5*
Traditionalist Catholic	**72**	**28**	**4.4**
Centrist Catholic	**55**	**45**	**8.1**
Modernist Catholic	**31**	**69**	**5.0**
Latino Catholic	**31**	**69**	**4.5**
Other Christians	**80**	**20**	**2.7**
Other Faiths	**23**	**77**	**2.7**
Jews	**27**	**73**	**1.9**
ALL UNAFFILIATED	*28*	*72*	*16.0*
Unaffiliated Believers	**37**	**63**	**5.3**
Seculars	**30**	**70**	**7.5**
Atheists, Agnostics	**18**	**82**	**3.2**
ENTIRE ELECTORATE	**51**	**49**	**100.0**

Source: 2004 National Survey of Religion and Politics

Taken together, these findings demonstrate the importance of the "restructuring" of American religion, and the political relevance of the "politics of behaving
and belief" in the 2004 election. It also suggests that there was a good bit of truth
to the "God gap" widely discussed by journalists in the coverage of the 2004

campaign. Of course, the effects of traditionalism are more complex and subtle than the "God gap" news stories implied. For one thing, the "God gap" language missed the fact that people with less traditional views of God are not all "non-believers," but include people with a different understanding of faith. Thus, both George Bush and John Kerry had numerous religious constituencies in 2004. Furthermore, there are a lot of "people in the middle" in terms of traditionalism. Whatever it is called, the New Religion Gap was a very real thing in 2004.

Exploring the Attendance Gap

Unfortunately, very few surveys contain enough questions on religious practice and doctrine to develop the religious categories presented in tables 3.7 and 3.8. In fact, the NEP survey only has one such measure: worship attendance. Of course, as we have just seen, worship attendance is strongly associated with other measures of traditionalism, and as was shown in tables 1.2 and 1.3 (chapter 1), it was also strongly associated with the 2004 presidential vote. This raises a practical question: is worship attendance by itself a good measure of traditionalism?

Figure 3.1 strongly suggests that the answer is "yes." This figure plots the vote for President Bush for the six categories of attendance (the solid line) and the 10 deciles of a traditionalism scale (the dotted line) recalculated without worship attendance (but otherwise the same as in table 3.7).

Clearly, the more traditional the respondents, the more likely they were to vote for Bush in 2004—the less traditional, the more likely they were to vote for Kerry (dotted line). And notice how closely worship attendance paralleled this pattern (solid line). As one might expect, the full traditionalism scale—containing a variety of religious behaviors and beliefs—predicts the presidential vote a bit better than worship attendance by itself. Nonetheless, worship attendance was a good proxy for the traditionalism scale.

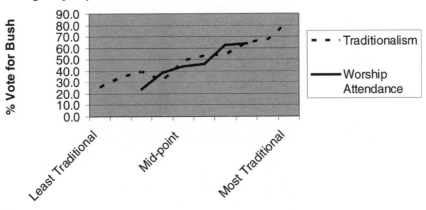

Figure 3.1   Traditionalism Scale, Worship Attendance, and 2004 Presidential Vote

Source: 2004 National Survey of Religion and Politics

Table 3.9   Worship Attendance and the Presidential Vote, 2004

		Two-Party Vote			Voter Coalitions	
	Size	**Bush**	**Kerry**	Turnout	*Bush*	*Kerry*
More than once a week	*17.4*	63.7	36.3	**64.9**	*22.9*	*13.7*
Once a week	*25.9*	62.8	37.2	**67.1**	*36.5*	*22.7*
1-2 a month	*15.9*	46.3	53.7	**61.5**	*14.3*	*17.3*
A few times a year	*16.1*	44.0	56.0	**56.4**	*12.2*	*16.3*
Seldom	*13.8*	38.8	61.2	**54.3**	*9.9*	*16.3*
Never	*10.9*	24.3	75.7	**53.4**	*4.2*	*13.6*
ALL	**100.0**	**51.2**	**48.8**	**60.9**	*100.0*	*100.0*

Source: 2004 National Survey of Religion and Politics

Table 3.9 displays the full range of the "attendance gap" using a post-election survey with six categories. These survey data differ a little from table 1.2 (in chapter 1) in that the attendance gap is not as symmetrical. For example, the "never attend" respondents gave Kerry stronger support than weekly attenders gave Bush—but also there were significantly fewer of them, so the Republicans came out marginally ahead.

This survey contains an estimate of voter turnout across the attendance categories (fourth column), and turnout also benefited Bush. About two-thirds of the weekly attenders went to the polls—roughly 14 percentage points greater than the never attenders. As a consequence, the weekly attenders made up nearly three-fifths of all Bush's ballots. This figure was significantly larger than weekly attenders for Kerry (a bit more than one-third of all his ballots) and about twice the proportion Kerry received from the seldom and never attenders combined (three in ten of all his ballots). Clearly, the attendance gap favored Bush in the 2004 election. (However, such a gap could favor a Democratic candidate that did a bit better among the less observant.)

Table 3.10 explores the attendance gap in a little more detail by expanding table 1.3 to show the attendance gap in all of the religious traditions, using the NEP data. These results must be viewed with great caution because the number of cases is very small in some of the religious groups. This table parallels table 3.8, and the pattern is even more striking: in every single case, weekly attenders voted more Republican than less than weekly attenders.

As one might expect, the attendance gap in Democratic constituencies, such as Latino Catholics, the Unaffiliated, and Black Protestants was relatively small. More of a surprise was the size of the gap in strong Republican constituencies, such as Evangelicals, Other Christians, and Latino Protestants. Thus, traditionalism made a big difference even in highly Republican religious communities. But here, too, religious tradition still mattered a great deal. Weekly attending Evangelicals were almost 19 percentage points more likely to vote for Bush than weekly attending Catholics (78.8 to 59.9 percent). Likewise, Mainline Protestants were always less Republican than Evangelicals—indeed, weekly

Table 3.10   The Attendance Gap by Religious Tradition, 2004

	Bush	Kerry	Attendance Gap
Evangelical Protestant	**78.8**	**21.2**	**10.6**
Weekly Attending Evangelicals	*82.5*	*17.5*	
Less Observant Evangelicals	*71.9*	*28.1*	
Other Christians	**74.0**	**26.0**	**18.7**
Weekly Attending Other Christians	*77.5*	*22.5*	
Less Observant Other Christians	*58.8*	*41.2*	
Latino Protestant	**56.6**	**43.4**	**19.3**
Weekly Attending Latino Protestants	*64.7*	*35.3*	
Less Observant Latino Protestants	*45.4*	*54.6*	
Non-Latino Catholic	**55.3**	**44.7**	**8.5**
Weekly Attending Catholics	*59.9*	*40.1*	
Less Observant Catholics	*51.4*	*48.6*	
Mainline Protestant	**53.3**	**46.7**	**5.2**
Weekly Attending Mainline Protestants	*57.3*	*42.7*	
Less Observant Mainline Protestants	*52.1*	*47.9*	
Latino Catholic	**36.9**	**63.1**	**2.5**
Weekly Attending Latino Catholics	*38.3*	*61.7*	
Less Observant Latino Catholics	*35.8*	*64.2*	
Unaffiliated	**27.1**	**72.9**	**5.7**
Weekly Attending Unaffiliated	*32.6*	*67.4*	
Less Observant Unaffiliated	*26.9*	*73.1*	
Jews	**23.4**	**76.6**	**12.5**
Weekly Attending Jews	*34.6*	*65.4*	
Less Observant Jews	*22.1*	*77.9*	
Other Faiths	*17.6*	*82.4*	*5.3*
Weekly Attending Other Faiths	*19.7*	*80.3*	
Less Observant Other Faiths	*14.4*	*85.6*	
Black Protestant	*13.5*	*86.5*	*8.4*
Weekly Attending Black Protestants	*16.9*	*83.1*	
Less Observant Black Protestants	*8.5*	*91.5*	
ALL	*51.0*	*49.0*	

Source: 2004 National Election Pool (NEP)

attending Mainliners vote less for Bush than the less observant Evangelicals (57 to 71 percent). And note that some of the religious traditions with the highest level of weekly attenders, including Black Protestants and Latino Catholics, voted heavily for Kerry.

The Attendance Gap: 2004 and 1944

As noted above, the New Religion Gap is a relatively recent phenomenon. What follows is a comparison of the effects of worship attendance on the presidential vote in 2004 and 1944, using the same over time survey data employed in the previous chapter.[31]

Table 3.11   Frequency of Worship Attendance, 2004 and 1944

	2004	1944
Attend:		
Weekly or more	43.3	42.9
Less than weekly	56.7	57.1
ALL	*100.0*	*100.0*

Source: 2004 National Survey of Religion and Politics, 1944 AIPO 335

As with religious affiliation, comparing religious behavior over a 60 year period is problematic. For one thing, few questions on religious practice were asked in the 1940s (and even fewer on religious beliefs), and when they are available, they are not strictly comparable to present day questions.[32]

Table 3.11 looks at one case where a minimum degree of comparability can be secured: weekly worship attendance in 2004 and 1944. The 2004 survey used here shows that 43 percent of adult Americans reported attending worship weekly. In the 1944 data, the figure was also about 43 percent, a figure that fits with the most comparable survey questions on worship attendance asked in the 1940s.[33]

Table 3.12 reports the relationship between worship attendance and the presidential vote in 2004 and 1944. In 2004, there was a sharp partisan difference based on reported attendance. Among reported weekly attenders, President Bush received more than three-fifths of the ballots and Senator John Kerry received less than two-fifths. In contrast, among the less observant, just two-fifths voted for Bush and three-fifths for Kerry. These findings are comparable to the 2004 NEP data in table 1.2.

The situation in 1944 was quite different: there was essentially no difference between the votes of reported weekly and less than weekly worship attenders. Indeed, about 46 percent of both the weekly and less than weekly attenders voted for Governor Dewey, the Republican nominee, and about 53 percent of both groups voted for President Roosevelt, a Democrat. Thus, there was a huge change for both parties over this 60 year period. For example, the GOP picked up nearly 17 percentage points among the reported weekly attenders—but lost the same amount among the less observant.

Table 3.12   Worship Attendance and the Presidential Vote, 2004 and 1944

| | 2004 | | 1944 | |
	Rep	Dem	Rep	Dem
Attend:				
Weekly or more	63.1	36.9	46.4	53.6
Less than weekly	40.0	60.0	46.1	53.9
ALL	*51.2*	*48.8*	*46.2*	*53.8*

Source: 2004 National Survey of Religion and Politics, 1944 AIDO 3.35

Table 3.13   Worship Attenders and Presidential Voter Coalitions, 2004 and 1944

| | 2004 | | 1944 | |
	Rep	**Dem**	**Rep**	**Dem**
Attend:				
Weekly or more	59.5	36.4	43.1	42.8
Less than weekly	40.5	63.6	56.9	57.2
ALL	*100.0*	*100.0*	*100.0*	*100.0*

Source: 2004 National Survey of Religion and Politics, 1944 AIPO 335

How important was frequency of attendance to the party's vote coalitions? Table 3.13 reports the percentage of the Republican and Democratic vote in 2004 and 1944. For President Bush, nearly three-fifths of all his ballots came from reported weekly worship attenders and the remaining two-fifths from less observant voters. The less observant were marginally more important for Senator Kerry, accounting for more than two-thirds of his ballots, while weekly attenders accounted for less than two-fifths. But back in 1944, President Roosevelt and Governor Dewey received the same proportion of the vote from weekly and less than weekly attenders—a little more than two-fifths from the former and more than one-half from the latter.

These findings reveal that the attendance gap did not exist 60 years ago, but was quite prominent in 2004. When exactly did this voter gap first emerge? Figure 3.2 plots the net Republican advantage of reported weekly attenders from 1944 to 2004 (the Democratic vote percentage is subtracted from the Republican vote percentage, so that a Republican advantage is a positive number and a Democratic advantage a negative number).[34]

Figure 3.2 shows that the attendance gap in the presidential vote appeared suddenly in 1972, rising from essentially zero to about 10 percentage points. It next

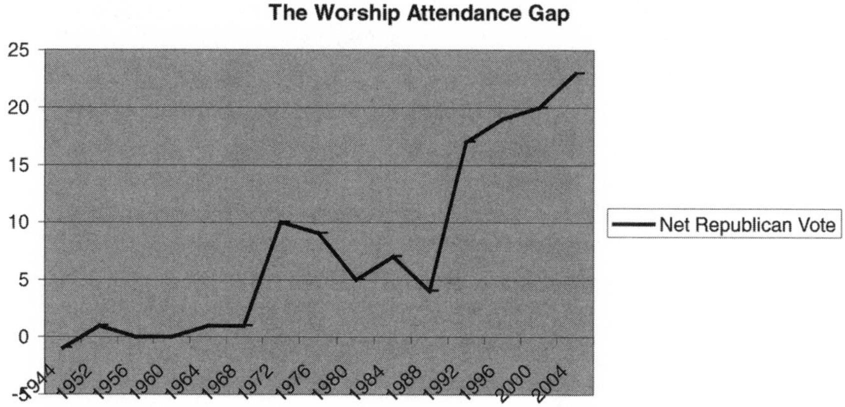

The Worship Attendance Gap

Figure 3.2   The Worship Attendance Gap, 1944-2004

Source: 2004 National Survey of Religion and Politics, 1944 AIPO 335 declined a bit during the rest of the 1970s and 1980s, reaching a low point in 1988 with about 4 percent. Then in 1992, the gap suddenly widened again and continued to grow until 2004. Thus, the attendance gap emerged in the same time that scholars began to notice the "restructuring" of American religion and the appearance of the "culture wars" in national politics.

The attendance gap was the largest during the highly polarized politics of the first years of the twenty-first century, including the 2004 election. Indeed, a glance back at figures 2.1 and 2.2 (in chapter 2) reveals that the attendance gap appeared at the time when Mainline Protestants and Catholics moved toward an even division of the presidential vote, and when Evangelicals and the Unaffiliated respectively moved into the Republican and Democratic ranks.

Conclusions

In sum, religious behavior and belief have become important factors in explaining the vote in American presidential elections. The concept of religious traditionalism is a useful way to reduce the great complexity of religious behavior and belief so as to more easily assess their political impact. In recent times, religious traditionalism has become associated with the Republican vote, while less traditional voters have tended to favor the Democrats. Indeed, one reason for the attendance gap is that worship attendance reflects the effects of traditionalism across religious communities. Thus, worship attendance can be used as a proxy for traditionalism when other aspects or measures of behavior and belief are missing. (And on a practical note, pollsters who fail to ask worship attendance in their surveys do so at their own peril.)

The New Religion Gap is of recent vintage, emerging in tandem with the "restructuring" of American religion and the appearance of the "culture wars" in 1972. However, the Old Religion Gap based on religious tradition has not disappeared. Instead, the "politics of behaving and believing" have added a new complexity to party coalitions based on the Old Religion Gap. In the next chapter, we turn to a key factor in coalition building: issues, priorities, and positions among voters.

— 4 —

The Meaning of the Religion Gaps:
Issues and Coalitions

Religion was clearly an important factor in the 2004 presidential election, both the Old Religion Gap based on religious tradition and the New Religion Gap based on religious traditionalism. These religion gaps attracted great attention in large measure because of what they implied about the meaning of the close contest. For many observers the most important consideration was the issue priorities and positions of religious voters, a concern well illustrated by the debate over the role of "moral values." As was shown in table 1.5 and 1.6 (in chapter 1), "moral values" were, in fact, a top priority for a large minority of voters who strongly backed President Bush. However, other larger minorities of voters had economic and foreign policy priorities, which influenced their vote as well.

Students of democracy have long put a special focus on the political attitudes of the electorate in general and its components parts. After all, the vote communicates the public's will about the direction of government and the future content of public policy. And taking stands on issues is one of the most important ways that candidates appeal to voters and build large enough voter coalitions to win elections. However, voting is often a very blunt instrument for communicating policy preferences, especially in the context of coalition politics, where diverse groups may support the same candidate for many different reasons. Thus, the debate over the significance of the "values voters" in the 2004 election was well placed, if fraught with confusion.

This chapter seeks to clarify the political meaning of the religion gaps by reviewing the issue priorities and positions of religious communities, and how they fit into electoral coalitions. It begins by exploring the 2004 "moral values" controversy in more detail, and then reviews the role of issue priorities in the 2004 Republican and Democratic electoral coalitions. Next, it traces changes in issues priorities between 1944 and 2004. The chapter then reviews the issue positions of religious voters in 2004, and finally, it turns to broader political identifications, ideology, and partisanship, with a look back to the past and how religious communities have changed politically. This material describes the issue content of the Old and New Religion gaps.

The Question of "Moral Values"

Even before the 2004 balloting was completed, extensive criticism was directed at the issue priorities question in the NEP, the source of the controversy in the first place. Some critics claimed the "moral values" terminology was vague, so that respondents had no clear sense of what it meant, particularly when compared to the other seven more specific options in the question, such as the war in Iraq or health care.[1] In addition, it was argued that the term "moral values" could apply to a wide variety of matters, such as personal characteristics of the presidential candidates or social justice, and not just the "hot button" social issues.[2] For these reasons, the "moral values" results were questionable, and thus the initial snap judgments about the significance of "moral values" were seriously overstated. Certainly, one could not readily assume that "moral values" meant abortion and same-sex marriage, a common assumption in the initial reports.

While these criticisms of the NEP question have some merit, they apply more to the initial interpretation of the "moral values" results than the results themselves. They certainly do not invalidate the basic NEP findings on issue priorities, which are supported by other surveys. Thus, it is worth exploring this question in a little more detail.

Defining "Moral Values"

What did the voters mean by "moral values" in the context of the 2004 election? A post-election survey of voters conducted by the Pew Research Center (PRC) offers some answers to this question.[3] The NEP question on the issue priorities was replicated, and then respondents were asked an open-ended follow-up question on what they meant by the term "moral values." Table 4.1 presents the results of the follow-up question, breaking out respondents who chose "moral values" in the first question, those choosing other issue priorities, and then the combination of both sets of respondents.

The results are quite revealing. Two-fifths of the "moral values" voters named a specific social issue, such as abortion, marriage, and embryonic stem cell research (first column). A little less than one-third mentioned "religion" or "traditional" or "family" values, a vaguer set of responses, but ones that fit well with the social issues. Thus, more than two-thirds of the "moral values" voters defined it in a fashion consistent with the initial interpretation on Election Night.

Table 4.1   Defining "Moral Values"

Moral Values Means:	"Values Voters"	Other Voters	Combined
Specific Social Issues	41.1	20.7	28.7
Religion, Traditional Values	29.5	39.5	35.6
Candidate Character	19.6	17.4	18.2
Other Issues	8.5	8.5	8.5
Political Responses	1.4	13.8	9.0
ALL	**100.0**	**100.0**	**100**

Source: 2004 Pew Research Center Post-Election Survey

However, in partial confirmation of the critics, about one-third of the "moral values" voters meant something else by the term. Almost one-fifth named candidate characteristics, such as honesty and trustworthiness, and many connected these qualities to Bush and Kerry (and some even brought up former President Clinton). To a purist, such responses may appear not to be about issues. However, the election was in fact a choice between two candidates, and applying issue priorities to the candidates would make perfect sense to some voters. Thus, many of these responses also fit well with the social issue category, albeit without a clear policy content. If these responses are counted along with specific mentions of social issues and traditional morality, then some nine of ten "moral values" voters defined the term as the conventional wisdom assumed.

Less than one-tenth of the "moral values" voters mentioned some other kind of issue, such as economic equality, helping the poor, or health care. A persuasive and even powerful case can be made for thinking of such matters as "moral values." However, few "moral values" voters used the term in that way. A final handful of these respondents offered a response that commented on the political aspects of "moral values." For example, some mentioned the "religious right" or "wedge issues," but the largest proportion said that the topic should not be an issue. These responses strongly suggest that the respondents understood "moral values" as related to social issues, albeit in a negative way.

A slightly different pattern occurred among respondents that did not identify "moral values" as a voting priority (the second column in table 4.1). Here one-fifth listed a specific social issue, but two-fifths mentioned religion or "traditional" values. Nearly one-fifth also named candidate characteristics. Thus, more than three-quarters of the respondents who did not consider "moral values" a priority defined it as related to social issues in one way or another.

It is interesting to note that the same percentage of these respondents listed another kind of issue (8.5 percent). But the biggest difference between the "moral values" and non-moral values voters was the proportion of the "political responses," given by about one-seventh of these voters. Most of these comments argued that "moral values" should not be a political issue. Of course, these voters acted on their own advice and chose issue priorities other than "moral values" as the basis of their vote.

The Number of the "Values Voters"

Thus "moral values" had a fairly clear meaning to voters in the 2004 election, and the term referred to social issues and "traditional" values or associations linked to social issues. No doubt, this meaning was partly the result of the politics of the 2004 campaign and the preceding elections. So the initial judgments about the election results were not entirely wrong, however incomplete they may have been in other respects.

But this raises another question: how many moral values voters were there in 2004? Table 4.2 presents several estimates of the number of "values voters" found in different surveys.[4] For ease of presentation, the issue priorities were reduced to three options: "moral values," foreign policy, and economic issues (as in table 1.6 in chapter 1).

The first column reports the NEP results, showing that 23.6 percent of the 2004 voters had "moral values" priorities. Although this response was the single largest of the seven options offered in the question, it is worth noting that significantly more voters picked foreign policy (36.2 percent) and economic issue priorities (40.2 percent). Thus, the initial judgment on the importance of "moral values" was clearly overstated, as the critics claimed.

Note, however, that there was remarkable agreement in the proportion of the "values voters" across these surveys. The PRC post-election replication of the NEP question actually produced a higher estimate than the NEP itself—27.8

Table 4.2   The "Values Voters" in 2004: Size and Presidential Vote

	NEP	PRC1	PRC2	AMER1	AMER2
Issue Priorities					
"Moral Values"	23.6	27.8	26.0	26.1	39.4%
Foreign Policy	36.2	37.9	46.2	38.0	63.7%
Economic Policy	40.2	34.2	27.8	35.7	46.9%
	100	**100**	**100**	**100**	
Issue Priorities and the Vote					
"Moral Values"					
Bush	82	88	83	70	61
Kerry	18	12	17	30	39
Foreign Policy					
Bush	60	51	42	55	50
Kerry	40	49	58	45	50
Economic Policy					
Bush	26	24	17	31	34
Kerry	74	76	83	69	66

Source: See Note 4
Legend: NEP = 2004 National Election Pool PRC1 = 2004 Pew Research Center, NEP Replication PRC2 = 2004 Pew Research Center, Open-ended AMER1 = 2004 National Survey of Religion and Politics, Issue Priorities AMER2 = 2004 National Survey of Religion and Politics, Issue "very important" to vote.

percent (second column). The PRC survey also asked an open-ended question on voter priorities (third column). When these specific responses are recoded using the definition of "moral values" presented in table 4.1, it produced an estimate of 26 percent for the "values voters."

The fourth column in table 4.2 looks at another type of question on issue priorities (AMER1). Here, the respondents were first asked how important social, foreign policy, and economic issues were to their vote. These questions mentioned specific issues, in effect addressing the criticism that the NEP question was too vague.[5] After assessing the relative importance of these kinds of issues, the respondents were then asked which type of issue was most important to their vote. This second question produced an estimate of 26.1 percent for the "values voters."

The fifth column in table 4.2 reports the percentage of the respondents that said that each of these kinds of issues was "very important" to their vote in the initial set of questions (AMER2). Here, the percentages do not add to 100 percent because voters could assign importance to more than one issue. These data reveal that almost two-fifths of voters saw "moral values" as "very important" to their vote—a much larger estimate for the number of "values voters" than the other measures in the table. But consistent with the other surveys, many more voters said foreign policy and economic issues were "very important" to their vote.

In addition, the 2004 exit poll conducted by the *Los Angeles Times* produced results that support these patterns. This survey also presented respondents with a list of issues, in this case 10, and asked them to choose up to two that were important to their vote. One of the options was "ethics and moral values" and a comparable analysis produced an estimate of 30.0 percent for the "values voters."[6]

These various measures of "values voters" had the same relationship to the presidential vote, as shown in the second part of table 4.2 (and similar to table 1.6 in chapter 1). Here, the table presents the Bush and Kerry vote for each of the three kinds of issue priorities.

Bush always won the "values voters" by large margins, no matter how these voters were measured. In contrast, Kerry always won the "economic policy voters" by similarly large margins. There was much more variation for the "foreign policy voters," with Bush and Kerry each winning big in one of the formulations (in the first and third columns, respectively), and more closely divided results in the remaining three. These results surely reflect the relative weight of different aspects of foreign affairs captured by the various kinds of questions asked. Of course, this pattern also holds for "moral values" and economic policy, as indicated by the relative size of Bush and Kerry's majorities across the table.

In sum, the "moral values" voters were a real phenomenon in the 2004 election, representing roughly one-quarter of voters. This large minority of the electorate had a clear preference for Bush over Kerry. But most voters had other issue priorities. Indeed, the "economic policy voters" had a strong preference for Kerry over Bush, and "foreign policy voters" were more divided.

Issue Priorities and the Presidential Voter Coalitions in 2004

How much impact did the "values voters" have on the election results? And what was their relationship, and that of other kinds of issue voters, to the Old and New Religion gaps?

Tables 4.3 and 4.4 explore these questions by presenting the NEP data in more detail (essentially combining and expanding tables 1.5 and 1.6 in chapter 1). The first three columns of these tables list the issue priorities of each religious community (and the three columns add across the page to 100 percent). So, for example, in table 4.3, 62.2 percent of Weekly Attending Evangelicals were "moral values" voters.

The last three columns present the proportion of all presidential ballots accounted for by the issue priorities in each religious category. So, for example, in table 4.3, "moral values" voters among Weekly Attending Evangelical Protestants accounted for 14.3 percent of all of Bush's ballots. All of the figures in the last three columns sum down to the bolded figures for the Republican, Swing, and Democratic constituencies—and then this set of figures sums to 100 percent (of the Bush vote).

The Republican Coalition. Table 4.3 presents this information just for the Bush voters (51 percent of the respondents that cast a ballot for Bush or Kerry). A good place to begin is with "moral values." Voters with such priorities were not the most important part of the Bush coalition. In fact, only four religious communities had a plurality with "moral issue" priorities. Three were Republican constituencies: Weekly Attending Evangelical Protestants (62.2 percent naming "moral values"); Latino Protestants (54.2 percent); and Other Christians (42.7 percent). And one was a Democratic constituency, Weekly Attending Black Protestants (76.7 percent).

However, more than one-third of the Bush voters in all the other Republican constituencies had "moral values" priorities, a pattern that held for just one other Democratic constituency (Less Observant Black Protestants at 40 percent). The Bush voters in all the other religious communities were much less likely to have "moral issue" priorities, including the Swing constituencies.

How much did Bush benefit from the "moral issue" priorities? Overall, 37.5 percent of all his ballots came from "moral values voters," with 28.7 percent coming from Republican religious constituencies and 5.8 percent from Swing and 3.0 from Democratic constituencies. And a total of 14.3 percent of all Bush's votes in this regard came from one such source, Weekly Attending Evangelical Protestants. Other major contributors in this regard were Weekly Attending Catholics (5.0 percent) and Less Observant Evangelicals (3.8 percent).

To put these figures in perspective, the contribution of the "moral values" votes among Weekly Attending Evangelicals to the total Bush vote was about

Table 4.3   The Republican Coalition in 2004

	% of Group's Vote:			% of All Bush Ballots		
	moral values	*foreign policy*	*economic policy*	*moral values*	*foreign policy*	*economic policy*
Republican Constituencies						
Weekly Attending Evangelical Protestant	**62.2**	25.6	12.2	14.3	5.9	2.8
Other Christians	**42.7**	36.0	21.3	2.2	1.9	1.1
Less Observant Evangelical Protestant	35.8	**42.8**	21.4	3.8	4.5	2.3
Weekly Attending Catholics	40.2	**42.5**	17.3	5.0	5.3	2.1
Weekly Attending Mainline Protestants	35.3	**48.0**	16.8	1.9	2.6	0.9
Latino Protestants	**54.1**	32.9	12.9	1.5	0.9	0.4
				28.7	**21.1**	**9.6**
Swing Constituencies						
Less Observant Mainline Protestants	24.4	**51.6**	24.0	3.8	8.0	3.7
Less Observant Catholics	16.1	**58.6**	25.3	2.0	7.2	3.1
				5.8	**15.2**	**6.8**
Democratic Constituencies						
Latino Catholics	23.1	38.5	38.5	0.7	1.1	1.1
Unaffiliated	13.0	**60.1**	26.9	0.8	3.7	1.7
Jewish	5.7	**60.0**	34.3	0.1	0.7	0.4
Other Faiths	27.3	36.4	36.4	0.2	0.3	0.3
Weekly Attending Black Protestants	**76.7**	14.0	9.3	1.1	0.2	0.1
Less Observant Black Protestants	40.0	20.0	40.0	0.2	0.1	0.2
				3.0	**6.0**	**3.7**

Source: 2004 National Election Pool (NEP)

equal to the contribution of all the other Republican constituencies' "moral values" voters combined.

Overall, foreign policy priorities were more important to the Bush vote than "moral values." For one thing, foreign policy priorities featured prominently in seven religious communities: three Republican, two Swing, and two Democratic constituencies. In addition, foreign policy priorities attracted one-third or more of the Bush voters in all but three groups (and all three were characterized by moral values priorities.)

Bush received a total of 42.3 percent of his ballots from voters with foreign policy priorities: 21.1 percent came from Republican constituencies, 15.2 percent from Swing, and 6.0 from Democratic constituencies. Indeed, the top two sources of Bush votes in this regard were the Less Observant Mainline Protestants (8.0 percent) and Less Observant Catholics (7.2 percent). However, Weekly Attending Evangelical Protestants were the third largest source of foreign policy votes with 5.9 percent.

To put these figures in perspective, the Swing constituencies' contribution to the total Bush vote in this regard was about the same size as the "moral values" contribution of Weekly Attending Evangelical Protestants.

What about economic policy priorities? These were much less important to Bush's coalition. In no religious constituency were such priorities prominent among the Bush voters (although there was a tie among Latino Catholics, Other Faiths, and Less Observant Black Protestants).

Economic policy priorities accounted for just 20.1 percent of all Bush ballots, about evenly divided between Republican constituencies (9.6 percent) and Swing plus Democratic constituencies (6.8 percent). In this regard, it was the Swing constituencies that made the largest contribution to the total Bush ballots, 6.8 percent—a bit more than the foreign policy contribution of Weekly Attending Evangelicals.

Of course, given the closeness of the election, all of these votes mattered to Bush. Indeed, these data show the skillful use of issue priorities to build what was literally a "minimum winning coalition." "Moral values" were critical to securing strong support from Weekly Attending Evangelicals as well as the backing of other religious constituencies. Foreign policy and economic issue priorities were also critical for securing victory among the Swing constituencies, which were largely unaffected by "moral values." Thus, Bush built a diverse religious coalition, using different issue appeals to tie together religious voters defined by both the Old and New Religion gaps.

The Democratic Coalition. Table 4.4 offers analogous information on the Kerry vote coalition (49 percent of all the ballots cast for Kerry or Bush). The order of the religious groups is reversed for ease of presentation. In fact, the Kerry coalition was in some respects the opposite of the Bush coalition.

Clearly, the key to the Kerry coalition was economic policy priorities. A majority of the Kerry voters in all but one religious constituency had such priorities. The one exception was Jews, where the economy was a close second

Table 4.4 The Democratic Coalition in 2004

	% of Group's Vote:			% of All Kerry Ballots:		
	moral values	foreign policy	economic policy	moral values	foreign policy	economic policy
Democratic Constituencies						
Less Observant Black Protestants	6.6	18.9	**74.5**	0.4	1.3	5.0
Weekly Attending Black Protestants	6.0	21.9	**72.1**	0.4	1.6	5.3
Other Faiths	12.6	30.8	**56.6**	0.6	1.5	2.8
Jewish	14.4	**43.2**	42.3	0.5	1.6	1.6
Unaffiliated	12.7	35.0	**52.3**	2.4	6.7	10.0
Latino Catholics	5.9	26.8	**67.3**	0.3	1.4	3.5
				4.8	**14.0**	**28.0**
Swing Constituencies						
Less Observant Catholics	9.5	30.3	**60.2**	1.2	3.7	7.3
Less Observant Mainline Protestants	8.6	31.2	**60.2**	1.3	4.8	9.2
				2.5	**8.5**	**16.5**
Republican Constituencies						
Latino Protestants	6.3	25.0	**68.8**	0.1	0.5	1.5
Weekly Attending Mainline Protestants	12.3	31.6	**56.1**	0.5	1.2	2.2
Weekly Attending Catholics	2.5	35.0	**62.5**	0.2	2.9	5.1
Less Observant Evangelical Protestants	4.8	19.2	**76.0**	0.2	0.8	3.2
Other Christians	5.3	36.8	**57.9**	0.1	0.7	1.1
Weekly Attending Evangelical Protestants	8.3	24.4	**67.3**	0.4	1.3	3.6
				1.6	**7.4**	**16.7**

Source: 2004 National Election Pool (NEP)

to foreign policy. And such priorities produced 61.2 percent of all the Kerry ballots. As one might expect, the largest portion of these votes were contributed by Democratic religious constituencies, 28.0 percent. Here the single largest source of votes was the Unaffiliated, with a contribution of 10 percent of Kerry's votes, although if combined the two Black Protestants groups contributed about the same amount (10.3 percent).

But note that Kerry actually received more economic policy votes from among the Swing and Republican constituencies, 33.2 percent of all his ballots. Here, the Swing constituencies were crucial. For example, Less Observant Catholics contributed nearly as many Kerry ballots as the Unaffiliated or Black Protestants (9.2 percent).

Kerry also picked up a significant number of votes from the Republican religious constituencies on economic policy. The single biggest source was Weekly Attending Catholics, which at 5.1 percent contributed as many Kerry votes as Weekly Attending Black Protestants. And taken together, both groups of Evangelical Protestants contributed 6.8 percent of all Kerry's votes.

Foreign policy priorities were markedly less important to the Kerry campaign, accounting for 29.9 percent of all his ballots. Only Jews had a plurality with such priorities, but foreign policy voters accounted for more than 30 percent of the Kerry votes in seven additional religious groups, including both Swing constituencies and three Republican constituencies. Overall, the Democratic constituencies provided 14 percent of Kerry's foreign policy votes, while another 15.9 percent came from swing and Republican constituencies. Here, the top contributors were the Unaffiliated, Less Observant Mainliners, and Catholics.

In contrast, "moral values" mattered very little to the Kerry coalition, accounting for just 8.9 percent of all his ballots. Indeed, such priorities scored in the double digits in just four religious groups, three Democratic (Jews, the Unaffiliated, and Other Faiths) and one Republican (Weekly Attending Mainline Protestants).

To put these figures in context, the contribution to the Kerry ballots from all "moral values" voters among the Democratic constituencies (4.8 percent) was less than the economic issue ballots provided among Weekly Attending Catholics (5.1 percent).

Given the closeness of the contest, modest gains in any of these issue areas could have put John Kerry in the White House. For instance, he might have squeezed out more votes from the economic policy voters. However, such priorities were already the mainstay for his coalition and he did pick up a significant contribution from the Swing and Republican constituencies in this regard. Indeed, any increased support on economic policy might well have required changes in his approach to foreign policy or "moral values," on the grounds that neutralizing Bush's appeals on these matters would have freed up voters to support Kerry on economic policy. Although the Kerry coalition was less diverse than the Bush coalition, he also used issue appeals to tie together religious groups defined by both the Old and New Religion gaps.

These findings clearly reveal the great complexity of the electoral coalitions in 2004, which cautions against facile interpretations of the election's meaning. The stress on "moral values" in the Election Night interpretations made an important point: Bush exploited the New Religion Gap to pick up crucial votes. However, the critics of the Election Night interpretations made two important points as well. First, Bush exploited the Old Religion Gap to secure votes on foreign and economic policy, and this source of votes was as important overall as "moral values." And second, the Kerry campaign exploited the combination of the Old and New Religion gaps to secure votes based on economic issues.

Issue Priorities over Time

Thus, "moral values" were one important element in assembling the 2004 electoral coalitions, especially on the Republican side, but other issues and priorities served this purpose as well. How does this issue agenda compare to similar agendas in past elections?

Unfortunately, the issue priority questions in the NEP have not been asked in a consistent fashion in past elections.[7] To look back at issue priorities over a significant length of time one has to turn to open-ended questions, such as when survey respondents are asked to list the "most important problems facing the nation" and their verbatim answers are recorded. Data of this sort can be pieced together from 1944 to 2004, and recoded into economic, foreign policy, and social issue priorities.[8]

In 1944, 66 percent of Americans said economic issues were the most important. Many voters looked toward the end of the Second World War and were concerned about the economic situation, wondering if the nation would return to the hard economic times of the Great Depression. Another 28 percent of the public was concerned about foreign policy matters, given the altered state of world affairs. Social issues were hardly mentioned, accounting for just 4 percent of the respondents. This figure involves a generous definition of social issues, including various forms of public disorder (such as substance abuse and crime).

Comparable figures for 2004 show that economic issues were much less salient than in 1944, at about two-fifths of the public. Foreign policy had about the same level of concern as in the past, a bit more than one-quarter of the answers. However, social issue concerns, defined in this broad way, were important to more than one-fifth of the respondents—a five-fold increase over 1944. It is important to keep this change in perspective: although the increase was large, only a minority of Americans reported social issue priorities by this measure.

How and when did these issue priorities change? Figure 4.1 plots the level of economic, foreign policy, and social issue concerns from 1944 to 2004. Economic issues started out high in 1944 and then declined until 1972, the low point in this series. Then, in response to the economic troubles of the late 1970s, these concerns rose again, remaining fairly high until the 1990s, when a steady decline began.

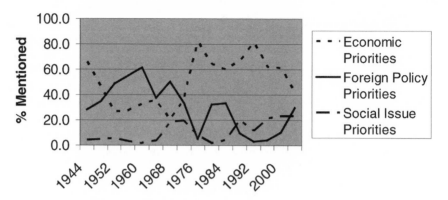

Figure 4.1   Issue Priorities, 1944-2004

Source: See note 8

Foreign policy concerns presented something of a mirror image, starting out lower in 1944 and rising during the Cold War. There was a sharp decline in the 1970s, only to be followed with an up spike again in the 1980s. Then, foreign affairs declined in importance in the 1990s and moved up again after the 2000 election.

In these data, social issues were always salient to many fewer people. They were hardly measurable until the 1960s, when they suddenly expanded, peaking in 1972. They then slowly declined until the 1980s and then rebounded in the 1990s. So, economic and foreign policy concerns have been common in American politics, fluctuating with events. But social issue concerns are relatively new.

This pattern for social issues parallels the advent of the New Religion Gap. Figure 4.2 explores this parallel a little more fully. It also plots social issue concerns over time, but adds comparable priority data for one religious community, Weekly Attending Evangelical Protestants, and also includes the attendance gap data from figure 3.2 (net Republican vote by worship attendance, see chapter 3). The three lines closely parallel one another.

These patterns strongly suggest that the New Religion Gap was at least in part the result of the rise of social issue priorities. This trend began with the cultural turmoil of the 1960s, encapsulated in the 1972 presidential election, then declined for the rest of the 1970s and 1980s, only to return after 1988 and continue thereafter. Scholars who have investigated the rise of social issues in American politics have drawn similar conclusions.[9]

The graph for Weekly Attending Evangelical Protestants is instructive, partly because this religious community received so much attention in 2004 (and indeed for the two previous decades), but also because it illustrates an important point about the political agenda. Changes in the issue priorities of just a few groups of voters can alter political coalitions and influence the results of close elections.

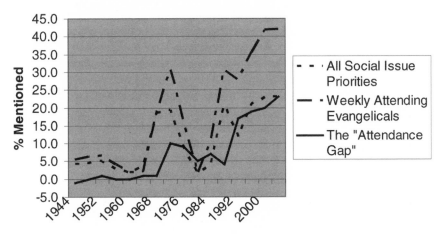

Figure 4.2   Social Issue Priorities and the Attendance Gap, 1944-2004

Source: See note 8

Weekly attending Evangelicals and other religious traditionalists developed social issue priorities and gradually shifted into the Republican Party, as was shown in figures 2.1 and 2.2 (in chapter 2). These data suggest that social issue priorities have become an element of party coalitions along with the rise of the New Religion Gap, and supplementing the impact of the Old Religion Gap.

Religious Communities and Issue Positions in 2004

Thus far the discussion has focused on issue priorities and their consequences. But issue priority does not reveal anything directly about the issue positions of religious voters. Fortunately, the NEP contains a number of issue questions on social, foreign, and economic policy, and it is worth describing the results in some detail.

Social Issues. Table 4.5 presents attitudes on two "hot button" social issues, marriage and abortion, listed by the religious categories. Overall, voters in the 2004 election had fairly moderate positions on social issues. For instance, on the subject of marriage, less than two-fifths believed that there should be "no legal recognition" of same-sex couples, but nearly as many preferred the recognition of civil unions and one-quarter favored same-sex marriage. On abortion, about one-sixth wanted abortion to be "illegal in all cases," while better than one-quarter preferred it to be "illegal in most cases." A bit more than one-third favored abortion to be "legal in most cases" and about one-fifth said abortion should be "legal in all cases."

Although the Republican religious constituencies tended to be more conservative on social issues, there was a good bit of variation among them. The two most Republican groups, Weekly Attending Evangelicals and the Other

Table 4.5 Religion and Social Issues, 2004

	Views of Marriage:			Views of Abortion:			
	No legal recognition	Civil unions	Legally marry	Illegal in all cases	Illegal in most cases	Legal in most cases	Legal in all cases
Republican Constituencies							
Weekly Attending Evangelical Protestants	**72.7**	24.0	3.3	34.6	**48.2**	13.4	3.7
Other Christians	**64.2**	29.3	6.5	20.5	**57.4**	16.4	5.7
Less Observant Evangelical Protestants	**47.5**	39.8	12.7	14.4	33.6	**40.2**	11.8
Weekly Attending Catholics	36.9	**44.3**	18.8	**33.4**	29.8	27.2	9.6
Weekly Attending Mainline Protestants	38.6	**40.9**	20.5	11.3	25.8	**40.3**	22.6
Latino Protestants	**53.8**	26.3	20.0	24.1	**32.9**	27.8	15.2
Swing Constituencies							
Less Observant Mainline Protestants	23.9	**43.6**	32.5	5.5	17.1	**49.3**	28.1
Less Observant Catholics	24.3	**43.8**	31.9	7.0	27.4	**41.4**	24.2
Democratic Constituencies							
Latino Catholics	31.2	**43.5**	25.4	17.4	19.6	28.3	**34.8**
Unaffiliated	11.5	34.2	**54.4**	4.8	10.1	**48.0**	37.2
Jewish	2.7	27.0	**70.3**	1.3	5.2	40.3	**53.2**
Other Faiths	30.4	30.4	**39.1**	10.4	19.4	**40.3**	29.9
Weekly Attending Black Protestants	**66.2**	24.5	9.4	28.1	26.7	**28.9**	16.3
Less Observant Black Protestants	**37.2**	35.9	26.9	5.0	16.3	**46.3**	32.5
ALL	**37.8**	36.4	25.8	16.2	**27.3**	35.3	21.2

Source: 2004 National Election Pool (NEP)

Christians, had strong majorities against same-sex marriage and restrictions on abortion. But note that even in these groups, only a minority favored the banning of abortion outright. Of course, these were the religious groups with the strongest "moral values" priorities.

The other Republican constituencies were less conservative on these issues. Less than one-half of the Less Observant Evangelicals favored no legal recognition for same-sex couples, and they also preferred that abortion be legal in most cases. Weekly Attending Catholics and Mainline Protestants were more moderate still, with a plurality accepting same-sex marriage. However, Weekly Attending Catholics were quite conservative on abortion, while their Mainline Protestant counterparts were more liberal. Latino Protestants were a bit more conservative on these matters than Less Observant Evangelicals on abortion, but a tad less so on marriage.

The two swing constituencies, Less Observant Mainliners and Catholics, tended toward the liberal side of these issues, particularly when compared to their more observant co-religionists. A plurality of both groups favored civil unions and about one-third same-sex marriage. And on abortion, a plurality favored keeping abortion legal in most cases, and roughly one-quarter preferred it to be legal in all cases.

The Democratic religious constituencies also showed some diversity on these issues. Latino Catholics were on balance liberal on these social issues, resembling the Less Observant Catholics. Three groups were strongly to the left on marriage and abortion: the Unaffiliated, Jews, and the Other Faiths. However, Black Protestants were more conservative. For instance, two-thirds of Black weekly attenders opposed any legal recognition for same-sex couples and nearly two-fifths of the less observant held this view. On abortion, the weekly attenders are sharply divided, but are still the most pro-life of the Democratic constituencies. The less observant are much more pro-choice, resembling the Unaffiliated.

The complexity in these patterns results in large measure from the interaction of the Old and New Religion gaps. The most conservative issue positions appeared among the groups with higher levels of traditionalism, as seen in the differences between weekly attenders and the less observant. However, religious traditions still mattered as well, as illustrated by the differences between Evangelicals, Catholics, and Mainliners.

Foreign Policy Issues. Table 4.6 reports opinion on two related foreign policy issues: approval of the Iraq war and whether the Iraq war was part of the broader war on terrorism. Overall, the 2004 electorate was sharply split on the war in Iraq, with a little more than one-half approving or strongly approving, and slightly less than one-half disapproving or strongly disapproving. A somewhat larger majority saw the Iraq war as part of the war on terrorism.

Approval of the Iraq war tended to be strong among the Republican constituencies and the disapproval strong among the Democratic constituencies. Indeed,

Table 4.6 Religion and Foreign Policy, 2004

	View of Iraq War				Iraq War is:	
	Strongly approve	Somewhat approve	Somewhat disapprove	Strongly disapprove	Part of the war on terrorism	Separate from the war on terrorism
Republican Constituencies						
Weekly Attending Evangelical Protestants	**46.8**	31.4	9.3	12.4	**83.8**	16.2
Other Christians	**43.5**	30.1	9.8	16.7	**75.6**	24.4
Less Observant Evangelical Protestants	**43.1**	30.8	7.8	18.4	**72.8**	27.2
Weekly Attending Catholics	**29.9**	26.8	19.0	24.3	**59.1**	40.9
Weekly Attending Mainline Protestants	**33.0**	23.9	16.0	27.1	**51.2**	48.8
Latino Protestants	**37.3**	24.8	8.1	29.8	**61.3**	38.8
Swing Constituencies						
Less Observant Mainline Protestants	**31.4**	22.4	15.2	31.0	**54.2**	45.8
Less Observant Catholics	**28.1**	28.5	15.9	27.5	**58.3**	41.7
Democratic Constituencies						
Latino Catholics	25.0	23.6	18.9	**32.5**	33.1	**66.9**
Unaffiliated	13.9	15.2	18.5	**52.4**	37.8	**62.2**
Jewish	17.1	12.7	23.4	**46.8**	33.8	**66.2**
Other Faiths	11.4	9.7	23.4	**55.4**	32.4	**67.6**
Weekly Attending Black Protestants	8.2	19.2	19.2	**53.4**	35.7	**64.3**
Less Observant Black Protestants	5.3	8.8	26.8	**59.2**	33.8	**66.2**
ALL	**29.3**	**23.9**	**15.5**	**31.3**	**56.5**	**43.5**

Source: 2004 National Election Pool

five of the six Democratic groups had majorities that strongly disapproved of the war, with the sixth group, Latino Catholics, more evenly divided.

Here, there was more variation among the Republican constituencies. While pluralities of all such groups strongly approved of the Iraq war, the level of strong disapproval more than doubled between the Weekly Attending Evangelicals and Weekly Attending Mainline Protestants. As one might imagine, the Swing constituencies were closely divided, but with majorities approving of the war and slim pluralities strongly approving. Recall that it was the Swing constituencies and Weekly Attending Mainline Protestants who were most likely to report foreign policy priorities.

An even sharper pattern occurs on the terrorism item: all of the Republican and Swing constituencies agreed that the Iraq war was part of the war on terrorism, and all of the Democratic constituencies disagreed. There was only modest variation among the Democratic groups, and more differences among the Republican groups. Of particular note were Weekly Attending Mainline Protestants, with a bare majority in agreement. Indeed, on this issue both Mainline Protestant groups differed sharply from Evangelicals. But note that here there was little difference between more and less observant Catholics.

The interplay of the Old and New Religion gap is once again evident in these data on foreign policy, although the patterns are weaker than on the social issues. The strongest support for the wars in Iraq and on terrorism occurred with a combination of religious tradition and traditionalism: Weekly Attending Evangelical Protestants. And different combinations of worship attendance and affiliation were associated with degrees of opposition to these wars.

Economic Issues. Table 4.7 reports opinions on two questions closely related to economic policy. Unfortunately, the best economic policy questions in the NEP could not be cross-tabulated with religion because they were asked on different versions of the exit poll questionnaires. However, the two items are quite revealing: whether George Bush favored "ordinary Americans" or "large corporations," and the degree of concern about the availability of health care. Overall, a majority of the electorate said that Bush favored large corporations, while seven of every ten were "very concerned" about the availability of health care.

The Republican constituencies were sharply divided on President Bush's economic biases. Large majorities of Weekly Attending Evangelicals, Other Christians, and Less Observant Evangelicals said that Bush favored ordinary Americans. However, only a slim majority of Latino Protestants held this view and a slim majority of Weekly Attending Catholics believed that Bush favored large corporations. About three-fifths of Weekly Attending Mainline Protestants and the two Swing constituencies also agreed that Bush had a big business bias. And even larger majorities of the Democratic constituencies saw Bush in this fashion.

On the availability of health care, a majority of every constituency claimed to be "very concerned." But the size of the majority increased almost in lockstep from Weekly Attending Evangelicals to Weekly Attending Black Protestants,

Table 4.7   Religion and Economic Issues, 2004

	George Bush Favors:		Availability of Health Care:		
	Ordinary Americans	*Large corporations*	*Very concerned*	*Somewhat concerned*	*Not very concerned*
Republican Constituencies					
Weekly Attending Evangelical Protestants	**76.7**	23.3	**57.9**	32.3	9.8
Other Christians	**62.8**	37.2	**56.3**	34.9	8.7
Less Observant Evangelical Protestants	**58.9**	41.1	**68.5**	22.7	8.8
Weekly Attending Catholics	48.5	**51.5**	**71.2**	23.1	5.7
Weekly Attending Mainline Protestants	39.7	**60.3**	**68.0**	25.0	7.0
Latino Protestants	**51.3**	48.8	**65.4**	17.9	16.7
Swing Constituencies					
Less Observant Mainline Protestants	41.1	**58.9**	**73.0**	21.9	5.2
Less Observant Catholics	40.5	**59.5**	**71.9**	22.1	6.0
Democratic Constituencies					
Latino Catholics	25.0	**75.0**	**75.4**	18.7	6.0
Unaffiliated	21.7	**78.3**	**69.9**	24.5	5.6
Jewish	14.7	**85.3**	**76.9**	21.8	1.3
Other Faiths	27.5	**72.5**	**92.9**	7.1	0.0
Weekly Attending Black Protestants	16.8	**83.2**	**91.7**	7.6	0.7
Less Observant Black Protestants	10.1	**89.9**	**84.0**	9.9	6.2
All	**43.2**	**56.8**	**70.4**	**23.1**	**6.5**

Source: 2004 National Election Pool (NEP)

with only modest discrepancies along the way. Here, too, there was some variation among the Republican constituencies, but once again, uniformity among the Democratic groups. Recall that it was these Democratic constituencies that were most likely to have economic issue priorities.

Neither of these economic questions were policy issues, and concern over health care might not translate into support for a particular health care proposal. Nonetheless, these questions reveal the political importance of economic issues. Although the pattern is weaker than for social issues, the combination of the Old and New Religion gaps is nonetheless associated with it. With regard to the former, note the difference between the Weekly Attending and Less Observant Catholics on Bush's class bias. And with regard to the latter, note the difference between Weekly Attending Evangelicals and Jews on the availability of health care.

Religious Communities, Ideology, and Partisanship

Elections are influenced by short-term factors, such as issue priorities and positions, but they are also influenced by long-term political identifications of voters. Two important identifications are self-identified ideology and partisanship, and so it is valuable to look at the religious communities in terms of these basic political attitudes. And because ideology and partisanship have long-term influence, it is especially useful to compare the results for 2004 to 1944, using some of the same surveys employed in chapters 2 and 3.[10]

Ideology. Table 4.8 presents self-identified ideology for the religious communities in 2004 and 1944, separating out "conservatives," "moderates," and "liberals." The meaning of the terms "conservative" and "liberal" have changed substantially since 1944, so these results have to be interpreted with great care. Nonetheless, they reveal how these religious traditions situated themselves on the political spectrum in two different political eras, one characterized by the Old Religion Gap and one where the New Religion Gap had appeared.

In this 2004 survey, two-fifths of American adults claimed to be "conservative," about one-third "moderate," and a little more than one-quarter "liberal." Not surprisingly, the conservatives were concentrated among the Republican religious constituencies. Weekly Attending Evangelicals were the most conservative (63.8 percent), followed by Less Observant Evangelicals (52.3 percent). Here is a good example of the New Religion Gap. In contrast, fewer of the Other Christians and Latino Protestants claimed to be conservative, with pluralities claiming to be moderates. Here are examples of the importance of the Old Religion Gap.

Weekly Attending Catholics and Mainline Protestants had pluralities of conservatives, providing a sharp contrast with their less observant co-religionists among the Swing constituencies. The Less Observant Mainliners were on balance conservative, but far less so than the weekly attenders. Meanwhile, the Less Observant Catholics preferred to call themselves liberals, a sharp

Table 4.8   Religion and Ideology, 2004 and 1944

	2004			1944		
	Conservative	Moderate	Liberal	Conservative	Moderate	Liberal
Republican Constituencies						
Weekly Attending Evangelical Protestant	63.8	23.8	12.4	32.0	40.2	27.7
Other Christian	31.2	40.8	28.0	32.6	17.4	50.0
Less Observant Evangelical Protestant	52.3	29.2	18.5	25.4	39.1	35.5
Weekly Attending Catholic	49.0	28.7	22.3	20.2	43.4	36.4
Weekly Attending Mainline Protestants	46.3	25.2	28.5	31.9	36.5	31.6
Latino Protestant	36.2	38.1	25.7	*	*	*
Swing Constituencies						
Less Observant Mainline Protestants	39.2	29.9	30.9	26.5	43.4	30.1
ALL	**40.1**	**31.7**	**28.2**	**25.4**	**40.1**	**34.5**
Less Observant Catholics	31.8	32.1	36.1	18.0	52.8	29.2
Democratic Constituencies						
Latino Catholics	35.2	29.1	35.8	*	*	*
Unaffiliated	24.1	36.9	39.0	20.7	38.8	40.5
Jews	22.4	21.1	56.6	16.7	34.3	49.0
Other Faiths	19.3	40.4	40.4	*	*	*
Weekly Attending Black Protestants	32.6	46.8	20.6	15.6	41.0	43.4
Less Observant Black Protestants	26.7	38.0	35.3	12.1	45.1	42.9

Source: 2004 National Survey of Religion and Politics; 1944 National Election Study

contrast with the more observant Catholics. Here, one sees both the Old and New Religion gaps at work.

The Democratic constituencies were more likely to identify as liberal; a solid majority of Jews chose this label, as did a plurality of the Unaffiliated and the Other Faiths. However, Latino Catholics were evenly divided, with a slight plurality of liberals, while the Black Protestant groups had a plurality of moderates. But among Black Protestants, almost one-third of the weekly attenders were conservatives and more than one-third of the Less Observant were liberals.

The situation in 1944 presents a sharp contrast. In that year, just one-quarter of the electorate claimed to be conservative, two-fifths were moderate, and more than one-third were liberals. Indeed, most of the Republican constituencies in 2004 identified as liberals in 1944, including Weekly Attending Catholics, Less Observant Evangelicals, and Other Christians. Weekly Attending Mainline Protestants were evenly divided between conservatives and liberals. Indeed, only the Weekly Attending Evangelicals were on balance conservative—but by just a small amount.

The 2004 Swing constituencies were also on balance liberal, the Less Observant Mainliners a bit less than the Less Observant Catholics. And all the Democratic constituencies of 2004 were solidly liberal in 1944, including the Unaffiliated, Jews, and both groups of Black Protestants.

Between 1944 and 2004, religious traditionalism became linked to political conservatism. This pushed the weekly attenders in a conservative direction and the less observant in a liberal direction. It also changed the orientation of some religious traditions. But note that religious groups less affected by these religious changes remained largely unchanged in their ideology, such as the Unaffiliated and Jews.

Partisanship. Table 4.9 reports the self-identified partisanship of the religious communities in 2004 and 1944, separating out Republicans, Independents, and Democrats. The meaning of party identification has changed much less than ideology over this period, although the nature of party coalitions has changed a good bit. In 2004, a little over one-third of the adult population identified as Republicans, about one-fifth as independents, and more than two-fifths as Democrats.

The order of the religious constituencies in this table and others were identified by their votes in the 2004 election with the NEP survey results (see table 1.3 in chapter 1). However, it is gratifying that another survey largely confirms this ordering with self-identified partisanship. By far, the most Republican group in this regard was Weekly Attending Evangelical Protestants, and three other groups had a plurality of Republicans: Less Observant Evangelicals, Weekly Attending Catholics, and Weekly Attending Mainline Protestants. However, two groups that were solidly in George Bush's column at the ballot box did not on balance identify as Republicans: the Other Christians (plurality independent) and Latino Protestants (plurality Democrats).

As with ideology, the Swing constituencies showed different patterns. The Less Observant Mainliners were closely divided with a very slight advantage for

Table 4.9   Religion and Partisanship, 2004 and 1944

	2004			1944		
	Republican	Independent	Democrats	Republican	Independent	Democrats
Republican Constituencies						
Weekly Attending Evangelical Protestant	64.8	11.9	23.3	37.1	14.8	48.0
Other Christian	34.7	35.9	29.4	44.3	27.3	28.4
Less Observant Evangelical Protestant	48.3	19.3	32.4	27.9	21.3	50.8
Weekly Attending Catholic	45.7	16.2	38.1	16.4	24.0	59.6
Weekly Attending Mainline Protestants	49.8	16.9	33.3	46.5	15.1	38.3
Latino Protestant	38.6	17.2	44.1	*	*	*
Swing Constituencies						
Less Observant Mainline Protestants	40.7	18.0	41.3	42.1	23.4	34.5
ALL	**36.1**	**20.5**	**43.4**	**33.1**	**23.1**	**43.8**
Less Observant Catholics	35.8	14.9	49.3	18.2	30.7	51.1
Democratic Constituencies						
Latino Catholics	15.1	23.6	61.3	*	*	*
Unaffiliated	24.6	32.9	42.5	27.6	31.0	41.4
Jews	21.4	10.7	67.9	10.8	31.4	57.8
Other Faiths	8.8	36.8	54.4	*	*	*
Weekly Attending Black Protestants	13.0	17.3	69.8	23.0	24.6	52.5
Less Observant Black Protestants	8.6	18.5	73.0	12.1	60.4	27.5

Source: 2004 National Survey of Religion and Politics; 1944 National Election Study

the Democrats. Meanwhile, the Less Observant Catholics had almost a majority of Democrats. And all of the Democratic constituencies identified with the party they voted for in 2004, usually with strong majorities. The one exception was the Unaffiliated, which had a solid plurality of Democrats.

The differences between 1944 and 2004 are quite interesting. The overall partisan division was almost the same: about one-third Republican, roughly one-fifth independents, and more than two-fifths Democratic in 1944. But what has changed is the partisanship of the particular religious communities. Many of the Republican constituencies in 2004 were in the Democratic camp, including Weekly Attending Catholics and both groups of Evangelical Protestants. Indeed, only the Mainline Protestants and Other Christians identified on balance as Republicans, a pattern that also held for one of the 2004 Swing constituencies, Less Observant Mainline Protestants.

In contrast, the Less Observant Catholics were for the most part Democrats—as were Jews and Weekly Attending Black Protestants. The Unaffiliated had a plurality of Democrats, very much as in 2004. The Less Observant Black Protestants favored the Democrats on balance, but most were independents.

This realignment of religious communities since 1944 brings this discussion full circle. The rise of the New Religion Gap interacted with the Old Religion Gap to forge important changes in party identification. Traditionalist religious groups moved slowly toward the GOP, and their opposites either stayed Democratic or gravitated in that direction. By 2004, a new set of electoral coalitions were in operation, organized around a diverse issue agenda of "moral values" and foreign and economic policy.

Conclusions

This chapter has reviewed the role of issue priorities and positions in the votes of religious communities in 2004, with occasional glances into the past. It began by exploring the Election Night controversy over "moral values" in more detail, finding that the "values voters" were a real phenomenon, but that other issue priorities mattered as well. A careful look at the contribution of issue priorities revealed how each presidential candidate exploited the Old and New Religion gaps. Bush used diverse issue appeals, including "moral values" and foreign and economic policy to assemble a complex coalition of religious groups, while Kerry relied largely on economic appeals to do the same.

A look back at issue priorities over time reveals that the diverse agenda in the 2004 election is of recent vintage, resulting from the expansion of social issues in the political agenda. Indeed, the increase in the salience of social issues closely parallels the appearance of the New Religion Gap. The combination of the Old and New Religion gaps was associated with attitudes on social, foreign, and economic policy in the 2004 campaign. They were also associated with ideology and partisanship, as well as changes in these broad political identifications over time. Of course, religion is not the only demographic factor that matters in elections, and the next chapter puts the religion gaps in social context by looking at gender, age, and income.

5

The Religion Gaps in Social Context: Gender, Age, and Income

Thus far we have shown that religion was an important factor in the 2004 election, both the "politics of belonging" and the Old Religion Gap and the "politics of behaving and believing" and the New Religion Gap. And as shown in table 1.7 (in chapter 1), the affiliation and attendance gaps were larger than many better-known voter gaps, including the gender gap, the generation gap, and the income gap. Indeed, only the race gap was larger in 2004—but race and ethnicity are closely linked to religious affiliation.

Of course, these other demographic factors were also important to the 2004 vote as well. Was the political impact of religion in part a reflection of these other factors? Do these factors undermine or reinforce the effects of religion on politics? How has the impact of these other factors changed over time in comparison to the impact of religion? Such questions readily come to mind because of everyday associations between religion and other social attributes. For example, congregational life is in large part about families and children, where gender and age are important considerations. In addition, many people turn to religion for help in coping with the stresses of daily life, including those caused by age and social class. So, it would be surprising indeed if religion were not related to other demographic factors.

The goal of this chapter is to explore the role that the key demographic factors of gender, age, and income play in the links between religion and politics. The text first describes the distribution of each factor among religious communities, then discusses its direct link to the vote, now and in the past, and finally reviews the joint impact of religion and the factor in question on the 2004 vote. While taking these other demographic factors into account does not eliminate the influence of religion on the vote, it does reveal much about the social context in which religion is connected to politics.

Gender and Religion

Gender has long been closely associated with religion. For one thing, human sexuality presents large and persistent challenges in the human experience, and religion has often been part of the response. Religious beliefs help define how men and women should behave sexually, and religious practices frequently reinforce these beliefs. The well-known changes in gender roles that occurred in the twentieth century were in many ways challenges to the gender roles that had been defined by traditional religious beliefs, generating extensive conflict within religious communities. Indeed, controversies related to gender were central to the "culture wars." But religion matters for another reason quite apart from gender-based disputes: women are and have long been more active in religious life than men. Thus, there is reason to believe that there will be different gender profiles among religious groups.[1]

The Distribution of Gender by Religion

Table 5.1 looks at the distribution of gender by religious category in the 2004 NEP data. (For ease of presentation, the religious categories are listed by religious tradition.) In this survey, women outnumbered men 53.9 to 46.1 percent among 2004 voters. But this gender division was not evenly distributed across the religious categories. For one thing, women made up a large majority of the weekly worship attenders in all the religious traditions. For example, roughly three-fifths of weekly attending Black Protestants, Mainline Protestants, Catholics, and Evangelical Protestants were female. This pattern held for the smaller religious categories as well (although because of the small number of cases, they are not subdivided by attendance here). And note that men were more common among the less observant in every tradition and were a majority of the Unaffiliated. There were two exceptions to this pattern: Evangelical Protestants had more women at both levels of attendance, while men were most common among Jews, even the most observant (a finding that may reflect the small number of respondents).

The Gender Gap

Thus, women were more common in the religious groups that voted more Republican in 2004. This pattern is interesting because of the Democratic bias of the gender gap.[2] As shown in table 1.7 (in chapter 1), the gender gap was 7.3 percentage points in the 2004 NEP data, a figure smaller than either of the affiliation or attendance gaps of 22.8 and 17.0 percentage points, respectively.

Table 5.1   Religion and Gender

	Male	Female	
Weekly Attending Evangelical Protestants	42.1	57.9	**100**
Less Observant Evangelical Protestants	45.5	54.5	**100**
Weekly Attending Mainline Protestants	39.4	60.6	**100**
Less Observant Mainline Protestants	48.2	51.8	**100**
Latino Protestants	45.0	55.0	**100**
Weekly Attending Black Protestants	35.7	64.3	**100**
Less Observant Black Protestants	50.0	50.0	**100**
Weekly Attending Catholics	41.1	58.9	**100**
Less Observant Catholics	50.7	49.3	**100**
Latino Catholics	49.8	50.2	**100**
Other Christians	43.1	56.9	**100**
Jews	53.8	46.2	**100**
Other Faiths	41.5	58.5	**100**
Unaffiliated	52.3	47.7	**100**
ALL	**46.1**	**53.9**	**100**

Source: 2004 National Election Pool (NEP)

Like the New Religion Gap, the gender gap is of recent vintage. Table 5.2 shows the development of the gender gap between 2004 and 1944 (using the same data employed for the previous overtime comparisons).[3] In these data, the 2004 gender gap was 5.7 percentage points in favor of Democrat Kerry over Republican Bush. But back in 1944, there was no gender gap at all: both Democrat Roosevelt and Republican Dewey received essentially the same percentage of the male and female vote.

Figure 5.1 plots the gender gap over time (calculated as net Democratic vote) and compares it to the attendance gap (calculated as net Republican vote). This graph shows that the gender gap emerged at about the same as the attendance gap. In the 1950s and 1960s, a modest gender gap favored the GOP, but it shifted

Table 5.2   The Gender Gap, 2004 and 1944

	2004		1944	
	Bush	Kerry	Dewey	FDR
Male	54.1	45.9	45.8	54.2
Female	48.4	51.6	45.7	54.3
ALL	**51.1**	**48.9**	**45.7**	**54.3**
The Gender Gap	*5.7*		*0.1*	

Source: 2004 National Survey of Religion and Politics; 1944 AIPO 335

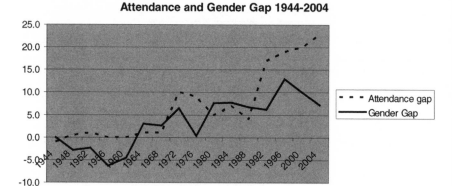

Figure 5.1   The Gender and Attendance Gaps, 1944-2004

Source: National Election Studies, 1944-2004

dramatically toward the Democrats in 1972. Both the gender and attendance gaps continued to grow over the rest of the century, albeit in an uneven fashion. However, the gender gap peaked in 1996, and then declined in 2000 and 2004, while the attendance gap continued to expand. The temporal similarity suggests that both the gender and attendance gaps were a product of the cultural turmoil of this era, when the "restructuring" of American religion was underway and the "culture wars" emerged.

The Gender Gap within Religious Communities

Table 5.3 portrays the joint impact of religion and gender on the 2004 presidential vote by dividing the religious categories into men and women. The right-hand column reports the gender gap within each religious group; a positive figure indicates that men voted more Republican than women and a negative figure notes the opposite.

The first thing to notice is that for most of the religious traditions the gender gap is *positive*, meaning that males voted more Republican and females more Democratic. In fact, just two of these gender gaps were negative and both were quite small (weekly attending Black Protestants and the composite Other Faiths category).

Overall, weekly attenders tended to exhibit smaller gender gaps than their less observant co-religionists. Indeed, the smallest gender gaps occur among groups that exhibited high levels of religious traditionalism: Weekly Attending Evangelical and Black Protestants, Other Christians, and Latino Protestants. In contrast, the largest gender gaps tended to occur among groups with relatively low levels of religious traditionalism, such as among Jews, Less Observant Mainline Protestants, the Unaffiliated, and Less Observant Black Protestants.

Weekly attending Mainline Protestants and Catholics were located toward the middle of the range of gender gaps. From this perspective, Weekly Attending

Table 5.3   Religion, Gender, and the 2004 Vote

		Bush	Kerry	Gender Gap
Weekly Attending Evangelical Protestants	*Male*	84.7	15.3	**3.6**
	Female	81.1	18.9	
Less Observant Evangelical Protestants	*Male*	75.3	24.7	**6.5**
	Female	68.8	31.2	
Weekly Attending Mainline Protestants	*Male*	63.1	36.9	**8.9**
	Female	54.2	45.8	
Less Observant Mainline Protestants	*Male*	59.9	40.1	**15.4**
	Female	44.5	55.5	
Latino Protestants	*Male*	57.3	42.7	**2.7**
	Female	54.6	45.4	
Weekly Attending Black Protestants	*Male*	15.8	84.2	**-1.7**
	Female	17.5	82.5	
Less Observant Black Protestants	*Male*	13.6	86.4	**9.7**
	Female	3.9	96.1	
Weekly Attending Catholics	*Male*	66.5	33.5	**10.7**
	Female	55.8	44.2	
Less Observant Catholics	*Male*	54.9	45.1	**7.1**
	Female	47.8	52.2	
Latino Catholics	*Male*	40.3	59.7	**7.6**
	Female	32.7	67.3	
Other Christians	*Male*	75.3	24.7	**3.2**
	Female	72.1	27.9	
Jews	*Male*	31.7	68.3	**17.5**
	Female	14.2	85.8	
Other Faiths	*Male*	17.2	82.8	**-1.0**
	Female	18.2	81.8	
Unaffiliated	*Male*	32.4	67.6	**10.8**
	Female	21.6	78.4	
ALL		**51.0**	**49.0**	**7.3**

Source: 2004 National Election Pool (NEP)

Catholics present a modest anomaly, having a somewhat larger gender gap than one might otherwise expect—about the same size as the Unaffiliated.

In any event, these patterns suggest that religious traditionalism reduces the independent impact of gender on the vote, and the absence of traditionalism increased the independent impact of gender on the vote, allowing for greater variation between men and women. (Alternatively, one could argue that gender reduces the effects of religious traditionalism on the vote.)

This pattern can be seen clearly if one looks at just worship attendance and gender, as displayed in figure 5.2: weekly attending men voted the most for Bush in 2004, followed by weekly attending women, less observant men, and finally less observant women, who voted the least for Bush in 2004.

It could be that religious traditionalism inculcates a consistent set of values among both men and women. A modest test of this possibility is the impact of marriage and children on the relationship among religion, gender, and the vote. At the beginning of the twenty-first century, being married and having children is something of a "traditional value," and scholars have found a "marriage gap" in voting behavior.[4] When the patterns in table 5.3 are subject to control for marital status, married persons nearly always voted more for Bush than their unmarried co-religionists. And there was a similar effect for respondents reporting children at home, with parents more for Bush and the childless more for Kerry (data not shown).[5]

However, the basic differences in table 5.3 do not diminish when marriage and children are taken into account: males consistently voted more Republican than their female counterparts, weekly attenders were more Republican than their counterparts, and the differences between the religious traditions persisted. Thus, gender and religion represent different kinds of social distinctiveness, which are politically relevant and deeply intertwined.

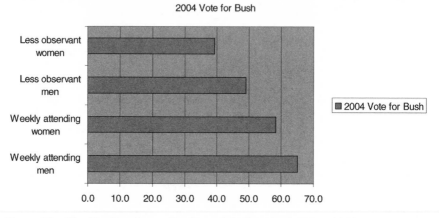

Figure 5.2   Worship Attendance, Gender, and the Presidential Vote, 2004
Source: 2004 National Election Pool (NEP)

Age and Religion

Like gender, age has long been closely associated with religion. Problems associated with age—from conception to the grave—are a persistent preoccupation in the human experience. Religious institutions have shared this preoccupation at a practical level as well as in the loftier realms of practice and doctrine. Scholars have noted two effects of age on religion among adults.[6] One is a "life-cycle" effect: young adults typically become less active in organized religion as they make their way into the world, but many return to organized religion once they have established families and have children. Many people then remain religiously active as they become senior citizens. The second effect is "generational." The era in which a person comes of age can produce distinctive perspectives on religion and other matters. So, for instance, Catholics who grew up in the 1950s before Vatican II experienced a different style of Catholicism than their co-religionists who came of age after Vatican II in the 1970s.[7] Given these effects, one would expect there to be different age profiles among religious groups in the electorate.

The Distribution of Age by Religion

Table 5.4 looks at the age of the religious categories in the 2004 NEP data, separating out five age groups (18 to 29, 30 to 39, 40 to 49, 50 to 64, and over 65 years). Although a bit crude, these five categories capture a bit of both life-cycle and generational effects.[8]

The 18 to 29 year olds are sometimes called "Generation Y." They were young adults in 2004 and came of age in the 1990s when religious "restructuring" was a fact of life. They made up about one-sixth of the electorate, reflecting in part the lower voter turnout among this age group. Meanwhile, the 30 to 39 year olds were at the age of typical family formation in 2004 and came of age in the 1980s, just when the religious "restructuring" was underway. They accounted for a bit more than one-sixth of the electorate in 2004. The 40 to 49 year olds were in middle of child-rearing and came of age in the 1970s; they made up a little more than one-fifth of 2004 voters in this survey. Often treated as a single group, dubbed "Generation X," these two categories experienced the beginnings of the religious "restructuring."

The largest group in year span (and numbers in this survey) is the 50 to 64 year old category, making up more than one-quarter of the electorate. This category encompasses most of the "baby boom" generation. Located between child rearing and retirement in 2004, they came of age in the 1950s and 1960s. Finally, the 65 or older group were retirement age in 2004 and came of age in the 1940s or before—including the "greatest generation" of the World War II era and their younger siblings. This category also made up about one-sixth of the 2004 electorate.[9]

Table 5.4   Religion and Age, 2004

	18 to 29 years	30 to 39 years	40 to 49 years	50 to 64 years	65 or older	Total
Weekly Attending Evangelical Protestants	12.4	16.7	22.5	28.8	19.6	**100**
Less Observant Evangelical Protestants	12.2	14.1	26.3	28.4	19.0	**100**
Weekly Attending Mainline Protestants	10.2	13.2	22.6	29.8	24.2	**100**
Less Observant Mainline Protestants	13.8	16.2	24.4	29.2	16.4	**100**
Latino Protestants	30.1	14.4	21.6	24.6	9.3	**100**
Weekly Attending Black Protestants	20.8	19.9	23.9	24.6	10.8	**100**
Less Observant Black Protestants	28.6	23.5	20.6	20.6	6.7	**100**
Weekly Attending Catholics	10.2	12.6	21.6	27.9	27.7	**100**
Less Observant Catholics	17.4	22.5	23.5	27.6	9.0	**100**
Latino Catholics	29.2	23.7	15.9	21.0	10.2	**100**
Other Christians	19.9	14.7	22.3	27.8	15.3	**100**
Jews	10.3	12.4	17.6	30.9	28.8	**100**
Other Faiths	16.5	21.8	24.2	33.1	4.4	**100**
Unaffiliated	25.6	22.8	22.3	22.0	7.3	**100**
ALL	**16.9**	**17.9**	**22.7**	**27.0**	**15.5**	**100**

Source: 2004 National Election Pool (NEP)

The religious groups had distinctive age profiles in table 5.4. For example, Evangelical Protestants closely resembled the electorate as a whole, with slightly fewer young voters and slightly more senior citizens. There was no difference by level of worship attendance. The composite Other Christians category came even closer to the overall age profile, which may reflect its internal diversity.

In contrast, Mainline Protestants, Catholics, and Jews departed from the overall age profile in two ways. First, the weekly attenders contained more senior citizens and fewer respondents under the age of 40. The less observant groups showed a reverse pattern: fewer senior citizens and more twenty- and thirty-something voters.

Yet another pattern occurred among the racial and ethnic minorities. Black Protestants, Latino Protestants, and Catholics all had a much higher incidence of younger respondents, especially those under 40, and they also had fewer senior citizens. Here, there were only modest differences by worship attendance. For example, weekly attending Black Protestants were just a little older than their less observant co-religionists. The composite Other Faiths category resembled this pattern as well, but with a bulge in the 50 to 64 year category. Finally, the Unaffiliated also had a larger number of younger voters and fewer senior citizens.

The Generation Gap

On the surface, these patterns fit with the conventional view of the generation gap, with younger voters most common in many religious groups that voted Democratic in 2004. But even a cursory glance at these data reveals a good bit of complexity: many of the Democratic groups characterized by greater youth are racial and ethnic minorities, while Evangelical Protestants were evenly balanced. In fact, age did not have a consistent effect on the 2004 vote: Senator Kerry won the very youngest voters, but also the very oldest.

Partly due to this complexity, the generation gap was not very large in 2004. As shown in table 1.7 (in chapter 1), the generation gap was 4.4 percentage points, far smaller than the attendance gap (22.8 percentage points) and affiliation gap (17.0 percentage points).

Table 5.5 compares this version of the generation gap in 2004 to 1944. There was a small generation gap in both years. In these data, the generation gap in 2004 was six percentage points, with younger voters preferring Democrat John Kerry. Back in 1944, these data show a generation gap of just about the same size, 5.7 percentage points, with younger voters preferring Democrat Roosevelt.

However, there has been a great deal of change between 1944 and 2004, as demonstrated in figure 5.3, which compares the generation gap (measured by net Democratic vote) to the attendance gap (both gaps measured as net Republican vote). From 1944 to 1972, Democrats had an advantage among voters under 40. This advantage reached a high point in 1972 when the Democratic nominee, George McGovern, was associated with the youth "counter culture" of the 1960s. Of course, 1972 is when the attendance gap first appeared.[10] After 1972, the generation gap declined, and by 1980, Republican Ronald Reagan, the oldest person ever elected to the White House, enjoyed a

Table 5.5   The Generation Gap, 2004 and 1944

	2004		1944	
	Bush	Kerry	Dewey	FDR
Under 40 years	46.7	53.3	42.6	57.4
Over 40 years	52.7	47.3	48.3	51.7
ALL	**50.8**	**49.2**	**46.2**	**53.8**
The Generation Gap	*6.0*		*5.7*	

Source: 2004 National Survey of Religion and Politics; 1944 AIPO 335

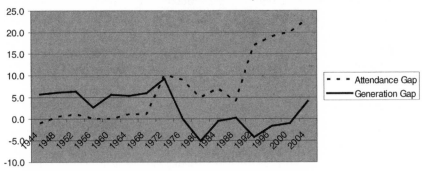

Figure 5.3   The Generation and Attendance Gaps, 1944-2004
Source: National Election Studies, 1944-2004

net advantage among *younger* voters (as seen by the negative sign). But in 2004, the generation gap returned to previous form, with the Democrats having a net advantage among younger voters. This shift paralleled the expansion of the New Religion Gap

The Generation Gap within Religious Communities

Table 5.6 reports the joint impact of religion and age on the 2004 presidential vote, reporting the size of the generation gap within religious categories in the right-hand column (a positive figure indicates that older voters were more Republican and a negative figure notes the opposite).

Surely the most interesting pattern in table 5.6 is the *negative* gaps: in many of the religious categories, it was the voters under 40 who voted more for Bush and less for Kerry. For example, for weekly attending Evangelical Protestants, 90 percent of voters under 40 backed Bush compared to just 80 percent of their co-religionists over 40. This produces a generation gap of -10.3 percentage points. This simplified measure of the generation gap masks the very youngest and oldest voters, but this choice makes little difference. For example, among weekly attending Evangelicals, 18 to 24 year olds voted 89 percent for Bush, while those over 75 years voted just 64 percent for Bush.

This pattern holds for less observant Evangelicals, weekly attending Black Protestants and Jews, and to a lesser extent for weekly attending Mainline Protestants, Catholics, and the Unaffiliated. Some of these groups showed quite small generation gaps in 2004, and there was some complexity to the underlying data.[11] And, of course, many of these religious groups voted on balance for Kerry rather than for Bush.

However, some groups fit the expected pattern of older voters casting more Republican ballots. The generation gaps have positive signs for Latino Protestants, Latino Catholics, and the Other Faiths. Other groups that tend to fit

Table 5.6   Religion, Age, and the 2004 Vote

		Bush	Kerry	Generation Gap
Weekly Attending Evangelical Protestants	*Under 40*	90.3	9.7	**-10.3**
	Over 40	80.0	20.0	
Less Observant Evangelical Protestants	*Under 40*	78.4	21.6	**-8.9**
	Over 40	69.5	30.5	
Weekly Attending Mainline Protestants	*Under 40*	58.4	41.6	**-1.4**
	Over 40	57.0	43.0	
Less Observant Mainline Protestants	*Under 40*	51.9	48.1	**0.2**
	Over 40	52.1	47.9	
Latino Protestants	*Under 40*	51.9	48.1	**10.3**
	Over 40	62.2	37.8	
Weekly Attending Black Protestants	*Under 40*	22.4	77.6	**-8.7**
	Over 40	13.7	86.3	
Less Observant Black Protestants	*Under 40*	7.5	92.5	**2.8**
	Over 40	10.3	89.7	
Weekly Attending Catholics	*Under 40*	60.4	39.6	**-0.6**
	Over 40	59.8	40.2	
Less Observant Catholics	*Under 40*	51.4	48.6	**0.3**
	Over 40	51.7	48.3	
Latino Catholics	*Under 40*	30.9	69.1	**11.0**
	Over 40	41.9	58.1	
Other Christians	*Under 40*	73.8	26.2	**1.6**
	Over 40	75.4	24.6	
Jews	*Under 40*	34.6	65.4	**-15.2**
	Over 40	19.4	80.6	
Other Faiths	*Under 40*	12.0	88.0	**8.9**
	Over 40	20.9	79.1	
Unaffiliated	*Under 40*	28.6	71.4	**-2.6**
	Over 40	26.0	74.0	
ALL		**51.0**	**49.0**	**4.4**

Source: 2004 National Election Pool (NEP)

this pattern in a more modest way were the Other Christians and the less observant Black Protestants, Catholics, and Mainline Protestants.

What accounts for these patterns? These data suggest that lifecycle and generation effects interact in different ways in the various religious traditions. Among
white Christians, and especially Evangelical Protestants, religious traditionalism
seems to have had a special effect on voters under 40, including the very youngest voters. This pattern may reflect a religious influence on their core values, but
it may also reflect internal cues and external political appeals from the closely divided politics of this era. By the same token, this kind of political influence may
also account for the "youth movement" among weekly attending Black Protestants and Jews, groups that were and still are very Democratic.

In contrast, older traditionalists grew up in a less polarized time when the partisan bias of the country was Democratic. The traces of this generational effect
may help account for the lower vote for Bush among older voters—even for
those who gave him a majority of their ballots in 2004.

As one might expect, voters under 40 in less traditional religious communities
were less susceptible to the effects of religion. Or put another way, in the absence
of religious traditionalism, younger voters are more open to other influences,
which often push them in a Democratic direction—but sometimes toward the
Republicans. This factor may be especially important for younger immigrants,
who encounter a wide range of new experiences, such as Latinos and the Other
Faiths. In these cases, the greater Republican vote of voters over 40 may reflect
residual effects of a more traditional upbringing or other non-religious influences
that may lead older voters in a more conservative direction.[12]

In sum, age was deeply intertwined with religion in 2004, producing contra-
dictory political effects, and thus reducing its overall impact on the vote. In many
respects, these patterns reflect the transition from an era dominated by the Old
Religion Gap to one where the New Religion Gap is important as well.

Income and Religion

Like gender and age, socio-economic class has a long association with religion. The struggle to make a living has been a constant part of the human experience, and religion has regularly helped individuals cope with that struggle.
Most religious communities have beliefs concerning appropriate economic rela-
tions between people, including the responsibilities toward the poor, although
these beliefs vary widely. The best general statement of the relationship between
class and religion is still Richard Niebuhr's *Social Sources of Denominationalism*, in which he notes that the religious response to class differences produced
working-class, middle-class, and upper-class denominations.[13]

Of course, disputes over the distribution of income have been a staple of
American politics, and religious communities have been deeply involved in those
disputes as well, whether it was the "gospel of hard work" and individual

responsibility or the "social gospel" and collective responsibility. In this regard, some scholars have noted that religion can be an "opiate for the masses," but others have seen it as a "prophetic voice" for social reform.[14] So, from both a sociological and political perspective, there is good reason to expect that religious communities would have different class profiles.

The Distribution of Income by Religion

Table 5.7 looks at the distribution of income by religious category in the 2004 NEP data. For ease of presentation, annual family income was grouped into five categories. The lowest was incomes of less than $30,000, a group that includes impoverished voters as well as many working-class people, accounting for a little more than one-fifth of the sample. The second group covers annual family incomes of $30,000 to $50,000, covering lower middle-class voters, and also making up a bit more than one-fifth of the electorate. The third category captures

Table 5.7   Religion and Social Class in 2004

	Under $30,000	$30 to $50,000	$50 to $75,000	$75 to $150,000	Over $150,000	Total
Weekly Attending Evangelical Protestants	23.1	21.9	26.9	23.5	4.6	**100**
Less Observant Evangelical Protestants	27.3	22.4	22.0	24.3	4.0	**100**
Weekly Attending Mainline Protestants	13.3	24.1	26.4	29.3	6.9	**100**
Less Observant Mainline Protestants	20.5	19.2	25.5	26.9	7.9	**100**
Latino Protestants	33.2	17.3	25.5	17.3	6.7	**100**
Weekly Attending Black Protestants	28.4	23.9	21.9	22.4	3.4	**100**
Less Observant Black Protestants	42.0	27.4	13.4	14.7	2.6	**100**
Weekly Attending Catholics	19.6	20.3	21.7	29.5	8.9	**100**
Less Observant Catholics	14.2	22.5	24.8	28.9	9.6	**100**
Latino Catholics	29.7	25.0	23.8	15.8	5.7	**100**
Other Christians	27.3	23.7	20.5	23.7	4.8	**100**
Jews	10.9	14.7	17.1	34.1	23.2	**100**
Other Faiths	28.5	25.1	22.2	20.1	4.1	**100**
Unaffiliated	26.7	24.0	19.8	20.5	9.0	**100**
All	**23.0**	**22.1**	**23.2**	**24.6**	**7.1**	**100**

Source: 2004 National Election Pool (NEP)

the "middle" of the middle-class, voters with annual family incomes between $50,000 and $75,000; this group was about the same size as the previous one. The upper-middle class is found in the fourth group, with annual incomes of $75,000 to $150,000. Made up of business managers and professionals, this category made up about one-quarter of the electorate. The final group is a measure of the upper-class, those with incomes over $150,000 a year, accounting for less than one-tenth of the sample.[15]

Although there are few sharp distinctions in these data, they reveal a number of different patterns. Evangelical Protestants closely mirrored the overall distribution of income in the 2004 electorate, as they did with age. Here, the weekly attenders had slightly fewer upper-class members and a larger number in the middle category. Meanwhile, Less Observant Evangelicals also contained fewer upper-class voters, but this deficit was balanced by a larger number in the working-class category.

Some religious groups matched or exceeded the affluence of the electorate as a whole, including Jews, the Unaffiliated, Mainline Protestants, and Catholics. Among Mainline Protestants, there was an interesting difference in the income profile by worship attendance. Weekly attenders had markedly fewer working-class respondents and a greater proportion of middle- and upper middle-class voters, while the less observant had a bimodal pattern, nearly matching the entire electorate with regard to the working-class voters, but also having more in the top two income categories as well. The Unaffiliated showed this same pattern, only more pronounced, exceeding the entire electorate in the proportion of *both* working-class and upper-class members.

In this regard, Catholics were quite a bit different from Mainline Protestants. The Weekly Attending Catholics also exceeded the entire electorate in the proportion of upper income members, but contained more working-class voters as well. But the biggest difference was among the Less Observant Catholics: they were among the leaders in terms of the proportion of upper-class voters and were among the religious categories with the fewest working-class members. In this respect, the Less Observant Catholics resembled Weekly Attending Mainline Protestants.

Other groups were markedly less affluent, and chief among them were religious minorities. Black Protestants and the Latino groups exceeded the entire electorate in the proportion of working-class people. But here there was some variation as well. On the one hand, the Less Observant Black Protestants were the least affluent of all the religious categories, with some two-fifths in the working-class category. And, on the other hand, Weekly Attending Black Protestants had fewer working-class adherents and more middle-class members. Interestingly, the two composite categories of Other Christians and Other Faiths resembled the income distribution of Weekly Attending Black Protestants. Finally, the Latino groups also had fewer working-class members than Black Protestants, but also had more upper-class adherents (resembling the Unaffiliated in this regard).

The Income Gap

Thus, income differences cut across the religious categories, with many of the religious groups exhibiting a considerable dispersion of income. From these data, one might conclude that *both* high and low incomes were linked to religion in one fashion or another. However, some of the religious groups that voted most Republican were less affluent, while some that voted Democratic were quite well off.

Overall, income was an important factor in the 2004 vote. As shown in table 1.7 (in chapter 1), the income gap was 12.3 percentages points, larger than the gender (7.3 percentage points) and generation gaps (4.4 percentage points), but smaller than the affiliation (22.8 percentage points) and attendance gaps (17.0 percentage points).

Unlike the gender or attendance gaps, the income gap is a long-standing division in American politics, with lower income voters preferring the Democrats and higher income voters the Republicans. However, comparing income at different points in time is quite difficult. Not only have there been massive changes in the economy, there have been major and necessary changes in how such questions are asked in surveys. To get a sense of how the political impact of income has changed over time, we were forced to use subjective measures of class asked of respondents, which are less precise than measures of income.[16] For this reason, the data presented here must be viewed with special caution.

Table 5.8 shows the "class" gap in 2004 and 1944. In 2004, there was a class gap between lower and upper-class voters of 13.1 percentage points—about the same as the 12.3 percentage points in the NEP data. Back in 1944, the figure was 21 percentage points. This comparison suggests that class divisions have subsided over time, but remain important nonetheless.

Figure 5.4 plots the class gap in the presidential vote from 1944 to 2004 in terms of net Democratic advantage and compares it to the attendance gap (measured as net Republican advantage). Although there is considerable variation, the class gap was substantial before 1972, when it took a dramatic decline, at just about the time the attendance gap appeared. No doubt this dip reflects the special circumstances of President Nixon's landslide victory over George McGovern, when many working-class people voted Republican.

Table 5.8   Class and the Presidential Vote, 2004 and 1944

	2004		1944	
	Bush	**Kerry**	**Dewey**	**FDR**
Lower Income	43.1	56.9	33.3	66.7
Higher income	56.3	43.7	54.3	45.7
All	**50.8**	**49.2**	**45.7**	**54.3**
The Class Gap	*13.2*		*21.0*	

Source: 2004 National Survey of Religion and Politics; 1944 AIPO 335

Class and Attendance Gaps, 1944-2004

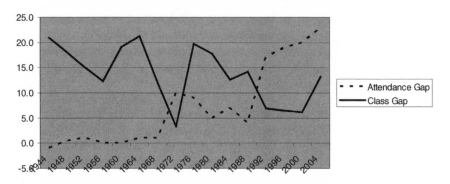

Figure 5.4   Social Class and Worship Attendance Gaps, 1944-2004

Source: National Election Studies, 1944-2004

The class gap then returned to a high level for the rest of the 1970s and the 1980s, as the attendance gap diminished. Next, the class gap declined in the 1990s—just as the attendance gap resumed its upward movement. Finally, the class gap moved back up in 2004, supporting the notion that this election was especially divisive, combining elements of both cultural and class conflict. Thus, a class gap appears to have had a constant impact on the vote over time, temporarily subsiding when the New Religion Gap expanded and religious "restructuring" was under way.

The Income Gap within Religious Communities

Table 5.9 reports the impact of both religion and income on the 2004 presidential vote, reporting the size of the income gap within religious categories in the right-hand column (where a positive figure indicates that upper income voters were more Republican than lower income voters and a negative figure notes the opposite).

There is a clear and uniform pattern to the income gaps in table 5.9: they are relatively large and almost uniformly positive (the one negative gap is for the composite category of Other Faiths). Thus, higher income members of nearly all religious communities voted more Republican than their lower income co-religionists, who voted more Democratic. A good example is Evangelical Protestants, who showed an income gap of 9 percentage points for weekly attenders and 10 percentage points for the less observant. Some 77 percent of the weekly attenders with incomes of less than $50,000 a year voted for Bush—but 86 percent of weekly attenders with incomes over $50,000 backed the President. However, the religious differences persist: Less Observant Evangelicals with high incomes also cast some 77 percent of their ballots to Bush, equal to the weekly attenders with low incomes.

The income gaps were much larger in other religious groups. For example, the gap was 17 percentage points among weekly attending Catholics and Other

Table 5.9   Religion, Class, and the 2004 Vote

		Bush	Kerry	Class Gap
Weekly Attending Evangelical Protestants	Under $50,000	76.9	23.1	**9.1**
	Over $50,000	86.0	14.0	
Less Observant Evangelical Protestants	Under $50,000	66.9	33.1	**10.0**
	Over $50,000	76.9	23.1	
Weekly Attending Mainline Protestants	Under $50,000	46.7	53.3	**16.0**
	Over $50,000	62.7	37.3	
Less Observant Mainline Protestants	Under $50,000	46.4	53.6	**9.9**
	Over $50,000	56.3	43.7	
Latino Protestants	Under $50,000	51.4	48.6	**4.9**
	Over $50,000	59.4	40.6	
Weekly Attending Black Protestants	Under $50,000	16.2	83.8	**0.4**
	Over $50,000	16.8	83.2	
Less Observant Black Protestants	Under $50,000	7.7	92.3	**2.2**
	Over $50,000	9.9	90.1	
Weekly Attending Catholics	Under $50,000	49.3	50.7	**17.0**
	Over $50,000	66.3	33.7	
Less Observant Catholics	Under $50,000	46.5	53.5	**8.1**
	Over $50,000	54.6	45.4	
Latino Catholics	Under $50,000	34.9	65.1	**7.2**
	Over $50,000	42.1	57.9	
Other Christians	Under $50,000	64.7	35.3	**17.3**
	Over $50,000	82.0	18.0	
Jews	Under $50,000	14.5	85.5	**13.1**
	Over $50,000	27.6	72.4	
Other Faiths	Under $50,000	17.3	82.7	**-0.8**
	Over $50,000	16.5	83.5	
Unaffiliated	Under $50,000	25.1	74.9	**4.8**
	Over $50,000	29.9	70.1	
ALL		**51.0**	**49.0**	**12.3**

Source: 2004 National Election Pool (NEP)

Christians, 16 percentage points among Weekly Attending Mainline Protestants, and 23 percentage points among Jews. Put another way, without the higher income members among Weekly Attending Catholics and Mainline Protestants, Bush would not have obtained a majority of these religious communities at the polls. But here, too, the influence of religion persists: if upper income Jews had voted Republican in 2004 at the same rate as upper income Mainline Protestants, Bush would likely have received a majority of the Jewish vote.

Smaller income gaps appear among Less Observant Mainline Protestants and Catholics, roughly on par with Evangelicals. The Latino groups had more modest income gaps than the Unaffiliated. These results are a bit surprising since there is a wider disparity of income within these groups (see table 5.7). The smallest income gap was found among Black Protestants and the Other Faiths. Of course, all these religious communities were solidly in the Democratic camp in 2004.

This evidence suggests that religion tends to reduce the effects of income differences. (Of course, the reverse case can be made as well: income differences tend to reduce the effects of religious differences.) This tendency can be seen by the fact that groups with strong religious identities based on belonging show smaller income gaps. However, unlike gender and age, religious traditionalism does not appear to play as strong a role: the biggest income gaps occur in some of the groups characterized by high levels of traditionalism, such as Weekly Attending Mainline Protestants and Catholics. Meanwhile, many of the groups characterized by an absence of traditionalism, such as among Less Observant Catholics and the Unaffiliated, show lower income gaps.

Income is not the only measure of social class, with occupation and education regarded as key components as well.[17] The NEP data do not contain a good measure of occupation, but they do have a standard measure of education attainment. As shown in table 1.7 (in chapter 1), the education gap was not very large in 2004, largely because education has an uneven connection to the vote: voters with both the lowest and highest levels of education were more likely to cast a Democratic ballot, while those at the middle levels voted more Republican.

As a consequence, education adds a level of complexity to patterns presented in table 5.9, a full exploration of which is beyond the scope of the present discussion. However, one effect is that high levels of education reduce the income gap somewhat, especially among the higher income people—for example, producing more Democratic votes among voters who are both affluent and well-educated. It may be that professional occupations have a similar effect.[18] As a consequence, the markers of upper-class status—income, occupation, and education—do not have uniform effects on the vote. Such influences may help account for the fact that the income gap was relatively small for some religious groups, such as Less Observant Mainline Protestants.

However, none of the measures of class alter the underlying impact of religion on the vote. Class appears to represent a separate source of social distinctiveness not as closely intertwined with religion as gender or age. And changes in the political impact of class seem less related to the "restructuring" of religion, although temporal declines in the class gap paralleled the largest increases in the New Religion Gap.

Taken together, this evidence suggests that "class interests" may well operate differently from "cultural interests," sometimes undercutting the political effects of religion and sometime reinforcing them. In this sense, the religion, gender, and generation gaps all represent a similar kind of political cleavage, and social class another kind all together.

The Religion Gaps and Demography: Summary of Effects

What was the net effect of demography on the religion gaps in the 2004 election? Statistical analysis of the joint impact of religion, gender, age, and income (as well as other demographic variables) using the NEP data does not eliminate the effects of religion on the vote, showing that religion is not just a proxy for these other forms of demography. Indeed, religion remains one of the largest and most powerful demographic variables in predicting the 2004 presidential vote. Other factors, particularly gender and income, also had independent effects.[19] The final results of this analysis closely resemble the simple measure of the "voter gaps" presented in table 1.7 (in chapter 1). A similar analysis of recent elections reveals that religion typically has had an independent impact when other demographic variables are taken into account, although religion was not always as powerful an influence as in 2004.[20]

Table 5.10 provides a simple exposition of the results of this statistical analysis. It compares the Bush proportion of the two-party vote for each religious community to the Bush vote of two groups within these communities: less affluent women and affluent men[21] (the third and fifth columns of the table report the net difference from the actual Bush vote). These groups tended to be consistently opposed to and supportive of President Bush, respectively.

These findings neatly summarize the overall effects of these other demographic factors on the Bush vote of the religious communities. The less affluent women voted *less* Republican in 2004 in every religious group. Likewise, affluent men voted *more* Republican in every case. These differences are often quite large, although some are modest. And in keeping with the previous discussion, there is considerable variation in the size of these vote differences across the religious communities. However, in most religious communities, there were very large differences between the less affluent women and their less affluent male counterparts, essentially compounding the gender and income gaps. For example, note that there was a 30 percentage point difference among weekly attending Catholics, and the doubling of the Bush support among the Unaffiliated between the two groups.

However, these demographic differentials did not on balance eliminate the religious differences in the 2004 presidential vote. For example, weekly attending Evangelical Protestants were the strongest Bush supporters overall, and

Table 5.10   Effect of Demography on the 2004 Bush Vote

	Bush Vote: Actual	Bush Vote: Less Affluent Women	Difference: Less Affluent Women	Bush Vote: Affluent Men	Difference: Affluent Men
Weekly Attending Evangelical Protestant	82.1	72.0	-10.1	93.8	11.7
Less Observant Evangelical Protestant	71.7	55.3	-16.4	79.4	7.7
Weekly Attending Mainline Protestants	57.2	42.0	-15.2	60.3	3.1
Less Observant Mainline Protestants	52.0	38.7	-13.3	61.5	9.5
Latino Protestants	55.9	31.0	-24.9	69.5	13.6
Weekly Attending Black Protestants	16.8	10.5	-6.3	21.2	4.4
Less Observant Black Protestants	8.4	2.0	-6.4	10.5	2.1
Weekly Attending Catholics	60.0	40.2	-18.2	70.7	10.7
Less Observant Catholics	51.6	44.6	-7.0	63.0	11.4
Latino Catholics	36.7	29.0	-7.7	56.1	19.4
Other Christians	73.0	58.9	-14.1	94.3	21.3
Jews	23.4	0.0	-23.4	43.3	19.9
Other Faiths	17.0	14.9	-2.1	20.0	3.0
Unaffiliated	27.7	15.6	-12.1	41.1	13.4
All	**51.2**	**42.6**	**-8.6**	**55.9**	**4.7**

Source: 2004 National Election Pool (NEP)

remain the strongest Bush supporters among less affluent women; weekly attending Black Protestants were among the religious groups most opposed to Bush and this pattern did not change. The most important exceptions were Catholic women and Mainline Protestant men, where the differences by worship attendance largely disappear in the two outlying groups. However, both religious traditions largely maintain their relative position in the ranking of Bush supporters.

Conclusions

The questions posed at the beginning of this chapter can now be answered. First, the political impact of religion in the 2004 election is by and large not a reflection of other demographic factors, such as gender, age, or income. Indeed, in statistical analyses of these data, religion remains a powerful independent factor in the vote, although other aspects of demography mattered to the vote as well. The patterns persist despite the close associations between gender, age, and income. In part, this reflects the fact that different religious communities have different demographic profiles.

The connection of each of these factors to the vote changed during the last half of the twentieth century. The gender gap parallels the emergence of the New Religion Gap, reflecting the connection of gender to the cultural conflict of this era. The generation gap shows a similar pattern, declining over the period precisely when the New Religion Gap appeared. The income gap was more constant over time and not as closely linked to cultural conflict, although it did decline when the New Religion Gap made its biggest advances. It is worth noting that all three gaps increased in importance during the highly polarized 2004 election.

These other demographic gaps occur within the context of religious communities, sometimes undermining the effects of religion and at other times reinforcing them. For example, there is a gender gap within most religious communities, with women voting more Democratic. There are also generation gaps in most of these communities, but the direction of the gap varies, so that sometimes younger voters were more Republican and sometimes more Democratic. The size of the gender and generation gaps was often related to religious traditionalism. Finally, there was also a persistent income gap within almost all the religious communities, with higher income voters preferring the Republicans and lower income voters preferring the Democrats. The size of the income gap was related to religious tradition, but not to religious traditionalism.

These findings reveal the rich social context in which religion influences political choices. Religious communities are indeed closely intertwined with gender, age, and income, and their characteristic politics are influenced by these demographic factors. But the combination of religious traditions and traditionalism also influences the political impact of gender, age, and, to a lesser extent, income, by providing a powerful context for the forging of individuals' connections to politics. In the next chapter, we will review one social context that is especially important to presidential elections: region.

6

The Religion Gaps in Regional Context

The previous chapters have described the impact of religion on the 2004 presidential vote, both the Old Religion Gap among religious traditions as well as the New Religion Gap reflecting religious traditionalism and defined by worship attendance. These patterns represent a sharp departure from the middle of the twentieth century, and by the early twenty-first century, they were tightly entwined with other aspects of demography, including gender, age, and income. However, these conclusions apply to the United States as a whole, and can be misleading if applied uncritically to particular regions or states. Thus, it is useful to consider the relationship between religion and politics at the sub-national level, where presidential campaigns are actually waged and won.

Contrary to popular perception, no American office-holders are formally elected at the national level. Even the president is chosen in 50 state elections (plus the District of Columbia), where the results are combined through the Electoral College. In addition, all U.S. Senators are elected by state and all the members of the U.S. House of Representatives are chosen within state boundaries, not to mention scores of state and local officials. Furthermore, the machinery for all elections is administered at the local level, under a complex mix of local, state, and federal law. These facts have never been lost on politicians and their operatives, who are well aware of the location of the operational units of American campaigns.

The relationship of this political reality to religion can be usefully captured by looking at regions, groups of adjacent states that have similar histories, economies, and religious communities. The latter is central to everyday thinking about region, recently encapsulated in the distinction between "red" and "blue" states. Indeed, to many people the solidly "red" South is synonymous with Evangelical Protestantism, while the deep "blue" Northeast is linked to Catholics and Jews. Candidates, party leaders, and interest group activists know about these regional religious characteristics and plan their political activities accordingly.

The goal of this chapter is to put the Old and New Religion gaps in regional context. It begins with a brief discussion of major regions within the United States, their role in the 2004 election, and how these patterns differ from 1944. Then, the text reviews the religious communities and the 2004 presidential vote region by region. Finally, it looks at the regional distribution of issue priorities, with a special focus on the much debated "moral values" in 2004. The Old Religion Gap matters in all the regions, but the New Religion Gap is most evident in the most politically competitive regions.

Regions and the Presidential Vote

A good place to begin is with an overview of regions and the presidential vote in 2004. Table 6.1 presents the two-party vote by eight major regions (instead of the more typical four), dividing them into "red" (solidly for Bush), "purple" (evenly divided), and "blue" (solidly for Kerry) regions. The regional definitions used here come from the Religion by Region project of the Leonard E. Greenberg Center for the Study of Religion and Public Life at Trinity College. This project's key insight is that regions have distinctive civic cultures that reflect the size and distribution of religious communities as well as the long-standing relationships among them. Such regional cultures tend to replicate themselves over time, retaining their political distinctiveness despite major demographic and political shifts.[1] Table 6.1 arranges these eight regions from the most "red" to the most "blue," with two "purple" regions in between.

Table 6.1   Regions and the 2004 Vote

	Bush	*Kerry*
Red Regions		
Southern Crossroads	59.5	40.5
Mountain West	58.7	41.3
South	56.4	43.6
Purple Regions		
Midwest	51.1	48.9
Pacific Northwest	47.9	52.1
Blue Regions		
Pacific	45.3	54.7
Mid-Atlantic	45.1	54.9
New England	41.4	58.6
ALL	**51.0**	**49.0**

Source: 2004 National Election Pool (NEP)

Region and the Presidential Vote in 2004 and 1944. The most Republican of the "red" regions in 2004 is a novel combination, labeled the "Southern Crossroads" (found at the top of table 6.1) It comprises the Southwest (Arkansas, Louisiana, Oklahoma, and Texas) plus Missouri. Former Texas Governor George W. Bush came from this region, so it is no surprise that he won three-fifths of the two-party vote there. The other two "red" regions are more familiar: the "Mountain West" (Arizona, Colorado, Idaho, Montana, New Mexico, Utah, and Wyoming), where Bush won almost three-fifths of the vote, and the "South" (Alabama, Florida, Georgia, Kentucky, Mississippi, North and South Carolina, Tennessee, Virginia and West Virginia), where Bush obtained a solid majority. In 2004, Bush won all the states in these regions. Together, these regions make up what might be called the Republican "sun belt" coalition.

At the bottom of table 6.1, the most Democratic of the "blue" regions was "New England" (Connecticut, Maine, Massachusetts, New Hampshire, Rhode Island, and Vermont). Massachusetts Senator John F. Kerry came from this region, so it is hardly surprising that he garnered nearly three-fifths of the two-party vote there. Kerry also won a solid majority in the two other "blue" regions, the "Middle Atlantic" (Delaware, Maryland, New Jersey, New York, and Pennsylvania) and the "Pacific" (California, Hawaii, and Nevada). Kerry was victorious in all of the states in these regions except Nevada. Together, these regions make up the Democratic "bicoastal" coalition.

The "purple" regions in the center of table 6.1 were almost evenly divided. Kerry prevailed in the "Pacific Northwest" (Alaska, Oregon, and Washington) by a slim majority, with only Alaska voting Republican. This region is sometimes included in the Democratic "bicoastal" coalition, but it is more competitive politically. Finally, Bush carried the "Midwest" with just 51 percent of the vote (Illinois, Indiana, Iowa, Kansas, Michigan, Minnesota, Nebraska, North and South Dakota, Ohio, and Wisconsin). Overall, Bush prevailed in seven (Ohio, Indiana, Iowa, and the four plains states) and Kerry in four (Illinois, Michigan, Minnesota, and Wisconsin) of these states. These "heartland" states were contested by both parties in 2004.[2]

The Potential Electorate in 2004 and 1944. Table 6.2 reports key voting characteristics of these eight regions in 2004 and 1944.[3] As can be seen in the first column of the table, the regions vary enormously in the relative size of the voting age population, a measure of the potential electorate in 2004.[4] In this regard, the South was the largest region, containing a little more than one-fifth of the potential electorate. When combined with the Southern Crossroads and Mountain West, the "red" regions accounted for more than two-fifths of the potential electorate in 2004.

In contrast, the largest of the "blue" regions was the Middle Atlantic, with about one-sixth of the potential electorate. All together, the "blue" regions made up less than one-third of the voting age population. Finally, the two "purple" regions accounted for almost one-quarter of the potential electorate. The Midwest was larger (and the second largest region in the country) at one-fifth of the

Table 6.2 Region and the Vote, 2004 and 1944

	2004				1944			
	% Potential Electorate	% Actual Electorate	% Bush	% Kerry	% Potential Electorate	% Actual Electorate	% Dewey	% FDR
Red Regions								
Southern Crossroads	13.0	12.5	59.5	40.5	12.2	8.7	35.2	64.8
Mountain West	5.8	5.5	58.7	41.3	2.9	3.4	41.7	58.3
South	22.6	23.1	56.4	43.6	17.5	9.8	28.9	71.1
Purple Regions								
Midwest	20.5	23.9	51.1	48.9	28.4	34.7	51.3	48.7
Pacific Northwest	3.6	3.8	47.9	52.1	2.2	2.6	48.6	51.4
Blue Regions								
Pacific	13.3	9.6	45.3	54.7	5.9	6.7	41.3	58.7
Mid-Atlantic	16.2	16.0	45.1	54.9	24.2	26.4	45.7	54.3
New England	5.0	5.6	41.4	58.5	6.7	7.7	53.2	46.8
ALL	**100.0**	**100.0**	**51.1**	**48.9**	**100.0**	**100.0**	**46.2**	**53.8**

Source: See note 7

voting age population, while the Pacific Northwest was much smaller at less than one-twentieth.

These 2004 population patterns differed substantially from 1944. For one thing, there have been significant changes in the relative size of the voting age population by region (the fifth column in table 6.2).[5] All the 2004 "red" regions gained relative population, especially the Mountain West. Overall, these regions increased from about one-third of the potential electorate in 1944 to more than two-fifths in 2004.

The 2004 "blue" regions showed a more mixed pattern. The Pacific region more than doubled in relative size between 1944 and 2004, while New England and especially the Middle Atlantic lost population in relative terms. The aggregate result was that the 2004 "blue" regions showed only a modest decline in their share of the potential electorate. The 2004 "purple" regions showed a similar mixed pattern: the Pacific Northwest grew in relative terms, while the Midwest experienced a sharp decline. So in aggregate, these "purple" regions showed a substantial decrease in their share of the national voting age population over the period.

These changes in relative population can be substantially explained by migration. The major migratory pattern got underway after the Second World War when Americans began a steady movement from the northern "frost belt" into the southern and western "sun belt." This ongoing population shift built up the major metropolitan areas in the South, Southern Crossroads, Mountain West, and Pacific regions as well as the Pacific Northwest. As a consequence, the Midwest, Middle Atlantic, and New England all lost population in relative terms. These shifts accompanied significant changes in the economy, settlement patterns, and social life. A second migratory pattern was immigration from abroad. While new immigrants arrived in all the regions (and with them the new religious communities discussed in chapter 2), the "sun belt" gained the most, especially from Latin America and Asia.

The Actual Electorate in 2004 and 1944. The second column in table 6.2 reports the actual electorate in 2004, that is, the citizens who actually went to the polls. Four regions, the South, Midwest, Pacific Northwest, and New England, "over-performed" in this regard (that is, their share of the actual vote cast was larger than their share of the voting age population because of relatively higher turnout). The four remaining regions, the Southern Crossroads, Mountain West, Pacific, and Middle Atlantic, "under-performed" at the ballot box (that is, their turnout was relatively lower.) These variations reflect the number of competitive states in the 2004 campaign as well as differences in socioeconomic status and political culture.[6]

The change in the actual vote between 1944 and 2004 was even more dramatic than the shifts in the potential electorate. In 1944, two of the 2004 "red" regions, the Southern Crossroads and the South, provided substantially fewer actual votes than their relative population size. In part this discrepancy reflects racial discrimination, which kept African-Americans and Latinos away from the polls.

But this pattern also results from the lack of political competition in these areas in the 1940s. The Mountain West provides an exception on all these counts: it provided more actual votes than its relative population size in 1944, had fewer minorities, and was more competitive. All told, these "red" regions provided a little more than one-sixth of the votes cast in 1944, less than one-half their share of the actual electorate in 2004 (almost two-fifths).

The 2004 "blue" states showed a different pattern: all of these states over-performed at the ballot box in 1944. Their total was more than two-fifths of the actual votes cast in 1944, substantially more than their proportion of the vote in 2004 (about one-third). However, the most dramatic change occurred in the Mid-west, the key "purple" region in 2004. In 1944, the Midwest provided nearly two-fifths of all the votes cast—nearly as many as the 2004 "blue regions" combined. This represented a substantial gain over the region's relative population size and reflects the political competitiveness of the Midwestern states in the 1940s. The other "purple" region, the Pacific Northwest, was also competitive and over-performed at the ballot box as well.

The Party Vote in 2004 and 1944. There were even more dramatic changes in the party vote by region between 2004 and 1944. For one thing, all of the 2004 "red" regions were strongly Democratic in 1944. The South was particularly so, with more than seven of every ten ballots cast for Roosevelt. The Southern Crossroads and Mountain West were less lopsided, but still solidly in the Democratic camp (64.8 and 58.3 percent, respectively). Thus, these regions became solidly "red" at the same time that they were gaining a larger share of the national vote. Overall, this pattern reveals cultural continuity combined with significant political change.

Once again, the 2004 "blue" states were different. The Pacific and Middle Atlantic regions maintained their Democratic leanings from 1944, with the for-mer modestly more Republican and the latter changing hardly at all. But New England shifted from the Republican column in 1944 to the Democratic column by 2004. Although the states within these regions have experienced diverse political trajectories, their links to the Democratic Party have solidified in the midst of the population gains and losses. Here, too, there is evidence of cultural continuity within regions despite great political change.

Finally, the "purple" regions changed hardly at all in these regards: in 1944 and 2004, the Midwest was slightly Republican, while the Pacific Northwest was slightly Democratic. Both regions were and remained closely competitive, with the shifting populations largely reinforcing the existing political alignments. Here is evidence of both cultural and political continuity.

Presidential Vote Coalitions in 2004 and 1944. Table 6.3 sums up all these changes by reviewing the relative contribution of the eight regions to the Republican and Democratic presidential vote coalitions in 2004 and 1944. As one might expect, there was a great deal of change in the Republican camp. In 2004, President Bush received some two-fifths of his ballots from the 2004 "red" regions and more than one-quarter from the "purple" regions. But back in

Table 6.3   Region, 2004 and 1944 Presidential Vote Coalitions

	2004		1944	
	Bush	Kerry	Dewey	FDR
Red Regions				
Southern Crossroads	14.4	10.5	4.8	7.6
Mountain West	6.3	4.7	3.8	4.6
South	25.2	20.6	4.5	9.5
Purple Regions				
Midwest	23.7	24.2	43.7	35.5
Pacific Northwest	3.5	4.1	1.9	1.7
Blue Regions				
Pacific	8.4	10.9	6.4	7.9
Mid-Atlantic	14.0	18.2	26.0	26.5
New England	4.5	6.8	8.9	6.7
ALL	**100.0**	**100.0**	**100.0**	**100.0**

Source: See note 7

1944, Governor Dewey received some two-fifths of his votes from 2004 "blue" states and more than two-fifths from the "purple" states. These shifts resulted from both demographic and political change.

There was more continuity in the Democratic camp. In 2004, Senator Kerry received a little less than two-fifths of his ballots from the 2004 "blue" regions, compared to just over two-fifths for President Roosevelt in 1944. Note that the 2004 "red" regions were more important to Kerry (providing about one-third of all his ballots) than for Roosevelt (about one-fifth). And in a parallel fashion, the Midwest provided relatively fewer Democratic votes in 2004 than in 1944. These patterns reflect the effects of migration, the expansion of the electorate, especially among African-Americans, as well as political change.

Region and Religion in 2004

Armed with the basic patterns of regional politics and change over time, we can now review the connections between religion and the 2004 presidential vote by region. These regional differences reflect both the size and distribution of religious communities within the regions, but also the civic cultures that structure the relationships between these communities. Such regional cultures often modify, but rarely completely erase, the overall impact of the Old and New Religion gaps on politics.[7] (See Appendix B for estimates of the size of the major religious communities by state.)

The "Red" Regions

The three "red" regions are part of the Republican "sun belt" coalition and were characterized by large populations of white Protestants and Other Christians. This pattern was a key factor in the politics of the region in 2004, and it helps explain lack of competitiveness in most of these states. However, President Bush enjoyed different winning coalitions in each region.

The Southern Crossroads. The states in this "reddest" of regions are often combined with the South (Texas, Oklahoma, Arkansas, and Louisiana) or the Midwest (Missouri). However, they are all boundary states, lying between the South, Midwest, and Mountain West, and also between the United States, Mexico, and the Caribbean. The Religion by Region project labels the Southern Crossroads as the "showdown states," long characterized by cultural confrontation and a degree of ethno-religious diversity.[8] Both George W. Bush and Bill Clinton hailed from this region. Table 6.4 reports this region's religious characteristics in 2004, revealing a broad and dominant coalition of white Christians in the Republican camp.

White Christians dominated the potential electorate of the Southern Crossroads. Taken together, Evangelical and Mainline Protestants, non-Latino Catholics, and the Other Christians accounted for nearly three-fifths of the potential electorate. Weekly Attending Evangelicals were the single largest group, with roughly one-sixth of the electorate, about the size of all Mainline Protestants and larger than all non-Latino Catholics. But there were important exceptions to this pattern: Latinos also made up about one-fifth of the potential electorate, with Latino Catholics accounting for two-thirds of the total. Black Protestants were about one-tenth and the Unaffiliated about one-eighth of the voting age population; Jews and Other Faiths were relatively rare.

The second column in table 6.4 reveals a sharp difference between the potential and actual electorate in 2004. Weekly Attending Evangelicals provided more than one-fifth of the votes cast, substantially higher than their proportion of the voting age population. This group was Bush's strongest constituency, giving him more than four-fifths of their votes (third column) and providing him with about three in every ten of his ballots (fifth column). Bush also received strong support from Less Observant Evangelicals and Mainliners, Latino Protestants, and the Other Christians. All of these groups performed well at the ballot box. Together, these groups contributed nearly three-quarters of Bush's 2004 ballots.

Interestingly, Bush did not do as well with Weekly Attending Mainline Protestants, the religious group to which he belongs, as an observant United Methodist. This group also under-performed at the ballot box. Still, he received two-thirds of their votes, roughly the same as for the two groups of non-Latino Catholics. So, these groups contributed to the Republican victory as well. It is worth noting that the New Religion Gap was only modestly evident in this region in 2004.

Table 6.4   Southern Crossroads, 2004

Religious Groups	Electorate: Potential	Actual	Two-Party Vote Bush	Kerry	Voter Coalitions Bush	Kerry
Weekly Attending Evangelical Protestant	17.0	22.0	**81.6**	**18.4**	29.0	10.6
Less Observant Evangelical Protestant	11.2	11.1	**74.2**	**25.8**	13.3	7.5
Latino Protestants	4.9	5.0	**74.2**	**25.8**	6.0	3.4
Weekly Attending Mainline Protestants	6.0	3.5	**66.1**	**33.9**	3.7	3.1
Less Observant Mainline Protestants	10.4	15.0	**70.8**	**29.2**	17.1	11.3
Weekly Attending Black Protestants	6.7	7.5	**16.4**	**83.6**	2.0	16.5
Less Observant Black Protestants	3.6	3.6	**10.0**	**90.0**	0.1	9.4
Weekly Attending Catholics	6.0	7.0	**68.0**	**32.0**	7.7	5.9
Less Observant Catholics	6.3	5.4	**63.5**	**36.5**	5.5	5.2
Latino Catholics	10.9	4.7	**41.0**	**59.0**	4.4	5.0
Other Christians	2.7	3.3	**89.7**	**10.3**	4.7	0.9
Jews	0.4	0.9	**31.3**	**68.4**	1.0	0.7
Other Faiths	1.9	2.8	**20.0**	**80.0**	0.9	5.9
Unaffiliated	12.0	8.2	**33.3**	**66.7**	4.4	14.4
ALL	100.0	100.0	**59.5**	**40.5**	100.0	100.0

Source: 2004 National Election Pool (NEP)

The Democrats were not without partisans in the Southern Crossroads, although the level of support was often lower than in other regions. Black Protestants, Other Faiths, and Jews strongly backed Kerry. Likewise, Latino Catholics and the Unaffiliated also voted Democratic; but note that these two groups seriously under-performed at the polls. This low level of participation may reflect the lack of competition in the Southern Crossroads in 2004. The Democrats had hoped to make Missouri and Arkansas into battleground states, but this prospect had faded long before Election Day. However, the religious and ethnic diversity of the region does offer some opportunity for Democratic candidates with appeal to moderate white Christians.

The 2004 patterns in the Southern Crossroads stand in stark contrast to 1944, when virtually all the region's religious communities voted strongly Democratic. Here the growth of this region's population has been associated with an increase in Republican voting. But this development did not occur in a straightforward fashion: Evangelicals and other white Protestants actually make up a *smaller* portion of the potential and actual electorates in 2004 than in 1944, reflecting the increased religious diversity of the region. However, these changes have served to make white Christians more distinctive politically, a fact the GOP has successfully exploited. The ethos of the "showdown states" has facilitated coalition building among white Christians, so that the region has become integral to the Republican "sun belt" coalition.

The Mountain West. The Mountain West has its own kind of religious pluralism. The Religion by Region Project describes it as "sacred landscapes in transition,"[9] noting several religious concentrations: Utah and the intermountain region (dominated by Latter Day Saints), Arizona and New Mexico (impacted by Catholics, Latinos, and Native Americans), and the Rocky Mountain states (influenced by Mainline Protestantism). In addition, rapid population growth has produced a large unaffiliated population. Table 6.5 reports this region's characteristics in 2004, revealing a special coalition of white Christians in the Republican camp.

Like the Southern Crossroads, the Mountain West was dominated by white Christians, with the Other Christian category especially important (about one-seventh of the potential electorate), led by the Latter Day Saints. When combined with Evangelical (about one-fifth) and Mainline Protestants (about one-sixth), these communities swelled to about one-half of the potential electorate. Catholics made up more than one-fifth of the voting age population, with Latinos the largest group, at roughly one-seventh of the population. Black Protestants, Jews and Other Faiths were less common, together about as numerous as Latino Protestants. However, the single largest group was the Unaffiliated, making up nearly one-fifth of the potential electorate.

Here, too, the actual and potential electorates differed in 2004. The Other Christians were vastly over-represented among actual voters and strongly backed Bush, providing nearly three of every ten of his ballots. A similar situation occurred for Weekly Attending Evangelicals, who provided the president with

Table 6.5   Mountain West, 2004

Religious Groups	Electorate:		Two-Party Vote		Voter Coalitions	
	Potential	Actual	Bush	Kerry	Bush	Kerry
Weekly Attending Evangelical Protestant	11.0	14.4	87.4	12.6	21.4	4.4
Less Observant Evangelical Protestant	9.7	6.5	84.0	16.0	9.3	2.5
Latino Protestants	3.8	2.7	61.9	38.1	2.9	2.5
Weekly Attending Mainline Protestants	4.6	2.9	50.0	50.0	2.4	3.5
Less Observant Mainline Protestants	11.8	15.5	46.2	53.8	12.1	20.3
Weekly Attending Black Protestants	0.9	1.2	22.2	77.8	0.4	2.2
Less Observant Black Protestants	0.5	2.0	33.3	66.7	1.1	3.2
Weekly Attending Catholics	4.6	5.7	70.5	29.5	6.8	4.1
Less Observant Catholics	5.3	7.5	46.6	53.4	5.9	9.8
Latino Catholics	13.9	4.0	16.1	83.9	1.1	8.3
Other Christians	13.2	19.6	88.1	11.9	29.3	5.7
Jews	0.8	0.3		100.0		0.6
Other Faiths	1.6	1.3	40.0	60.0	0.9	1.9
Unaffiliated	18.3	16.4	23.0	77.0	6.4	30.8
ALL	100.0	100.0	58.7	41.3	100.0	100.0

Source: 2004 National Election Pool (NEP)

another one-fifth of the Bush vote. Weekly Attending Non-Latino Catholics also over-performed at the polling places, and on balance backed Bush. In addition, the President obtained support from Less Observant and Latino Protestants, although both these groups under-performed at the polls.

Senator Kerry's strongest support came from religious minorities, but collectively they provided only about one-tenth of all his ballots in the region. Here it is important to note the very low electoral performance of Latino Catholics, who made up just 3.8 percent of the actual electorate. However, Kerry was bolstered by strong support from the Unaffiliated, who provided nearly one-third of all his ballots. And in contrast to the Southern Crossroads, Mainline Protestants voted on balance Democratic, with the weekly attenders evenly dividing their votes and the Less Observant backing Kerry. Kerry also did well with Less Observant Catholics. Indeed, these last three groups contributed another one-third of all the Democratic ballots. Thus, there is some modest evidence of the New Religion Gap in the Mountain West.

This variegated coalition allowed the Democrats to be competitive in Colorado, New Mexico, and Arizona in 2004, and offers the prospect for competitive elections in the future. However, these patterns represent a significant change from 1944. Then, Mainline Protestants made up over one-half of the potential electorate and voted on balance Republican. All the other religious groups voted Democratic. Since then, Mainliners have sharply declined in relative numbers and all the other religious groups have grown in size. These "sacred landscapes" are indeed in "transition" in the Mountain West, and for the moment they are part of the Republican "sun belt" coalition.

The South. The South is the most distinctive of the regions in cultural terms, a reality captured in the Religion by Region Project's description as "in the evangelical mode."[10] The South was settled early in the colonial period and was soon influenced by successive waves of Protestant revivals, becoming the most famous of the "Bible Belts" across the nation. This religious distinctiveness was reinforced by the institution of slavery, the Civil War, and the struggle for Civil Rights. These experiences produced a peculiar kind of religious diversity within the framework of highly traditional Protestantism, reinforced by postwar migration. As a consequence, the once "solid South" of the Democratic Party has become the "solid South" of the GOP. Table 6.6 reports this region's characteristics in 2004, revealing a solid coalition of white Protestants in the Republican camp.

The potential electorate in the South was dominated by white Protestants, with Evangelicals bulking much larger than in any other region. Overall, more than one-third of the voting age population were Evangelical Protestants, with weekly attenders the single largest group at one-fifth of the total. Mainline Protestants were also common, making up more than one-sixth. These religious communities, plus the Other Christians, accounted for more than one-half of the potential electorate. Like Evangelicals, Black Protestants were also more numerous in the South than any other region, making up one-sixth of the voting age population.

Table 6.6 The South, 2004

Religious Groups	Electorate: Potential	Electorate: Actual	Two-Party Vote Bush	Two-Party Vote Kerry	Voter Coalitions Bush	Voter Coalitions Kerry
Weekly Attending Evangelicals	20.5	21.5	**83.9**	**16.1**	*31.7*	*8.0*
Less Observant Evangelicals	14.2	9.4	**72.2**	**27.8**	*11.9*	*6.1*
Latino Protestants	1.8	1.0	**70.0**	**30.0**	*1.3*	*0.5*
Weekly Attending Mainline Protestants	6.7	4.9	**81.4**	**18.6**	*7.0*	*2.1*
Less Observant Mainline Protestants	10.6	12.4	**60.5**	**39.5**	*13.1*	*11.4*
Weekly Attending Black Protestants	9.6	8.2	**14.5**	**85.5**	*2.1*	*16.2*
Less Observant Black Protestants	6.6	5.1	**10.0**	**90.0**	*0.6*	*11.2*
Weekly Attending Catholics	3.7	8.0	**70.2**	**29.8**	*9.9*	*5.6*
Less Observant Catholics	6.5	8.0	**62.1**	**37.9**	*8.7*	*7.0*
Latino Catholics	3.9	2.8	**30.0**	**70.0**	*3.4*	*2.0*
Other Christians	2.0	3.6	**71.1**	**28.9**	*4.4*	*2.4*
Jews	1.1	3.2	**20.2**	**79.8**	*1.1*	*6.0*
Other Faiths	1.4	2.9	**18.5**	**81.5**	*0.9*	*5.4*
Unaffiliated	11.4	9.0	**23.1**	**76.9**	*3.7*	*16.1*
ALL	100.0	100.0	**56.4**	**43.6**	**100.0**	**100.0**

Source: 2004 National Election Pool (NEP)

The Non-Latino Catholic and Unaffiliated groups were the least common in this region, each at one-tenth of the potential electorate. Latinos and other religious minorities were also less numerous, summing to less than one-tenth of the voting age population.

Weekly Attending Evangelicals were the strongest Bush constituency in the South, followed closely by Weekly Attending Mainline Protestants. Together, these two observant groups provided almost two-fifths of all Bush's Southern ballots. But Less Observant Evangelicals and Mainliners also backed the President, albeit at a somewhat lower level, providing another one-quarter of his ballots. Latino Protestants, Other Christians, and non-Latino Catholics voted for Bush as well. Thus, there was only modest evidence of the New Religion Gap in 2004.

The South showed fewer discrepancies between the potential and actual vote in 2004. This fact may reflect the lack of competitive campaigns in most of the Southern states. Interestingly, Non-Latino Catholics and other religious minorities appear to have over-performed at the ballot box, a pattern that may reflect, in part, the fierce struggle for Florida in 2004. Indeed, if present demographic trends continue, the entire region may become increasingly like the Sunshine State.

The mainstay of the Kerry vote in the South was Black Protestants. Both the Weekly Attending and Less Observant strongly voted Democratic, with the less observant more so. Indeed, Black Protestants provided more than one-quarter of all Kerry's ballots. The Unaffiliated also backed Kerry strongly, as did the other religious minorities, combining to more than one-quarter of the Democratic ballots. It is this combination of minority faiths and less religious voters that prevented an overwhelming Republican victory in 2004. These patterns suggest that moderate Democratic candidates may be able to find some purchase in the future if they can appeal to moderate white Protestants.

The South showed the sharpest contrast from 1944, when President Roosevelt could count on very large majorities from all of these religious communities (except for Black Protestants, few of whom could vote due to segregation). Indeed, post-war migration and the expanded electorate created a more diverse religious landscape in the South, with a significant reduction in the relative number of white Protestants. But the result to date has been the slow development of a strong Republican coalition "in the evangelical mode," making the region part of the Republican "sun belt" coalition.

The "Blue" Regions

In 2004, the three "blue" regions were part of the Democratic "bicoastal" coalition, and they had a strikingly different religious composition than the "red" regions. Catholics were more numerous, and Less Observant Mainline Protestants and religious minorities played a larger role. John Kerry won solid victories with different religious coalitions in each of these regions.

New England. The New England region is often combined with the Middle Atlantic to form a "Northeast" region, but it has a distinctive civic culture. The Religion by Region Project described New England with the phrase "steady habits, changing slowly," a good term for the adaptation of the original ethos of "dissenting Protestant" to succeeding waves of immigrants, particularly Catholics.[11] Indeed, the tension between Mainline Protestants and Catholics was and still is a critical feature of the politics of this region, now reinforced by the continued arrival of immigrants. Table 6.7 reports this region's characteristics in 2004, revealing a broad alliance in the Democratic camp, centered on less traditional white Christians.

In 2004, Catholics accounted for nearly two-fifths of the potential electorate in New England, and Non-Latino Catholics more than one-third, the largest of any region in the country. However, the Unaffiliated were the single largest category, accounting for one-fifth of the voting age population. Religious minorities made up another one-sixth of the potential electorate, including Black Protestants, Latinos, Jews, and the Other Faiths. Mainline Protestants accounted for another one-sixth of the voting age population, while Evangelicals and Other Christians combined were slightly less numerous.

In 2004, two of these religious communities over-performed at the ballot box: Less Observant Mainline Protestants and Less Observant Catholics. Both voted strongly for Kerry, providing almost one-half of all of Kerry's New England ballots. Although the Unaffiliated under-performed at the ballot box, they also voted Democratic, providing another one-fifth of Kerry's total. All the religious minorities backed the Democrats, and Kerry did especially well with another group, Weekly Attending Mainline Protestants.

In contrast, Bush carried Weekly Attending Catholics with a solid majority and did very well among Weekly Attending Evangelicals. Indeed, these two observant groups provided three of every ten of Bush's ballots. The President also won the Less Observant Evangelicals and the Other Christians, but these groups under-performed at the polls. Thus, there was some modest evidence of the New Religion Gap in this region. Interestingly, nearly one-half of Bush's ballots came from the Less Observant Mainliners and Catholics. This fact suggests that Republicans can compete in New England by making inroads into the less traditional religious communities. Indeed, the GOP had hoped to contest New Hampshire and Maine in 2004.

The 2004 New England vote also contrasted sharply with 1944. In that election, Republican Dewey carried the region on the basis of white Protestants, led by the numerous Mainliners, but also including Evangelicals and the Other Christians. Roosevelt had strong support from Catholics, Jews, and the Unaffiliated. This dramatic shift reflects changes in demography as well as politics. Constrained by its "steady habits," New England has changed its partisanship slowly, and is now central to the Democratic "bicoastal" coalition.

The Middle Atlantic. Although the Middle Atlantic is often combined with New England because of recent political similarities, it has a different civic

Table 6.7   New England, 2004

Religious Groups	Electorate: Potential	Actual	Two-Party Vote Bush	Kerry	Voter Coalitions Bush	Kerry
Weekly Attending Evangelical Protestants	5.9	5.1	82.5	17.5	9.9	1.6
Less Observant Evangelical Protestants	6.1	1.9	80.0	20.0	3.6	0.7
Latino Protestants	2.7	1.7	30.8	69.2	1.2	2.0
Weekly Attending Mainline Protestants	3.7	5.0	33.3	66.7	3.9	5.8
Less Observant Mainline Protestants	12.3	21.1	42.4	57.6	21.0	21.2
Weekly Attending Black Protestants	2.4	0.4	33.3	66.7	1.2	0.2
Less Observant Black Protestants	2.5	1.4	36.4	63.6	0.6	1.6
Weekly Attending Catholics	14.9	14.8	60.3	39.7	21.0	10.2
Less Observant Catholics	19.7	26.2	45.9	54.1	28.2	24.7
Latino Catholics	3.9	1.9	20.0	80.0	0.9	2.7
Other Christians	2.0	1.2	55.6	44.4	1.5	0.9
Jews	1.0	2.2		100.0		3.8
Other Faiths	2.8	2.0	12.5	87.5	0.6	3.1
Unaffiliated	20.2	15.1	17.8	82.2	6.3	21.6
ALL	100.0	100.0	41.4	58.5	100.0	100.0

Source: 2004 National Election Pool (NEP)

culture. The Religion by Region Project described the region as "the fount of diversity."[12] This appellation reflects the ethno-religious diversity of the original colonies, including Dutch New York, Anglican New Jersey, Quaker Pennsylvania, Swedish Delaware, and Catholic Maryland. One result was an ethos of religious pluralism eventually recognized in Will Herbert's formulation of "Protestant, Catholic, Jew."[13] Later waves of immigration fit into the Middle Atlantic's civic culture more comfortably than in many other regions. Table 6.8 reports this region's characteristics in 2004, revealing a solid pluralistic alliance in the Democratic camp, based on religious minorities and less traditional Christians.

As with New England, Catholics were numerous in the Middle Atlantic, making up about one-third of the potential electorate and Non-Latino Catholics more than one-quarter. However, the Unaffiliated were also the single largest group, accounting for about one-sixth of the voting age population. And religious minorities were numerous as well: Black Protestants made up almost one-tenth of the potential electorate, and all the other minorities one-seventh. Indeed, the Middle Atlantic had the largest population of Jews of any region. Mainline Protestants accounted for less than one-fifth of the potential electorate, while Evangelicals and Other Christians accounted for about one-seventh.

In this region, Senator Kerry received his strongest support from religious minorities, including the Other Faiths, Black Protestants, the Unaffiliated, Jews, Latinos—and the Other Christians as well. Together, this cosmopolitan coalition provided more than one-half of the Democratic ballots. Kerry also did well among Weekly Attending and Less Observant Mainline Protestants, winning both groups, and the weekly attenders by a larger margin.

In the Mid-Atlantic, Bush's electoral strength was concentrated among Catholics. Bush carried three-fifths of Weekly Attending Catholics and a slim majority of the Less Observant. These groups over-performed at the ballot box and together provided almost one-half of all Bush's ballots. Evangelicals supported Bush (and especially the weekly attenders), but they did not perform especially well at the polls. Thus, there was some evidence for the New Religion Gap. It is worth noting, however, that almost one-fifth of Bush's vote came from Mainline Protestants. This pattern suggests that the right kind of Republican candidate can compete in the pluralistic ethos of this region. In 2004, Pennsylvania was competitive for just this reason.

Here, too, there was a contrast with 1944, when both presidential nominees hailed from this region, one the current and the other a former governor of New York. Republican Dewey carried Mainline Protestants by large margins in 1944, but also won Evangelicals and the Other Christians. In contrast, President Roosevelt won big among Catholics, Jews, and Black Protestants. Thus, the "fount of diversity" has adjusted to the demographic and political shifts of the last 60 years, and now is part of the Democratic "bicoastal" coalition.

The Pacific. California makes up nearly all of the population in the Pacific region, with Hawaii and Nevada fitting within the great diversity of the Golden

Table 6.8 Middle Atlantic, 2004

Religious Groups	Electorate: Potential	Actual	Two-Party Vote Bush	Kerry	Voter Coalitions Bush	Kerry
Weekly Attending Evangelical Protestants	6.5	6.4	82.8	17.2	12.3	2.0
Less Observant Evangelical Protestants	5.7	3.3	56.8	43.2	4.3	2.5
Latino Protestants	2.1	2.3	37.3	62.7	1.9	2.5
Weekly Attending Mainline Protestants	6.0	3.5	40.0	60.0	3.3	3.8
Less Observant Mainline Protestants	12.1	13.7	48.7	51.3	15.4	12.4
Weekly Attending Black Protestants	5.8	4.3	16.5	83.5	1.6	6.3
Less Observant Black Protestants	6.1	4.3	8.2	91.8	0.8	7.0
Weekly Attending Catholics	13.3	15.1	62.4	37.6	21.7	10.0
Less Observant Catholics	13.2	21.3	53.0	47.0	26.1	17.7
Latino Catholics	6.3	4.4	25.3	74.7	2.6	5.8
Other Christians	1.6	2.0	45.5	54.5	2.0	1.9
Jews	3.5	5.1	25.0	75.0	3.0	6.8
Other Faiths	2.5	3.9	11.4	88.6	1.0	6.1
Unaffiliated	15.3	10.4	16.2	83.8	3.9	15.3
ALL	100.0	100.0	45.1	54.9	100.0	100.0

Source: 2004 National Election Pool (NEP)

State. Nevada is often included in the Mountain West, and the Pacific Northwest is sometimes combined with California. However, the present definition reflects the special ethnic and religious diversity of these states, which the Religion by Region Project captured as "fluid identities."[14] Partly the product of rapid population growth, this "hyper-pluralism" resembles the Middle Atlantic, but with an even broader range of participants. The Pacific region is what makes the Democratic coalition "bicoastal." Table 6.9 reports this region's characteristics in 2004, revealing a solid pluralistic coalition based on religious minorities and the Unaffiliated.

Catholics made up three of ten potential voters in the Pacific, and Latino Catholics accounted for more than one-fifth. Here, too, the Unaffiliated were the single largest group, accounting for more than one-fifth of the total. Religious minorities are also numerous, making up more than one-sixth of the voting age population, with the largest proportion of the Other Faiths of any region. White Protestants were less common in this region, with Evangelicals making up a little less than one-sixth of the total and Mainliners about one-tenth.

Many of the religious minorities in the Pacific region voted strongly Democratic in 2004, including Jews, the Other Faiths, and Black Protestants. The Unaffiliated and Latino Catholics also backed the Democrats to a somewhat lesser extent, but the latter significantly under-performed at the ballot box. Still, all these groups combined for more than one-half of all Kerry's ballots in 2004. Both the Non-Latino Catholic and Mainline Protestant groups voted Democratic in this region, with the weekly attenders the most Democratic. In contrast, President Bush did well among Evangelical and Latino Protestants, and Other Christians.

These patterns were both a cause and a consequence of the lack of competition in the region. It is worth noting, however, that Bush won Nevada in 2004, and Hawaii was perceived as competitive in the dying days of the campaign. And interestingly, this region is less Democratic than in 1944, when President Roosevelt was competitive among white Protestants and won all the other religious communities. Viewed from this long perspective, the growth of the Pacific region has made it more hospitable to Republicans, so that candidates like Richard Nixon, Ronald Reagan, and Arnold Schwarzenegger could piece together winning coalitions. But in 2004, the "fluid identities" of the Pacific region coalesced in the Democratic camp, becoming part of the "bicoastal" coalition.

The "Purple" Regions

Because of each party's success in the "red" and "blue" regions, the 2004 election was settled in the closely contested "purple" regions, the Pacific Northwest and especially the Midwest. Each of these regions was characterized by a close balance among different and potentially rival religious communities. The New Religion Gap was especially evident in these highly competitive regions.

The Pacific Northwest. Although the Pacific Northwest is often combined with California and regarded as part of the Democratic "bicoastal" coalition, it has a

Table 6.9 Pacific, 2004

Religious Groups	Electorate: Potential	Electorate: Actual	Two-Party Vote Bush	Two-Party Vote Kerry	Voter Coalitions Bush	Voter Coalitions Kerry
Weekly Attending Evangelical Protestants	8.6	7.9	**81.5**	**18.5**	*14.6*	*2.6*
Less Observant Evangelical Protestants	6.7	6.9	**70.0**	**10.0**	*14.2*	*1.2*
Latino Protestants	6.1	5.7	**60.3**	**39.7**	*7.8*	*4.1*
Weekly Attending Mainline Protestants	2.5	1.5	**30.0**	**70.0**	*1.0*	*1.8*
Less Observant Mainline Protestants	7.8	15.6	**46.5**	**53.5**	*16.4*	*14.9*
Weekly Attending Black Protestants	2.9	2.1	**31.0**	**69.0**	*1.5*	*2.6*
Less Observant Black Protestants	2.8	1.6	**10.0**	**90.0**	*0.2*	*2.7*
Weekly Attending Catholics	4.1	6.7	**32.6**	**67.4**	*5.0*	*8.1*
Less Observant Catholics	6.4	10.8	**40.5**	**59.5**	*9.9*	*11.5*
Latino Catholics	20.9	9.9	**30.1**	**69.9**	*6.8*	*12.4*
Other Christians	3.6	3.9	**69.8**	**30.2**	*6.1*	*2.1*
Jews	1.6	3.8	**15.4**	**84.6**	*1.3*	*5.8*
Other Faiths	4.0	2.8	**17.9**	**82.1**	*1.2*	*4.2*
Unaffiliated	22.0	20.7	**29.9**	**70.1**	*14.1*	*26.0*
ALL	100.0	100.0	**45.3**	**54.7**	*100.0*	*100.0*

Source: 2004 National Election Pool (NEP)

distinctive civic culture. The Religion by Region Project dubbed it the "none zone" because it had the largest Unaffiliated population of any region, a fact that has led other observers to call it the "anti-Bible Belt."[15] The "none zone" is a product of rapid population growth in the post-war period and the religious diversity it fostered. This situation has created regular contention over a range of topics, from sexual behavior to environmentalism. Table 6.10 reports the region's characteristics in 2004, revealing a broad alliance in the Democratic camp, anchored by the Unaffiliated.

The Unaffiliated accounted for some 28 percent of the potential electorate in the Pacific Northwest. However, all Evangelical Protestants were nearly as numerous at 25 percent. Indeed, the combination of the Unaffiliated, Other Faiths and Black Protestants was almost exactly equal to the combination of Evangelicals, Other Christians, and Latino Protestants—at about 32.5 percent of the voting age population in each column. Catholics and Mainline Protestants each accounted for another one-sixth of the total.

As in other regions, Senator Kerry did well with the Unaffiliated, winning three-fifths of their votes and obtaining from this group three of every ten of his ballots. He also received strong support from religious minorities, but his second largest source of ballots was Less Observant Mainline Protestants (a little more than one-sixth), a group that voted Democratic at the same rate as the Unaffiliated. Kerry also won the Less Observant Catholics by an even larger margin.

Evangelical Protestants voted for Bush in this region, with the weekly attenders the most supportive; both Evangelical groups provided more than one-third of all Bush's ballots. The President also won Weekly Attending Catholics and Mainliners by a small margin. Thus, the New Religion Gap was strongly in evidence. In addition, the Republicans also did well with Other Christians and Latino Protestants. It is worth noting that Bush received one-third of all his ballots from Kerry's top two constituencies, the Unaffiliated and Less Observant Mainline Protestants. So, the GOP had a less traditional component to its voter coalition in the Pacific Northwest.

These 2004 patterns resemble the situation in 1944. Then, white Protestants were closely divided, with a slight edge to the Republicans, while Catholics and Other Christians strongly backed the Democrats. Population growth and increased religious diversity since 1944 has modified, but not eliminated such political divisions. Hence, there is every reason to expect that neither political party will soon establish a clear advantage in the "none zone."

The Midwest. In many respects, the Midwest is a microcosm of the nation as a whole, a fact noted by the Religion by Region Project with the question "America's common denominator?"[16] Looked at another way, this region also contains much of the country's religious diversity, with the major religious traditions nearly evenly balanced. The Midwest was settled by waves of internal migrants and a diverse set of European immigrants in the nineteenth century, and then became the location of periodic religious revivals. These factors produced some of the best examples of "ethno-religious" politics in the nineteenth and twentieth

Table 6.10 Pacific Northwest, 2004

Religious Groups	Electorate: Potential	Electorate: Actual	Two-Party Vote Bush	Two-Party Vote Kerry	Voter Coalitions Bush	Voter Coalitions Kerry
Weekly Attending Evangelicals	15.3	12.8	78.3	21.7	21.2	5.3
Less Observant Evangelicals	10.1	11.7	52.4	47.6	12.9	10.6
Latino Protestants	2.0	3.0	60.0	40.0	3.1	2.8
Weekly Attending Mainline Protestants	5.3	4.8	53.8	46.2	5.5	4.3
Less Observant Mainline Protestants	11.2	16.0	38.4	61.6	12.9	18.8
Weekly Attending Black Protestants	1.0	1.7	44.4	55.6	1.6	1.8
Less Observant Black Protestants	0.6	0.9		100.0		1.8
Weekly Attending Catholics	4.5	6.3	52.8	47.2	6.3	6.4
Less Observant Catholics	8.8	7.3	30.8	69.2	4.7	9.6
Latino Catholics	4.2	3.4	30.0	70.0	3.5	3.2
Other Christians	5.1	3.7	80.0	20.0	6.3	1.4
Jews	0.9	0.7		100.0	1.6	
Other Faiths	3.4	2.4		100.0		4.6
Unaffiliated	27.6	25.1	38.5	61.5	20.4	29.4
ALL	100.0	100.0	47.9	52.1	100.0	100.0

Source: 2004 National Election Pool (NEP)

centuries. In the midst of this diversity, Mainline Protestantism left a strong imprint on the rural parts of the region, as did the conservatism of German Catholics located in the "triangle" defined by Cincinnati, St. Louis, and Milwaukee. Table 6.11 reports the region's characteristics in 2004, revealing a complex alliance in the Republican camp, anchored by religious traditionalists.

In 2004, Evangelical Protestants were the largest religious tradition in the Midwest, accounting for one-quarter of the potential electorate. However, Mainline Protestants and Catholics were each nearly as numerous. Weekly Attending Evangelicals were one of the largest religious groups (14.6 percent), but about the same size as Less Observant Mainliners (14.7 percent) and the Unaffiliated (15.4 percent), the single largest group. Taken together, the religious minorities made up about one-tenth of the voting age population.

Much of the Midwest was closely contested in 2004, and partly as a consequence, there were only a few deviations between the potential and actual electorate. The New Religion Gap was strongly evident in this region. President Bush eked out a narrow victory with the strong support of Weekly Attending Evangelicals and solid backing from Weekly Attending Mainline Protestants and Catholics. Together, these groups provided the Republicans with more than two-fifths of their ballots. Bush also did well with Less Observant Evangelicals and Other Christians, for another one-seventh of all his ballots.

Meanwhile, Less Observant Catholics and Mainliners divided their votes almost evenly, with the former favoring Bush and the latter for Kerry. The Democrats added strong support from Black Protestants, other religious minorities, and the Unaffiliated. Indeed, together these groups provided nearly two-fifths of all Kerry's ballots.

The Midwest was also evenly divided in 1944. However, the basis of party support has changed. Then the Republicans were the party of Mainline Protestants, also receiving support from Weekly Attending Evangelicals and the Unaffiliated. Meanwhile, the Democrats drew heavy support from Catholics, Other Christians, and other religious minorities.

These patterns can be seen most clearly in two very competitive Midwestern states, Ohio (won by Bush) and Michigan (won by Kerry), presented in table 6.12. The New Religion Gap is clearly visible: Bush did better with the weekly attenders, with Kerry doing better with the Less Observant. And one can also see the Old Religion Gap as well, with Bush having the most backing from Evangelicals and doing less well with Catholics.

Indeed, the key to the 2004 election in both states was the relative size of the religion gaps. In Ohio, Bush got almost two-thirds of Weekly Attending Catholics, but just broke even with this group in Michigan. In the Buckeye State, Bush got a large majority from Mainline Protestants, but received two-thirds in the Wolverine State. Bush also did better with Weekly Attending Black Protestants in Ohio and broke even with the Other Christians, while Kerry benefited from higher support among these groups in Michigan. It is easy to see how even

Table 6.11 The Midwest, 2004

Religious Groups	Electorate: Potential	Actual	Two-Party Vote Bush	Kerry	Voter Coalitions Bush	Kerry
Weekly Attending Evangelicals	14.6	14.6	80.9	19.1	23.1	5.7
Less Observant Evangelicals	10.6	7.9	69.5	30.5	10.8	5.0
Latino Protestants	1.3	1.3	31.1	68.9	0.8	1.8
Weekly Attending Mainline Protestants	8.3	6.7	53.2	46.8	7.0	6.4
Less Observant Mainline Protestants	14.7	17.4	48.6	51.4	16.5	18.3
Weekly Attending Black Protestants	4.5	3.0	14.4	85.6	0.8	5.2
Less Observant Black Protestants	3.2	2.2	11.5	88.5	0.5	4.0
Weekly Attending Catholics	8.5	12.8	55.7	44.3	13.9	11.6
Less Observant Catholics	11.7	13.6	50.2	49.8	13.4	13.9
Latino Catholics	3.6	3.1	20.2	79.8	1.2	5.1
Other Christians	1.3	2.8	64.3	35.7	3.5	2.0
Jews	0.7	1.1	24.3	75.7	0.5	1.6
Other Faiths	1.6	1.5	26.4	73.6	0.8	2.3
Unaffiliated	15.4	12.0	30.4	69.6	7.1	17.1
ALL	100.0	100.0	51.1	48.9	100.0	100.0

Source: 2004 National Election Pool (NEP)

Table 6.12 Ohio and Michigan in 2004

	Ohio % Vote	Two-Party Vote Bush	Two-Party Vote Kerry	Voter Coalitions Bush	Voter Coalitions Kerry	Michigan % Vote	Two-Party Vote Bush	Two-Party Vote Kerry	Voter Coalitions Bush	Voter Coalitions Kerry
Weekly Attending Evangelicals	**15.6**	*81.6*	*18.4*	*24.6*	*5.9*	**14.5**	*79.8*	*20.2*	*24.0*	*5.7*
Less Observant Evangelicals	**9.1**	*64.4*	*35.6*	*11.2*	*6.6*	**6.3**	*64.6*	*35.4*	*8.5*	*4.4*
Weekly Attending Mainline Protestants	**6.4**	*56.1*	*43.9*	*7.0*	*5.8*	**5.4**	*68.6*	*31.4*	*7.4*	*3.2*
Less Observant Mainline Protestants	**15.6**	*45.4*	*54.6*	*13.8*	*17.7*	**14.0**	*50.6*	*49.4*	*14.7*	*13.5*
Weekly Attending Black Protestants	**2.7**	*22.9*	*77.1*	*1.2*	*4.3*	**5.2**	*13.3*	*86.7*	*1.5*	*9.0*
Less Observant Black Protestants	**3.8**	*11.9*	*88.1*	*0.9*	*6.8*	**3.9**	*7.7*	*92.3*	*0.6*	*7.3*
Weekly Attending Catholics	**12.2**	*65.0*	*35.0*	*15.6*	*8.9*	**14.1**	*49.7*	*50.3*	*14.6*	*13.9*
Less Observant Catholics	**14.9**	*47.0*	*53.0*	*13.6*	*16.4*	**16.1**	*47.1*	*52.9*	*15.6*	*16.5*
Other Christians	**4.6**	*49.4*	*50.6*	*4.4*	*4.8*	**4.1**	*39.3*	*60.7*	*3.2*	*4.7*
Other Faiths	**5.1**	*19.8*	*80.2*	*2.0*	*8.5*	**6.6**	*33.3*	*66.7*	*4.4*	*8.3*
Unaffiliated	**10.0**	*29.7*	*70.3*	*5.7*	*14.3*	**9.8**	*27.4*	*72.6*	*5.4*	*13.5*
ALL	**100.0**	**51.5**	**48.5**	100.0	100.0	**100.0**	**48.5**	**51.5**	100.0	100.0

Source: 2004 National Election Pool (NEP), Ohio and Michigan state surveys

modest changes in numbers would have altered the elections results. In this sense, the Midwest was indeed "America's common denominator" in 2004.

Region and Issue Priorities

One way to illustrate the political impact of these regional religious coalitions is to review voters' issue priorities as reported in the NEP (and discussed at length in chapter 4). Table 6.13 reports the issue priorities for the "red," "purple," and "blue" states, overall and for the religious categories.

The overall priorities for the three types of regions are listed across the bottom of table 6.13. "Moral values" was most common in the "red" regions, and declined in the "purple" and "blue" regions. In partial contrast, foreign policy priorities were most common in the "blue" regions, and less so in the other two. And, economic policy priorities were about as common in all three kinds of regions. This variation in "moral values" priorities—and the relative lack of variation of the other priorities—suggest that "moral values" may have had more of an impact on the election: Bush's success is directly related to the level of "moral values" priorities.[17]

One reason for these regional patterns in issue priorities is the distribution of religious communities. Although the patterns in this table are complex, they are also quite revealing. In all regions, "moral value" priorities were the special province of Weekly Attending Evangelical Protestants, with approximately one-half choosing such concerns over foreign or economic policy. As one might expect, the "red" regions scored higher in this regard than the "blue" regions. But interestingly, the "purple" regions had the largest amount (57 percent). This "purple" anomaly held for the Less Observant Evangelicals, Weekly Attending Black Protestants, and the Other Faiths as well. These data may reflect the intense political mobilization in these competitive regions in the 2004 campaign.

Latino Protestants also scored high on moral values in the "red" states, but were less likely to hold these priorities in the "purple" and "blue" states. A similar shift occurred among the Other Christians, and Weekly Attending Mainline Protestants and Catholics. Note the evidence of the New Religion Gap: the less observant mentioned "moral values" less often than their more observant co-religionists within each region. However, Jews and the Unaffiliated showed an opposite trend, with "moral values" becoming more important from the "red" to "blue" states. These figures may reveal the locale of some liberal "moral values" voters.

Foreign policy priorities showed more variegated patterns. Less Observant Mainline Protestants and Catholics paid great attention to foreign policy matters and more so in the "blue" regions. Meanwhile, Less Observant Evangelicals and Weekly Attending Catholics showed a similar pattern. Jews and the Unaffiliated were also concerned with foreign policy, but this interest declined from the "red" to "blue" regions. Although there was less regional variation on

Table 6.13 Religion, Region, and Issue Priorities

	Red States			Purple States			Blue States		
	moral values	foreign policy	economic policy	moral values	foreign policy	economic policy	moral values	foreign policy	economic policy
Weekly Attending Evangelicals	51.6	26.5	21.9	57.4	19.1	23.5	47.8	34.1	18.1
Less Observant Evangelicals	25.8	35.9	38.3	30.6	32.7	36.7	26.7	41.9	31.4
Latino Protestants	52.1	27.1	20.8	14.3	32.1	53.6	29.0	29.0	42.0
Weekly Attending Mainline Protestants	32.4	40.7	26.9	26.2	43.6	30.2	20.0	35.0	45.0
Less Observant Mainline Protestants	18.2	40.1	41.7	19.2	36.9	43.9	12.5	47.4	40.1
Weekly Attending Black Protestants	17.2	24.9	57.9	22.6	13.2	64.2	14.8	18.5	66.7
Less Observant Black Protestants	8.2	11.2	80.6	14.3	14.3	71.4	12.2	31.1	56.7
Weekly Attending Catholics	33.1	34.3	32.6	29.9	31.3	38.8	17.5	49.6	32.9
Less Observant Catholics	18.3	40.2	41.5	11.7	39.3	49.0	11.5	50.7	37.8
Latino Catholics	20.0	31.8	48.2	9.6	28.8	61.6	10.0	29.2	60.8
Other Christians	41.4	34.9	23.7	25.9	38.9	35.2	19.6	30.4	50.0
Jews	3.5	54.4	42.1	6.3	18.7	75.0	18.9	50.0	31.1
Other Faiths	15.5	24.1	60.4	18.8	34.4	46.8	11.3	33.8	54.9
Unaffiliated	9.7	44.1	46.2	10.6	42.1	47.3	18.7	36.0	45.3
ALL	27.8	33.9	38.3	25.0	33.1	41.9	18.0	41.1	40.9

Source: 2004 National Election Pool (NEP)

economic policy concerns, Black Protestants, Latino Catholics, Other Christians, and Other Faiths all had a very strong interest in such matters, which tended to increase from the "red" to the "blue" regions. Interestingly, the same pattern held for Weekly Attending Mainliners, who were strong Kerry supporters in the "blue" regions.

Conclusions

This chapter has put the religion gaps in regional context. Since presidential elections are waged and won at the sub-national level, the regions reveal much about the political impact of religion. Using eight regions defined by the Religion by Region Project, there were important differences in the 2004 presidential election between the "red" regions won by Bush, the "blue" regions won by Kerry, and the highly competitive "purple" regions where the election was resolved. These regional patterns often differ starkly from 1944, revealing the effects of both demographic and political change. Indeed, the solidly "red" regions in 2004 were Democratic strongholds 60 years before, while solidly "blue" New England was then Republican. And there was also evidence of political continuity: the "purple" Midwest was evenly divided in both eras.

Region matters politically in part because of enduring civic cultures, and these reflect in part the size and distribution of religious communities as well as the long-standing ways that they interact with one another. For example, the "red" regions were characterized by the presence of traditional white Christians, and these groups played a critical role in the Republican coalitions, which varied from region to region. Likewise, the "blue" regions had many more Catholics, less traditional Christians, and a wider variety of religious minorities. In contrast, the "purple" regions were characterized by a balance between major religious communities, and this fact contributed to the close partisan competition. These differences are reflected in the distribution of issue priorities of the voters in 2004.

The Old Religion Gap was in evidence in all of the regions. In fact, the dominant religious traditions helped explain the lack of competition in the solidly "red" and "blue" regions. And in many regions, the New Religion Gap defined by church attendance was only modestly evident. However, both religion gaps were strongly evident in the highly competitive "purple" regions. With these findings in mind, we now turn to a final factor in accounting for the links between religion and politics in 2004: the impact of the campaign itself.

7

The Religion Gaps in Action: Campaign Contact and Activism

One reason that religion figured so prominently in accounts of the 2004 election was the extensive efforts to mobilize religious voters. Indeed, the discussion by journalists of "fundamentalists," the "God gap," and "values voters" in explaining the results all presumed such campaign activities. And much of the consternation occasioned by the election outcome reflected the perceived divisiveness of the religious elements of the campaign—and much of the surprise came from the apparent success of these efforts, which were assumed to have re-elected President Bush. As was shown in table 1.8 (in chapter 1), voters reported a substantial level of campaign contact, especially in the "battleground" states. Both campaigns were apparently successful in targeting their religious constituencies defined by the Old and New Religion gaps.

Seeking the votes of religious people is hardly new in American elections.[1] Given the size and variety of religious communities in the United States, it was all but inevitable that they would be included among the building "blocs" of electoral coalitions. Of course, candidates have had a personal interest in appealing to congenial religious voters to win elections, and political parties and interest groups found it useful to mobilize key religious communities to further their political purposes. Religious communities were often active participants in this process, seeking to achieve their policy goals by working for candidates, joining political parties and interest groups, and forming their own specialized political organizations. And like other kinds of communities, they often sought to activate their own members politically. Although the style, level, and intensity of such "religious politics" have varied over time, religion has been deeply embedded in the regular electoral process.

The goal of this chapter is to describe the role of religion in presidential campaign activity in 2004, both as an object and source of mobilization efforts. It begins with an overview of religion in the campaign, followed by evidence on the incidence of campaign and congregational contacts in religious communities. Next, it considers the impact of such contacts on turnout and the presidential vote. Finally, it describes the religious characteristics of the political activists who waged the 2004 presidential campaigns. A look back over time suggests that congregational contacts are more common now than in the past and that the religious character of political activists has changed as well. This material highlights the impact of the Old and New Religion gaps on campaign politics.

Religious Mobilization in the 2004 Presidential Campaign

News accounts of the 2004 campaign noted three parallel campaigns to mobilize religious voters. First was the major presidential campaigns, in which the national party committees and allied interest groups all operated sophisticated voter registration and get-out-the-vote programs that targeted religious constituencies. Second, the specialized political organizations associated with both the Christian Right and the "religious left" sought to mobilize religious voters on behalf of each campaign. And third, there were efforts to activate voters within congregations by clergy and laity. Overall, the Republican side was more engaged and more effective in all these regards, but there was also considerable activity on the Democratic side as well.

The Presidential Campaigns. The Bush campaign made a concerted effort to mobilize religious voters in 2004. The President had regularly expressed his faith in both political and official settings, with perhaps the best known example being the naming in 2000 of his favorite political philosopher: "Jesus, because he changed my life."[2] His support for a ban on late-term abortions, the federal marriage amendment, and conservative federal judges was especially attractive to religious conservatives. These direct issue appeals were well integrated into the rest of the campaign, and judged to have been on balance successful.[3]

The Bush campaign's chief strategist, Karl Rove, was determined to increase turnout among Evangelical Protestants, in part to correct a perceived shortfall among such voters in 2000.[4] However, Rove's strategy extended beyond just Evangelicals to other religious traditions, including Catholics, Orthodox Christians, Jews, Black and Latino Protestants—and to weekly worship attenders in general. Evidence of the latter was a controversial program by the Republican Party to obtain church membership directories for purposes of voter registration.[5] But beyond this program, the Republicans put great emphasis on registering religious voters, for example, deploying 10 church registration coordinators in the crucial state of Ohio.

Such registration efforts were complemented by extensive targeting of religious voters, including direct mail, telephone calls, emails, and personal contact.[6] More importantly, the Republicans built an extensive grassroots organization, partly with the aid of the internet, and it included a special category of "Team Leaders" among social issue conservatives. Here, Republican religious activists were offered detailed instructions on how to mobilize their co-religionists.[7]

Senator Kerry and the Democrats also made appeals to religious voters. Kerry sometimes used religious language for this purpose, such as, "Let us pray. Let us move our feet. Let us march together and let us lead America in a new direction, toward that mountaintop which has always been our destination."[8] And his support for economic justice, environmental stewardship, and a multilateral foreign policy was attractive to religious liberals. But in contrast to Bush, these appeals were not as well integrated with the rest of the campaign, nor judged to have been as successful.[9]

Although both Bush (a United Methodist) and Kerry (a Roman Catholic) were at odds with the official positions of their own denominations on certain issues, the Kerry campaign was vexed by intra-church controversy. A debate among Catholics over the quality of Kerry's Catholicism reached a crescendo when some Catholic Bishops advocated denying communion to Catholic politicians, like Kerry, who publicly disagreed with the Church's teachings on abortion.[10] Although this tactic was opposed by a majority of Catholic laity, it complicated Kerry's efforts to attract Catholic votes. The Democratic Party had similar problems with religious outreach programs, including unsuccessful efforts to appoint a religious liaison at the DNC and a short-lived voter guide project.[11]

However, the Democrats aggressively pursued traditional relationships with key religious constituencies, including Black Protestants, Latino Catholics, Jews, and other religious minorities. A good example was the outreach to Black Protestants: Senators Kerry and Edwards campaigned nearly every Sunday in black Protestant churches, and these efforts were reinforced at the end of the campaign by former vice-president Al Gore's whirlwind visits to black congregations and former President Bill Clinton's conference call to hundreds of black ministers.[12] In addition, expanded grassroots activities by allied interest groups also reached many religious voters. Here, the extensive registration and get-out-the-vote programs of American Coming Together, the America Voters coalition, and organized labor were particularly important.

Specialized Political Organizations. In 2004, Bush received substantial support from the Christian Right.[13] Some of these groups, such as Let Freedom Ring, made a special effort to mobilize clergy, training them in how to conduct voter registration drives and discuss issues in churches without running afoul of the tax laws. A wave of voter registration programs were put into operation, including Redeem the Vote, Vote the Rock, Pastors for Bush, Americans of Faith, Restore America, and the Center for Reclaiming America. Other Christian Right organizations distributed voter guides in congregations, supplemented by DVDs about President Bush. Although the Christian Coalition suffered from organizational disarray at the national level, many of its state and local affiliates were quite active. For example, the Ohio Christian Coalition claimed to have distributed 2 million voter guides in that battleground state. Other groups also participated in voter guide distribution, such as Focus on the Family (and Focus on the Family Action), the Family Research Council, the Traditional Values Coalition, Concerned Women for America, and Vision America.

Many of these organizations as well as others engaged in more conventional campaign activity, and the latter included the Campaign for Working Families, the Susan B. Anthony List, the Madison Project, and the Right to Life Committees. The best known leaders of the Christian Right—Jerry Falwell, Pat Robertson, James Dobson, D. James Kennedy, Ralph Reed, and Gary Bauer—were all active during the campaign. In addition, there were special efforts among conservative Catholic organizations, such as the Catholic League, Priests for Life, and Catholic Answers, which produced a "Voter's Guide for Serious Catholics." Similar lay efforts were waged on a smaller scale in other religious communities historically allied with the Democrats, such as Black Protestants.

Many of these organizations were reinvigorated and new ones were created by the same-sex marriage issue, which burst on to the political agenda in 2004.[14] Organizations active on this issue included Focus on the Family Action, the American Family Association, Americans United to Preserve Marriage, and the Family Research Council and its state-level equivalents; these efforts were loosely coordinated by the Arlington Group. One result was the appearance of same-sex marriage bans on the ballot in 11 states, supported by special organizations formed to advocate their adoption. For example, the Ohio Campaign to Protect Marriage spent $1.2 million in the general election in support of the state marriage amendment. All of the anti-same-sex marriage proposals won at the polls.

The "religious left" was not as organized in the 2004 campaign as the Christian Right, but there was considerable activity nonetheless, and probably a sharp increase over previous elections.[15] Progressive Evangelical Jim Wallis of Sojourners and Call for Renewal campaigned around the country under the banner of "God is not a Republican—or a Democrat," and the Progressive Faith Media dispatched progressive religious leaders to speak in battleground states. Liberal Catholics were especially active, including Pax Christi USA's "Life Does Not End at Birth" campaign, and efforts by Catholics for Political Responsibility, Catholics for the Common Good, Catholics for Free Choice, Catholic Action Network, Call to Action, and Catholics of Kerry. These groups bought newspaper and radio advertisements and distributed leaflets in churches. The Iraq war was a major issue for many religious liberals; a good example was the "Dove Ad Appeal" sponsored by Church Folks for a Better America. New election initiatives included Mobilization 2004 Campaign, Faithful Democracy, Faithfulvote.org, and Vote all Your Values.[16]

Other liberal religious organizations active in the campaign in one way or another included the Clergy Network for Leadership Change, the Religious Coalition for Reproductive Choice, Let Justice Roll, Progressive Christians Uniting, the Center for American Progress, Res Publica, and the Interfaith Alliance. There was also activity among liberal Black Protestants, Jews, and other religious minorities. Many of these groups worked in concert with secular pro-choice, environmental, women's, civil rights, and gay rights organizations. And there were also special organizations formed to oppose the marriage amendments in the states. For example, Ohioans Protecting the Constitution raised and spent some $900,000 in the Buckeye state. Speaking from a secular perspective were People for the American Way, Moveon.org, and Americans United for the Separation of Church and State. The latter waged a campaign to discourage political activity in churches.[17]

Denominations and Congregations. Even a casual review of the news coverage of the 2004 campaign reveals extensive involvement of denominations and ecumenical organizations. For example, the Southern Baptist Convention (SBC), the nation's largest Protestant denomination, rolled out a massive voter registration campaign, "iVoteValues," in cooperation with local Baptist churches, Focus on the Family, and the Family Research Council. Many denominations or denominational agencies provided their members with information on the issues in the campaign, such as the U.S. Conference of Bishops' *Faithful Citizenship: A Catholic Call to Political Responsibility* pamphlet and the United Methodist Church's *Faithful Democracy* project. Ecumenical organizations like the National Council of Churches and the National Association of Evangelicals provided general information on issues as well as information on the appropriate role of religious people in the campaign.[18]

However, the most controversial campaign efforts occurred at the congregational level, where clergy and lay activists, sometimes locally motivated and sometimes stimulated by outside groups, sought to motivate their co-religionists to vote.[19] Indeed, programs to train clergy, distribute voter guides, and recruit grassroots activists often presumed such congregational efforts. It is unclear if such efforts created the New Religion Gap, but they certainly exploited it.

By 2004, these tactics had been common in Evangelical Protestant churches, where they probably benefited the Bush campaign. However, an even longer experience with congregational cues is found in minority congregations, especially among Black Protestants, efforts that probably benefited the Kerry campaign in 2004. While there appears to have been considerable discussion of the election in Mainline Protestant and Catholic congregations, their greater heterogeneity militated against effective congregational mobilization of this sort. It is important to note, however, that this kind of activity was far from uniform even in conservative Evangelical congregations.[20]

Religious Constituencies and Political Contacts in 2004

What effect did all this campaign activity have on religious voters? A first step in answering this question is to assess the type and incidence of political contacts among religious people in the 2004 campaign. Information on two kinds of contacts is readily available from surveys: "campaign contacts" (contact from candidate, party, or interest groups, including the specialized political organizations of religious groups) and "congregational contacts" (contacts with individuals from clergy or laity within congregations). For ease of presentation, the following tables arrange the religious constituencies by the two-party vote, ranging from the most Republican constituency through the swing constituencies to the most Democratic constituencies (as in table 1.4 in chapter 1).

Campaign Contacts in 2004

Table 7.1 offers some evidence on campaign contacts from the PRC post-election survey.[21] In this survey, voters were asked if they had been contacted by either presidential campaigns by means of telephone, in person, or email. The responses to these queries are presented in the first three columns; the final column presents the percentage of voters that reported being contacted in at least one of these ways. Although these types of contacts are hardly exhaustive (for example, contact by direct mail is not included),[22] this information is useful in assessing the reach of the presidential campaigns and their allies.

The most common contact was by telephone, reported by more than one-half of voters. These may have been automatic calls used by the presidential campaigns ("robo" calls), calls made by volunteer telephone banks organized by political parties and interest groups, or personal calls from grassroots activists.[23] The other types of contacts were much less common: one-seventh of the respondents reported in-person contacts and about the same number reported email contacts. In total, almost two-thirds of these voters reported at least one such contact.

Overall, there was a rough parity in the rate of telephone contacts between the Republican and Democratic religious constituencies (with a modest advantage for the Republicans). For example, the two highest scores were found on either side of the partisan divide: Weekly Attending Mainline Protestants (76.6 percent) and Jews (73.6 percent). Other groups with high levels of telephone contact were also drawn from both sides of the partisan divide, including the Other Christians, Less Observant Mainline Protestants, Weekly Attending Evangelicals, and the Other Faiths. In contrast, minority faiths tended to have low rates of telephone contacts, as with Latino Protestants (19.7 percent) and the two Black Protestant groups (26.6 and 22.8 percent, respectively). Here, Latino Catholics were an exception (60.7 percent), scoring above other minorities groups—and above Non-Latino Catholics as well.

In-person contacts also showed a similar rough balance (with a modest advantage for the Democratic constituencies). The highest rates of such contacts were also spread across the partisan divide, with the largest figures found among the Less Observant Black Protestants, Weekly Attending Mainline Protestants, Other Christians, and Latino Catholics. The lowest levels of personal contacts were

Table 7.1   Religious Constituencies and Campaign Contacts, 2004

	Telephone	In-person	Email	Total Contacts
Republican Constituencies				
Weekly Attending Evangelical Protestant	60.7	14.5	10.5	**66.5**
Other Christian	64.9	17.5	24.6	**68.4**
Less Observant Evangelical Protestant	47.8	12.5	8.5	**55.8**
Weekly Attending Catholic	51.4	10.2	11.8	**60.4**
Weekly Attending Mainline Protestants	76.6	18.7	13.8	**80.8**
Latino Protestant	19.7	6.0	17.9	**31.3**
Swing Constituencies				
Less Observant Mainline Protestants	65.3	13.1	13.8	**71.4**
Less Observant Catholics	56.3	10.3	12.9	**63.3**
Democratic Constituencies				
Latino Catholics	60.7	16.9	16.9	**66.7**
Unaffiliated	52.1	15.8	24.8	**66.6**
Jews	73.6	13.2	22.6	**79.2**
Other Faiths	60.0	12.3	15.6	**67.7**
Weekly Attending Black Protestant	28.9	12.5	14.1	**48.4**
Less Observant Black Protestant	22.8	27.5	10.8	**40.2**
ALL	**55.2**	**14.0**	**14.6**	**64.0**

Source: 2004 Pew Research Center (PRC) Post-Election Survey

among Latino Protestants, Weekly Attending and Less Observant Catholics, Weekly Attending Black Protestants, and Less Observant Evangelicals.

Like personal contacts, reported email contacts showed a similar partisan parity (also with a slight edge for the Democrats). The Unaffiliated, Other Christians, Jews, and Latino Protestants reported the most online contacts. The lowest figures were found among the Less Observant Evangelicals and Black Protestants, followed by Weekly Attending Catholics and Evangelicals.

The final column in table 7.1 presents the percentage of voters reporting at least one of these kinds of campaign contact. The now familiar balance is evident. The religious constituencies with the highest total contact were Weekly Attending Mainline Protestants, Jews, and Less Observant Mainliners (all above 70 percent), while the lowest groups were Latino Protestants, both groups of Black Protestants, and Less Observant Evangelicals (all below 60 percent). For Protestants, there were more reported contacts among the weekly attenders, but essentially no difference among Catholics. This evidence suggests the impact of the New Religion Gap alongside the Old Religion Gap.

It is likely that these figures include contacts from specialized political organizations of the Christian Right and the "religious left." Other survey evidence provides some information on contacts by such organizations.[24] Overall, some 8.3 percent of the electorate claimed to have been contacted by a "conservative Christian" group, and another 7.1 percent by another kind of "moral or religious" group. These figures are roughly comparable in size to overall reported contacts from labor unions (11.2 percent) and environmental groups (9.7 percent). And when combined, these special group contacts were about as numerous as personal campaign contacts in table 7.1.

As one might imagine, the contacts from conservative Christian organization were most common among the weekly worship attenders and Evangelical Protestants. However, the contacts from other "moral or religious" groups were also common among Weekly Attending Catholics, Jews, and Black and Latino Protestants. Mainline Protestants of all kinds lagged behind in this source of contacts.

In sum, both the presidential campaigns and their allies apparently had some success in contacting voters in key religious constituencies. In fact, each side achieved something close to parity in the incidence of contacting, with the unevenness among particular groups balancing out across the partisan divide. This conclusion certainly fits with accounts of the hard fought 2004 presidential campaign.

Congregational Contacts

Table 7.2 offers some evidence on reported congregational contacts among voters. Here the PRC post-election survey included questions on three kinds of contacts: the availability of information on candidates and also state ballot issues in houses of worship, and the incidence of clergy cues to vote for a particular candidate or issue. The two types of voter information probably included the voter guides distributed by specialized political groups as well as information provided by denominational agencies; the clergy cues probably included more than pulpit endorsements from the clergy, which are rare events, even in conservative churches.[25]

These questions were asked only of respondents who reported attending worship once a month or more (57 percent of the voters in this survey), but the table reports the responses as a percent of the entire population so such contacts could be compared to campaign contacts in the previous table. These measures do not exhaust the types of congregational contacts either, excluding for example the interaction between congregation members (but see table 7.8). Nevertheless, they are useful in assessing the scope of congregational contacts in 2004.

Overall, congregational contacts were much less common than campaign contacts. For example, roughly one-sixth of the respondents reported that candidate information was available in their houses of worship, and only one-tenth reported information on ballot issues (but ballot measures did not occur in all states in 2004). Only about one-twentieth of the respondents reported that their clergy

Table 7.2   Religious Constituencies and Congregational Contacts, 2004

	Information	*Issue*	*Clergy*	Total Contacts
Republican Constituencies				
Weekly Attending Evangelical Protestant	33.5	22.1	11.2	**39.1**
Other Christian	19.0	5.3	1.8	**21.1**
Less Observant Evangelical Protestant	9.4	5.8	1.8	**12.1**
Weekly Attending Catholic	30.6	17.2	15.9	**38.8**
Weekly Attending Mainline Protestants	12.0	9.0	2.4	**17.4**
Latino Protestant	20.9	7.5	13.4	**34.3**
Swing Constituencies				
Less Observant Mainline Protestants	0.8	2.3	1.0	**3.3**
Less Observant Catholics	8.7	8.0	4.2	**11.4**
Democratic Constituencies				
Latino Catholics	28.6	31.0	32.5	**51.2**
Unaffiliated	1.3	3.7	0.8	**3.7**
Jews	5.7	0.0	0.0	**5.7**
Other Faiths	7.7	3.1	6.2	**13.8**
Weekly Attending Black Protestants	37.5	19.5	3.9	**49.2**
Less Observant Black Protestants	9.8	6.9	0.0	**11.8**
ALL	**15.4**	**10.5**	**6.0**	20.5

Source: 2004 Pew Research Center (PRC) Post-Election Survey

had urged them to vote a particular way. When combined, about one-fifth of the electorate reported at least one kind of congregational contact. Hence, congregational contacts were about one-third as common as campaign contacts.

The incidence of contact reports increased with the frequency of worship attendance, so that for respondents who claimed to attend once a month or more, 27 percent reported candidate information, 19 percent ballot issue information, and 11 percent clergy cues.

Weekly Attending Black Protestants led the way with almost two-fifths reporting candidate information available in their churches. This group was followed by Weekly Attending Evangelical Protestants, Weekly Attending Catholics, Latino Catholics, and Protestants. Interestingly, the religious groups with the highest level of campaign contacts, Weekly Attending Mainliners and Jews, scored low in terms of congregational contacts.

A very similar pattern occurred for the availability of issue information in houses of worship, with Latino Catholics scoring the highest. Latino Catholics also reported the highest level of clergy voting cues, followed by Weekly Attending Catholics, Weekly Attending Evangelicals, and Latino Protestants (all above

10 percent). Such cues were rare among the other religious constituencies. Here Weekly Attending Black Protestants scored particularly low, something of a surprise given the prominent role clergy play in the black church.

When all the congregational contacts are combined (in the right-hand column), the highest rate of congregational contacting was reported by Latino Catholics (51.2 percent) and Black Protestants (49.2 percent), both strong Democratic constituencies. Some Republican constituencies had high rates as well: Weekly Attending Evangelicals (39.1 percent), Weekly Attending Catholics (38.8 percent), and Latino Protestants (34.3 percent). Although the rate of contacting was larger for these Democratic constituencies, the relevant Republican constituencies were more numerous.

Table 7.3 adds together total campaign and congregational contacts to provide a summary measure of reported political contacts (first column). Overall, 72 percent of the voters reported some kind of contact in this survey, with about one-half reporting just campaign contacts, one-eighth both kinds of contacts, and the remaining one-twelfth only congregational contacts. For some groups, such

Table 7.3   Total Voter Contacts, 2004

| | Contacts: | | |
| | | Campaign | | Congregational |
	Total	Only	Both	Only
Republican Constituencies				
Weekly Attending Evangelical Protestant	80.0	40.9	25.5	13.6
Other Christian	82.4	61.4	7.0	14.0
Less Observant Evangelical Protestant	62.1	50.0	5.8	6.3
Weekly Attending Catholic	72.6	33.9	26.5	12.2
Weekly Attending Mainline Protestants	82.4	65.3	15.6	1.8
Latino Protestant	58.3	23.9	7.5	26.9
Swing Constituencies				
Less Observant Mainline Protestants	73.0	69.7	1.8	1.5
Less Observant Catholics	68.5	56.8	6.4	5.3
Democratic Constituencies				
Latino Catholics	84.3	32.5	34.9	16.9
Unaffiliated	68.7	65.0	1.6	2.1
Jews	79.7	74.1	5.6	0.0
Other Faiths	70.8	56.9	10.8	3.1
Weekly Attending Black Protestants	72.6	23.4	24.2	25.0
Less Observant Black Protestants	50.0	38.2	2.0	9.8
All	**72.1**	**51.6**	**12.3**	**8.2**

Source: 2004 Pew Research Center (PRC) Post-Election Survey

as Weekly Attending Black Protestants, congregational contacts substantially made up for a lack of campaign contacts. In other cases, such as the Mainline Protestant groups, congregational contacts added relatively little to total contacts. And of course, for some religious constituencies, such as Weekly Attending Evangelicals, both kinds of contacts were important.

Partisan Bias in Total Contacts

Unfortunately, the information in the previous table does not include non-voters, nor does it indicate the direction of the contacts, whether they favored Bush or Kerry. Some evidence on this point from another survey with more complete information is provided in table 7.4.[26] The first column of the table offers an estimate of the total contacts in each of the religious constituencies, including both voters and non-voters. Although this information is not identical to the information in the previous table, the pattern of total contacts is similar by religious group. Overall, two-thirds of the adult population reported a contact of one kind or another in 2004.

The remaining columns in table 7.4 address the partisan bias of these reported contacts, breaking out respondents that reported contact only from the Bush campaign, only from the Kerry campaign, or from both campaigns. The final column presents a "net Bush advantage" in total contacting (a positive sign means that the group received more contacts from Bush and a negative sign more contacts from Kerry).

Overall, the balance of contacts was quite even between the campaigns, with Bush having a slight edge. These patterns are similar to table 1.8 (in chapter 1), which reported voter contact information from the NEP, and a slight advantage to Kerry. In fact, the Bush advantage in table 7.4 comes largely from congregational contacts, information not explicitly asked about in the NEP.

These findings reveal what appears to be highly successful campaign targeting by the presidential campaigns and their allies: all but one of the Republican constituencies showed a net Bush advantage in reported contact (and it was the composite Other Christians group); all but one of the Democratic constituencies showed a net Kerry advantage (and it was the composite Other Faiths category). And the swing constituencies were almost evenly divided. By and large, each side was able to reach the religious voters most congenial to its cause as well as compete for those that were persuadable.

The largest net Bush contacting advantage was found among Weekly Attending Evangelical Protestants—some 29.9 percentage points. It is also the largest net advantage of any group. Bush also had a relatively large advantage among Weekly Attending Catholics and Mainline Protestants, but less of an edge with Latino Catholics and Less Observant Evangelicals. Likewise, Kerry enjoyed double digit advantages in most of the Democratic constituencies. Note the even division of contacts among the Less Observant Mainline Protestants and Catholics, and contrast these results with their weekly attending co-religionists. These

Table 7.4   Religious Constituencies, All Contacts, and Contact Bias, 2004

	Total Contacts	Bush Contact	Both Contact	Kerry Contact	Net Bush Advantage
Republican Constituencies					
Weekly Attending Evangelical Protestant	79.6	39.9	29.7	10.0	**29.9**
Other Christian	66.1	20.4	23.1	22.2	**-1.8**
Less Observant Evangelical Protestant	53.5	19.7	17.4	16.4	**3.3**
Weekly Attending Catholic	74.3	37.1	19.0	18.1	**19.0**
Weekly Attending Mainline Protestants	75.7	31.4	25.5	19.0	**12.4**
Latino Protestant	52.8	25.0	11.1	16.7	**8.3**
Swing Constituencies					
Less Observant Mainline Protestants	63.8	22.0	21.4	20.4	**1.6**
Less Observant Catholics	66.4	24.4	16.5	25.6	**-1.2**
Democratic Constituencies					
Latino Catholics	71.5	17.0	35.8	18.7	**-1.7**
Unaffiliated	54.7	14.4	14.0	26.1	**-11.7**
Jews	82.7	25.0	15.4	42.3	**-17.3**
Other Faiths	40.5	21.6	8.1	10.8	**10.8**
Weekly Attending Black Protestants	66.0	11.4	26.8	27.5	**-16.1**
Less Observant Black Protestants	53.3	10.3	15.9	27.1	**-16.8**
ALL	**65.7**	**24.4**	**21.0**	**20.3**	**4.1**

Source: 2004 National Survey of Religion and Politics

data speak to the fierce political struggle for the support of these large religious communities.

As one might expect, the level and bias of political contacts varied by region. For one thing, respondents in the "battleground" states reported higher levels of political contact of all kinds, a pattern that also held for the "purple" regions as compared to the "red" and "blue" regions. Among the Republican constituencies, Bush enjoyed a large net advantage in the "red" and "purple" regions, and especially among weekly attenders. However, the advantage shrinks to almost nothing in the "blue" regions. For example, Bush had a contacting advantage among Weekly Attending Mainline Protestants in the "red" regions, but Kerry had an advantage in the "blue" regions. And this pattern reverses itself for the Democratic constituencies: in "blue" states Kerry enjoyed a large contacting advantage, while in the "red" and "purple" states, the Kerry advantage was smaller, often disappearing altogether. These data reveal the importance of region and regional subcultures to presidential campaigning (see chapter 6).

In conclusion, the Bush and Kerry campaigns essentially fought themselves to a stalemate with campaign contacts, each targeting key religious constituencies with some success. Although the greatest incidence of congregational contacts was among some Democratic constituencies, the Bush campaign enjoyed an overall advantage in congregational contacts. This reflects the importance of the New Religion Gap. Of course, the Old Religion Gap was also important, setting the baseline for the effects of worship attendance. A good example of how both religion gaps mattered was the pattern of contacting for Weekly Attending Evangelical Protestants. Indeed, the patterns tend to confirm the conventional wisdom on the critical role of this religious community in the Bush campaign.

Contacting, Turnout, and the Vote in 2004

The evidence on the incidence and partisan bias of contacting leads back to the original question: did all this contacting make a difference at the polls in 2004? Both commonsense and conventional wisdom suggests that it did, but measuring the precise impact of political contacting on the vote is a difficult and complicated task. After all, many factors affect the vote besides campaign contact, including other demographic factors and partisanship. Although a full consideration of these matters is beyond the scope of this chapter, some simple evidence on this point is worth reviewing.

Table 7.5 reports an estimate for voter turnout in 2004 using a post-election survey, with the religious categories and the measure of campaign contact used in table 7.4, divided into reported "contact" (of any kind) and "no contact."[27] In 2004, as in past elections, some religious communities voted at a higher rate than the electorate as a whole, including Jews, Weekly Attending Mainline Protestants, Catholics and Evangelicals, Other Christians, and Less Observant Mainliners. Meanwhile, others turned out at a lower rate, such as Latinos, Black Protestants, Other Faiths, and the Unaffiliated.

Much of this variation is explained by other demographic factors, such as income and education, or by political factors, like partisanship. The New Religion Gap was likely a factor as well, since weekly attenders uniformly voted at a higher rate than the less observant. But there was also some evidence that reported contact mattered too: in nearly every religious category, those who reported contact were more likely to go to the polls than those who reported no contact. For example, some four-fifths of Weekly Attending Evangelical Protestants who reported a contact showed up at the polls, compared to just three-fifths of those without a contact. There were just two exceptions to this pattern. One was the composite Other Faiths, where the "no contact" group voted at a higher rate, and the other exception was Weekly Attending Catholics, where there was essentially no difference in turnout by reported contact.

Table 7.5   Religious Constituencies, All Contacts, and Turnout, 2004

	Turnout	*Contact*	*No Contact*
Republican Constituencies			
Weekly Attending Evangelical Protestant	**67.8**	72.7	48.9
Other Christian	**65.1**	77.5	40.5
Less Observant Evangelical Protestant	**55.7**	74.3	34.3
Weekly Attending Catholic	**74.7**	75.0	73.4
Weekly Attending Mainline Protestants	**76.6**	82.5	57.6
Latino Protestant	**48.6**	60.5	35.3
Swing Constituencies			
Less Observant Mainline Protestants	**64.6**	73.3	49.1
Less Observant Catholics	**59.3**	65.8	45.7
Democratic Constituencies			
Latino Catholics	**43.1**	48.9	28.6
Unaffiliated	**52.1**	65.4	36.0
Jews	**86.5**	90.7	66.7
Other Faiths	**44.7**	40.0	47.8
Weekly Attending Black Protestants	**53.3**	57.6	45.1
Less Observant Black Protestants	**48.1**	59.6	34.7
ALL	**60.8**	**69.7**	**43.7**

Source: 2004 National Survey of Religion and Politics

Did the bias of contacts influence voters' choices once they came to the polls? Table 7.6 offers some evidence on this point, using the NEP data.[28] The table reports the Bush proportion of the two-party vote in each religious category, broken down by respondents who reported only Bush contacts, contacts from both sides, and Kerry-only contacts. The table also has a "no contact" column, which provides something of a baseline for assessing the impact of political contacting. (The Kerry figures are the reciprocal of the Bush numbers in the table.)

As one might expect, voters with Bush-only contacts tended to vote Republican and voters with Kerry-only contacts tended to vote Democratic, with those contacted by both campaigns usually falling in between. President Bush did very well among the Republican religious constituencies, receiving four-fifths or more of the ballots of the top five groups in the Bush-only column. All of these figures were substantially higher than the no-contact column, which nonetheless gave Bush solid majorities, suggesting that these groups were predisposed to vote Republican.

The pattern was mixed for respondents who heard from both sides: Bush received large majorities from the first three groups, but not for the next two, Weekly Attending Catholics and Mainline Protestants. And Bush did poorly in

Table 7.6   Religious Constituencies, All Contacts, and Voter Choice, 2004

	Contacted Bush Only	Contacted Both	Contacted Kerry Only	No Contact
Republican Constituencies				
Weekly Attending Evangelicals	93.4	74.1	50.0	*85.0*
Other Christians	87.5	76.5	36.8	*81.2*
Less Observant Evangelicals	90.9	73.1	30.0	*70.4*
Weekly Attending Catholics	82.4	46.0	38.9	*59.2*
Weekly Attending Mainline Protestants	80.0	40.0	18.8	*54.0*
Latino Protestants	58.3	71.4	0.0	*62.3*
Swing Constituencies				
Less Observant Mainline Protestants	79.1	33.8	12.7	*57.3*
Less Observant Catholics	83.3	40.9	17.2	*54.4*
Democratic Constituencies				
Latino Catholics	90.0	28.6	30.8	*26.5*
Unaffiliated	66.7	22.2	19.1	*30.5*
Jews	33.3	0.0	6.3	*22.2*
Other Faiths	50.0	72.7	0.0	*18.9*
Weekly Attending Black Protestants	33.3	26.3	2.9	*22.1*
Less Observant Black Protestants	90.0	16.7	0.0	*6.0*
ALL	**83.8**	**45.4**	**18.9**	*53.4*

Source: 2004 National Election Pool (NEP)

the Kerry-only column, winning just one-half of the Weekly Attending Evangelicals and losing the remaining groups by substantial margins.

The remaining Republican constituency, Latino Protestants, had a very odd pattern. Bush won a solid majority from the Bush-only voters, but it was less than the no-contact group—and even less than those contacted by both campaigns. And the Latino Protestants who heard only from Kerry gave Bush no votes at all.

The two swing constituencies showed a sharp gradient across the table, with Bush winning the first column decisively and Kerry doing the same in the third column. Here, Kerry won solid majorities of those contacted by both campaigns, but this success was not enough to put these constituencies in the Democratic column—in part because Bush had solid majorities among the no-contact respondents in these religious communities—a pattern that also suggests a predisposition toward the President.

Senator Kerry did quite well with the Democratic constituencies, scoring large wins in the Kerry-only column. He also did well in the both-contact and no-contact columns. However, the no-contact column reveals that Bush had some support among these Democratic constituencies. And the Republicans had solid wins among the small number of respondents in the Bush-only column.

This simple evidence appears to support the commonsense proposition that campaign and congregational contacts influenced the vote. With just a few exceptions, voters who reported being contacted turned out at higher rates, and also, with just a few exceptions, a partisan bias in contacting paid off in additional votes. On this last point, a contact bias appears to have mattered more in religious constituencies less firmly attached to the candidate's party.

These basic mechanisms appeared to work for both Bush and Kerry. However, Bush enjoyed higher levels of contact bias in the Republican constituencies, especially with Weekly Attending Evangelical Protestants. And although the level of contact was not always higher than for Democratic constituencies, the Republican groups were on balance larger. Here, congregational contacting appeared to make a difference, giving Bush a small but clear advantage. On the one hand, Bush's prime constituents were more available for such contacts because of their higher level of traditionalism, and Bush's allies were capable of reaching these religious voters. And on the other hand, Kerry's less traditional constituencies were not as available for this kind of contact, and his allies were less able to reach these religious voters.

Thus, it is reasonable to conclude that the conventional wisdom contained a good bit of truth: advantages in congregational contacting may well have allowed Bush to win additional votes in a very close election. However, such conclusions must be advanced with great caution, since the effects of socioeconomic status and partisanship are not taken into account in this simple presentation. Careful statistical analysis of these data tends to confirm these simple patterns, especially with regard to turnout.[29] It may well be that the extraordinary 2004 presidential campaign made few converts to either party, but rather maximized the participation of already committed partisans on both sides. Although the Kerry campaign and its allies were quite successful in contacting their key religious constituencies, deriving significant benefits at the ballot box, their efforts may have fallen a bit short.

Religious Constituencies and Campaign Activism in 2004

One final issue worth considering is the involvement of religious constituencies in the conduct of the 2004 presidential campaign. Table 7.7 reports on the religious characteristics of party campaign volunteers and delegates to the 2004 national party conventions. For purposes of comparison, the NEP data for Republican and Democratic voters is included in the far right-hand columns.

The information on campaign volunteers came from the PRC post-election survey.[30] Such volunteers have long been the backbone of campaign politics, but they were especially important in 2004 when the major parties and their allies recruited extensive networks of grassroots activists.[31] The information on the 2004 Republican and Democratic national convention delegates comes from the 2004 edition of a long-standing survey of party elites.[32] Convention

Table 7.7   Religious Constituencies and Campaign Activism, 2004

	Campaign Volunteers		Convention Delegates		Voters	
	Rep	*Dem*	Rep	*Dem*	Rep	*Dem*
Republican Constituencies						
Weekly Attending Evangelical Protestant	**22.9**	*5.4*	**23.1**	*3.0*	**24.4**	*6.5*
Other Christian	**4.3**	*4.5*	**5.0**	*7.4*	**5.7**	*2.1*
Less Observant Evangelical Protestant	**11.4**	*4.5*	**5.6**	*4.8*	**9.7**	*4.9*
Weekly Attending Catholic	**25.7**	*10.7*	**9.6**	*9.0*	**11.8**	*8.5*
Weekly Attending Mainline Protestants	**11.4**	*4.5*	**11.0**	*4.4*	**5.7**	*3.6*
Latino Protestant	**4.3**	*6.3*	**0.6**	*1.0*	**2.7**	*2.4*
Swing Constituencies						
Less Observant Mainline Protestants	**8.6**	*12.5*	**20.1**	*14.6*	**15.5**	*14.3*
Less Observant Catholics	**2.9**	*9.8*	**10.6**	*16.2*	**12.4**	*12.2*
Democratic Constituencies						
Latino Catholics	**0.0**	*3.6*	**3.0**	*3.0*	**3.1**	*5.7*
Unaffiliated	**4.3**	*17.0*	**3.6**	*14.0*	**6.0**	*15.4*
Jews	**4.3**	*8.9*	**2.2**	*6.4*	**1.0**	*4.2*
Other Faiths	**0.0**	*8.0*	**0.4**	*1.8*	**0.8**	*4.1*
Weekly Attending Black Protestants	**0.0**	*4.5*	**2.8**	*7.4*	**0.9**	*9.2*
Less Observant Black Protestants	**0.0**	*0.0*	**2.2**	*7.0*	**0.4**	*6.9*
ALL	**100.0**	**100.0**	**100.0**	**100.0**	**100.0**	**100.0**

Sources: See notes 30 and 32

delegates represent a good cross-section of the leaders and activists in the major political parties.[33] In one form or another, these were the individuals behind the contacting discussed above.

Republican Campaign Activists. A good place to begin is with the campaign volunteers. In this survey, the single largest group of Republican campaign activists was Weekly Attending Catholics, making up more than one-quarter of the total. This figure was twice as large as the Weekly Attending Catholics among GOP voters (in the far column)—and larger than all the Catholics among the Democratic volunteers. This finding is yet another indication of the intensity of the 2004 presidential campaign among Catholics.

Interestingly, the Catholic volunteers were a bit more numerous than Weekly Attending Evangelicals (22.9 percent) in the Republican ranks, but all Evangelicals combined were the largest group, making up more than one-third of the GOP volunteer corps. This figure was representative of the proportion of Evangelicals among GOP voters. Another one-fifth of the Republican activists were Mainline

Protestants, also about the same proportion as among GOP voters. However, the Mainline volunteers were more likely to be weekly attenders and the GOP voters to be less observant.

The remaining one-sixth of the Republican volunteers was a diverse mix of religious groups: Other Christians and the Unaffiliated (comparable to their proportions among GOP voters), and Latino Protestants and Jews (much larger than their proportions among the Republican electorate). Other religious minorities were very rare in the ranks of Republican volunteers.

What about the Republican delegates that re-nominated George W. Bush for president in 2004? The center column in table 7.7 reveals some differences with the GOP volunteer corps. The largest group of Republican delegates was Weekly Attending Evangelical Protestants, with nearly one-quarter of the total. These figures fairly accurately reflect their proportions among GOP volunteers and voters. Less Observant Evangelicals were less common among the delegates (5.6 percent), about one quarter the number of the weekly attenders. They were about one-half as numerous as their co-religionists among Republican volunteers and voters. In combination, Evangelical delegates made up more than one-quarter of the 2004 Republican convention—but still did not fully reflect the presence of Evangelicals in the Republican electorate.

The second largest group of GOP delegates was Less Observant Mainline Protestants, accounting for one-fifth of the total, followed by Weekly Attending Mainliners, at about one-tenth of the total. The former were more common than their co-religionists among GOP volunteers and voters; the latter matched the GOP volunteers in relative numbers, but were twice as numerous as their counterparts in the Republican electorate. If combined, Mainline Protestant groups were significantly over-represented among delegates compared to the volunteers and voters (roughly 3-to-2 in each case).

Taken together, Evangelicals and Mainline Protestants had a rough parity at the 2004 Republican convention (28 to 31 percent). Slicing the number another way, weekly attending white Protestants were more numerous than the less observant (34 to 26 percent).

Weekly Attending Catholics were less numerous among the Republican delegates than among the campaign volunteers (9.8 percent), but twice the number of their co-religionists among GOP voters. Meanwhile, Less Observant Catholics (10.6 percent) were about the same proportion as their counterparts among volunteers and voters. All told, Catholic delegates were ranked third behind the two large Protestant traditions at the 2004 Republican national convention.

The Other Christians accounted for one-twentieth of the GOP delegates, representing fairly accurately their co-religionists among Republican voters. The remaining religious categories combined for one-seventh of the Republican delegates. Interestingly, this figure was about the same size as these groups among GOP voters. Within these ranks, however, some groups were severely under-represented (the Unaffiliated, Latino Protestants) and some vastly over-represented (Black Protestants, Jews, Other Faiths); Latino Catholics were spot on. In any event, all of these groups were small. It is worth noting that the formally chosen Republican delegates were more representative of the GOP base in this regard than the self-selected campaign volunteers.

Democratic Campaign Activists. The Democratic campaign activists provide a contrast to the Republicans in several respects. In terms of campaign volunteers, the largest single group was the Unaffiliated (17 percent), a figure roughly comparable to the Unaffiliated among Democratic voters. The second largest group was Less Observant Mainline Protestants (12.7 percent), also roughly in line with the party's electorate. Weekly Attending Mainline Protestants were about one-third as numerous as the less observant (4.5 percent), and also roughly comparable to Democratic voters. Taken together, Mainline Protestants were about as numerous as the Unaffiliated in the Democratic campaign.

The Catholic volunteers show some of their historic link with the Democratic Party: Weekly Attending Catholics were the third largest group, almost matching their numbers in the Democratic electorate. These data also point to the polarization of Catholic politics in 2004. Less Observant Catholics were about as numerous (9.8 percent), also almost matching their counterparts among Democratic voters. All told, Catholics accounted for about one-fifth of the campaign volunteers, thus more numerous than Mainline Protestants or the Unaffiliated.

Non-Christians made up roughly another one-sixth of the Democratic volunteers, including Jews (8.9 percent) and Other Faiths (8.0 percent). These figures were twice the percentage of their counterparts in the Democratic electorate. In a similar fashion, the Other Christian volunteers (4.5 percent) are twice the size of their proportion among Democratic voters (2.1 percent).

Black Protestant and Latino volunteers combined for about one-seventh of the total (14.4 percent), about the same size as the non-Christians. The minority volunteers substantially under-represented their co-religionists in the Democratic electorate. Finally, Evangelical Protestants accounted for about one-tenth of the Democratic volunteers. Divided fairly evenly between weekly attenders and the less observant, they matched their co-religionists in the Democratic electorate fairly well.

What about the Democratic convention delegates that nominated John Kerry in 2004? Here, too, there were some differences with the party's volunteer corps. The single biggest group of convention delegates was Less Observant Catholics. Making up one-sixth of the total, they were a bit more numerous than their co-religionists among Democratic volunteers or voters. Weekly Attending Catholics were a little less numerous (9 percent) and matched their proportions in the other elements of the party more closely. All told, Catholics made up one-quarter of the Democratic delegates at the 2004 national convention.

The second largest group of delegates was Less Observant Mainline Protestants, at about one-seventh of the total, which closely matched their co-religionists in the Democratic volunteer corps and electorate. Weekly Attending

Mainliners were less common (4.4 percent), but also matched Democratic volunteers and voters fairly well. In sum, Mainline Protestants made up just about one-fifth of the delegates at the 2004 Democratic convention.

Unaffiliated delegates were also a large group among Democratic delegates, ranking third at one-seventh, a figure roughly comparable to their counterparts among Democratic volunteers and voters. The Black Protestant groups combined to be nearly as numerous among the delegates as the Unaffiliated, vastly exceeding their presence among volunteers, but closely approximating their co-religionists among Democratic voters. Latinos were less numerous among Democratic delegates than among volunteers or voters (4 percent), but when added to Black Protestants, the minority faiths approach one-fifth of all the Democratic delegates (and about the size of Mainline Protestants).

Non-Christians were less numerous among delegates than volunteers (8.2 percent), with Jews more nearly matching the proportion of Democratic voters, but the Other Faiths lagged behind in both respects. Here the Other Christians delegates were nearly as numerous as the non-Christians (7.4 percent). Many of these delegates were drawn from liberal faiths, such as Unitarian-Universalism, and were far more numerous than their counterparts among the Democratic volunteers and voters. When combined, the non-Christians and Other Christians also made up about one-sixth of the Democratic delegates in 2004, roughly on par with the Unaffiliated and Black Protestants.

In sum then, the major party activist corps reflected in large measure the voter coalitions of each party, although the campaign volunteers and national convention delegates each revealed a few important differences. Some of these differences, such as the large number of Catholic volunteers among Republican activists and the over-representation of Black Protestants with the Democrats may help explain some facets of the campaign. By the same token, the strong links between these kinds of activists and the religious base of each party helps explain the main thrust of each campaign. The Old and New Religion gaps were deeply embedded in the structure of the presidential campaigns, and the successful targeting of key religious constituencies came in part from co-religionists that were waging the campaigns.

A Look Back at the Past

How do the religious aspects of 2004 presidential campaigning compare to the past? This question is even more difficult to answer with the over time comparisons investigated in the previous chapters. Campaign politics has changed a great deal from the 1940s, and partly for this reason, pollsters now ask questions about campaigns that would not have occurred to their predecessors. Indeed, there is no comparable evidence on these matters in the 1940s, but there is some from the 1950s and 1960s. For our purposes, these limited data points fall before the advent of the New Religion Gap and thus can provide some sense of how the religious aspects of campaigns have changed.

New communication technologies have dramatically altered the way presidential candidates and their allies seek votes. Back in the 1950s, for example, in person contacts were much more common than in 2004 in large part due to the lack of alternatives. Telephone and television were just becoming staples of national campaigns, and of course, the internet had not yet been invented. But despite having new means to wage a campaign, the basics of campaign strategy were much the same. Candidates, political parties, and interest groups were just as interested in winning elections as they were at the end of the twentieth century, and just as concerned with targeting and contacting congenial voters.

Indeed, a careful look at voter contacting among religious communities circa the 1952 election suggests more continuity than change.[34] Both parties appeared to have been successful in reaching their religious constituencies. Of course, as has been shown in chapters 2 and 3, the parties' religious coalitions were different at the mid-point of the twentieth century, with an emphasis on religious tradition rather than traditionalism.

Surely one important difference is the nature of religious mobilization, both regarding internal cues and external appeals. In the earlier era, there is no evidence of tactics such as the distribution of voter guides in the congregations, nor were there many specialized political groups directed at mobilizing religious voters. One piece of telling evidence is that pollsters asked few questions about this aspect of religion and politics—so they must not have regarded it important. Of course, religion was certainly a part of national elections, and when it made front page news, such as with John F. Kennedy and Catholicism in 1960, surveys asked questions about it. Thus, there are a few questions that are useful for purposes of comparison.

Table 7.8 presents the results of three questions asked in 2004, 1964, and 1952. While not worded exactly the same way, they cover the same subject: the level of political discussion in congregations.[35] These data imply at least a minimum of congregational contacts about political matters, even if only informal cues.

In table 7.8, the patterns for religious discussion by and large fit the information on congregational contacting presented in table 7.2. First, note that about one-quarter of respondents reported political discussions in their houses of worship, a figure roughly comparable with the one-fifth that reported congregational contacts. Second, there was considerable variation by the Old and New Religion gaps. On the first count, Evangelicals and Black Protestants reported high levels of political talk, and on the second count, weekly attenders always reported more political discussion than their less observant co-religionists. For example, more than two-fifths of weekly attending Evangelical Protestants reported political discussions, compared to about one-fifth of Less Observant Evangelicals.

Interestingly, Jews also reported a high level of political discussion in 2004, despite the very low levels of congregational contacting reported in table 7.2. Perhaps existing political discourse means that congregational contacting is not relevant in synagogues. Or it could be that high levels of campaign contacting

Table 7.8   Political Discussion in Congregations, 2004, 1964, 1952

	2004	1964	1952
Republican Constituencies			
Weekly Attending Evangelical Protestants	44.3	13.2	14.8
Other Christians	28.4	15.4	15.4
Less Observant Evangelical Protestants	21.7	11.8	13.1
Weekly Attending Catholics	28.7	7.9	8.5
Weekly Attending Mainline Protestants	40.9	14.4	13.0
Swing Constituencies			
Less Observant Mainline Protestants	13.9	9.7	12.5
Less Observant Catholics	15.8	5.6	4.5
Democratic Constituencies			
Jews	42.3	40.9	9.2
Weekly Attending Black Protestants	35.3	43.0	24.2
Less Observant Black Protestants	26.4	35.5	33.8
ALL	**25.3**	**15.4**	**13.0**

Sources: See note 34

in the Jewish community, as shown in table 7.1, makes congregational contact less relevant. A similar pattern holds for Weekly Attending Mainline Protestants.

The most interesting comparisons are with 1964 and 1952. Note that the overall level of political talk was much lower in those years: about one-sixth in 1964 and less than one-seventh in 1952. Furthermore, the level of discussion was uniformly low among white Christians in both years, and also, there were only modest differences between weekly attenders and the less observant. Catholics scored particularly low, but this pattern persists in 2004, perhaps reflecting the large size of Catholic parishes.

Black Protestants reported a higher level of congregational discourse than white Protestants in 1964 and 1952. This pattern may reflect the special role of the Black church during the era of the civil rights movement. Jews showed a dramatic jump from 1952 to 1964, but this may reflect the particular questions asked in 1952 (where the word "church" was used instead of "church or synagogue").

These patterns must be viewed with great caution, of course. But they do suggest that congregations have become far more politicized in recent times, perhaps because congregational contacting has become more common and more systematized. And as was shown in chapter 4, this change may well reflect the rise of social issues in national politics. Such a conclusion is certainly consistent with the development of the New Religion Gap.

The involvement of religious communities in campaign politics has changed as well. Table 7.9 illustrates these changes by comparing the religious

Table 7.9 Religious Constituencies and Campaign Activism, 2004 and 1952

	Campaign Activists				Convention Delegates			
	2004		1952		2004		1952	
	Rep	Dem	Rep	Dem	Rep	Dem	Rep	Dem
Republican Constituencies								
Weekly Attending Evangelical Protestant	22.8	5.4	2.9	5.5	23.2	3.0	4.0	8.9
Other Christian	4.3	4.5	1.9	6.2	5.0	7.4	2.9	5.0
Less Observant Evangelical Protestant	11.4	4.5	12.6	9.0	5.6	4.8	3.7	7.8
Weekly Attending Catholic	25.7	10.6	14.6	24.1	9.6	9.0	6.3	15.3
Weekly Attending Mainline Protestants	11.4	4.5	21.5	11.8	11.0	4.4	39.2	28.1
Latino Protestant	4.3	6.3	*	*	0.6	1.0	*	*
Swing Constituencies								
Less Observant Mainline Protestants	8.6	12.4	33.0	18.6	20.2	14.6	34.6	17.7
Less Observant Catholics	2.9	9.8	1.0	7.6	10.6	16.2	3.7	11.8
Democratic Constituencies								
Latino Catholics	0.0	3.6	*	*	3.0	3.0	*	*
Unaffiliated	4.3	17.0	1.9	3.4	3.6	14.0	3.8	2.1
Jews	4.3	8.9	2.9	2.1	2.2	6.4	1.8	2.1
Other Faiths	0.0	8.0	*	*	0.4	1.8		
Weekly Attending Black Protestants	0.0	4.5	1.9	4.8	2.8	7.4	*	1.2
Less Observant Black Protestants	0.0	0.0	5.8	6.9	2.2	7.0	*	*
ALL	**100.0**	**100.0**	**100.0**	**100.0**	**100.0**	**100.0**	**100.0**	**100.0**

Source: See note 35

characteristics of campaign volunteers and national convention delegates in 2004 and 1952.

In 1952, Republican campaign volunteers were dominated by Mainline Protestants, who accounted for more than one-half of the total. And Mainliners were even more dominant among GOP national convention delegates, accounting for nearly three-quarters. Among the volunteers, the Less Observant were more numerous, but the opposite result occurred for the delegates. Catholics and Evangelical Protestants ran a poor second and third in both sets of activists, and all the other religious communities combined mustered only about the same proportion of these activists. This pattern certainly fits with the Republican religious coalition of that era (see chapter 2).

Note the stark differences between the Republican activist corps in 1952 and 2004. Catholics and Evangelicals had become the major sources of campaign volunteers, relegating Mainline Protestants to third place. Among convention delegates, Mainliners held on to second place, but just barely ahead of Catholics, with Evangelicals way out in front. In most respects, the GOP activist corps has diversified to include a broader range of religious communities. The apparent loss of Black Protestant activists in 1952 was balanced off somewhat by the increased number of Black Protestant delegates by 2004.

Similar changes have taken place among the Democrats. In 1952, almost one-third of the Democratic campaign volunteers were Catholics, and a majority of them—and the single largest religious group—were weekly worship attenders. However, Mainline Protestants were a close second, accounting for three in ten of the Democratic volunteers. The roles were reversed among the Democratic convention delegates, with Mainline Protestants nearing one-half of the delegates and Catholics at more than one-quarter. Evangelical Protestants ranked third in volunteers and delegates, with roughly one-sixth of each, largely because of the special place of Southern Democrats among the delegates. All of the other groups combined accounted for nearly one-quarter of the volunteers, but only one-tenth of the delegates.

By 2004, the Democratic activist corps had become even more diverse in religious terms. The role of Mainline Protestants declined dramatically among both volunteers and delegates, and the role of Catholics and Evangelicals diminished as well, especially among national convention delegates. In their place, a new set of religious groups appeared, led by the Unaffiliated, racial and ethnic minorities, and non-Christians.

Thus, the religious composition of the major party activists changed along with the religious coalitions among voters. At mid-century, the campaign activists were dominated by Mainline Protestants, with a significant Catholic presence. Other religious communities were much less consequential in these circles. Mainline Protestants and Catholics largely ran campaigns in a world where religious traditions were the most potent avenues for political mobilization, and appeals could be directed at traditions as a whole, without much concern for internal differences. This world is no more: the major party campaign activist corps contains complex coalitions of religious communities, defined by both the Old and New Religion gaps.

Conclusions

This chapter has investigated the role of religion in the presidential campaign activity in 2004. Journalists recorded extensive efforts to mobilize religious constituencies by the presidential candidates, their parties, and interest group allies, plus extensive activity by specialized political organizations of the Christian Right and the "religious left." In addition, there was considerable effort to activate voters at the congregational level. Survey evidence substantially confirms the large role of religion in the conduct of the campaign. There was extensive campaign contact with each party's religious constituencies, and although of lesser magnitude, there was also evidence of substantial congregational contact as well. The campaign contacts were nearly equal between the rival presidential candidates, but Bush had a small but significant advantage in congregational contact.

The incidence and partisan bias of political contacts appears to be associated with higher levels of turnout and support for particular candidates. Although these conclusions must be viewed with caution, they tend to support the conventional wisdom that the mobilization of religious voters on balance favored Bush. A key factor here was the exploitation of the New Religion Gap among religious traditionalists, but also careful attention to the Old Religion Gap among religious traditions. The high level of contact among Weekly Attending Evangelical Protestants is a good example of these tendencies.

In 2004, religious constituencies were well-represented among the major party campaign activists, including campaign volunteers and delegates to the national party conventions. By and large, these activists were representative of each party's religious coalition. Thus, the New and Old Religion gaps are deeply embedded in the campaign process. A look back over time suggests that congregational contacts are more common now than in the past, and the religious character of political activists has changed as well. The concluding chapter will speculate about the future role of religion in American politics.

8

The Religion Gaps and the Future

As was noted at the beginning of this book, the impact of religion on the 2004 election provoked consternation and surprise. The consternation was understandable, given the closeness of the outcome and intensity of the contest. But the surprise was hard to understand. Religion has mattered in American politics even before the founding of the republic, and more importantly, there was ample evidence that it would be important in the 2004 campaign. Furthermore, commentators and journalists recognized the crucial links between religion and politics in their discussion of the role of "fundamentalists," the "God gap," and the "values voters" in the campaign.

This book was written to illuminate the impact of religion on American elections so there would no longer be a surprise. The direction of religion and politics is difficult to predict, of course, and no guide can predict the future with complete accuracy. But observers can understand the basic patterns of the present and the recent past, and thus be prepared to investigate whatever happens next. Thus, it is worth summarizing the book's conclusions before offering some speculation about the future role of religion in American politics.

Summary of Conclusions

After reviewing the impact of religion on the 2004 presidential election "by the numbers," the text describes the Old and New Religion Gaps, and then explores the relationship of the religion gaps to issues and coalitions, other demographic traits, region, and campaign politics.

The Old Religion Gap. The "politics of belonging" has been and continues to be one of the most important ways that religion is connected to politics. This Old Religion Gap reflects the capacity of religious affiliation to influence how adherents vote. One reason the Old Religion Gap matters is that American religious communities have been and are extraordinarily diverse. A useful way to simplify this complexity for the purposes of political analysis is through the concept of a religious tradition.[1] This concept is the basis for "The ABCs of Religious Affiliation," which describes the major religious traditions in the United States at the turn of the twenty-first century.

The major religious traditions were important elements of presidential voter coalitions in 2004, and in a different configuration, they were even more important in 1944. In between these years, the partisan alignment of many of the major religious traditions has evolved (see chapter 2). One important reason for this change in the Old Religion Gap was the development of the New Religion Gap. (Tables 1.1 and 2.1 encapsulate these findings.)

The New Religion Gap. In recent times, the "politics of behaving and belonging" has become one of the important ways that religion is connected to politics. This New Religion Gap reflects the capacity of religious practice and doctrine to influence how the faithful vote. In the United States, religious behavior and belief are also quite diverse. A useful way to simplify this complexity for political analysis is the concept of religious traditionalism.[2] This concept is the basis for "The Checklist of Religious Practice and Doctrine," which describes the major elements of traditionalism in the United States at the turn of the twenty-first century.

Religious traditionalism was an important part of presidential voter coalitions in 2004, but not in 1944. Indeed, the New Religion Gap first appeared in 1972 (see chapter 3) in parallel with the "restructuring" of American religion and the much discussed "culture wars." Since the 1970s, the New Religion Gap has operated within the context of the Old Religion Gap, producing distinctive religious constituencies that are aligned with the Republican and Democratic parties. (Tables 1.3, 3.8, and 3.9 encapsulate these findings.)

In concrete terms, the coalition that re-elected George W. Bush was an alliance of Evangelical Protestants and Other conservative Christians (the Old Religion Gap) plus other weekly attending white Christians (the New Religion Gap), while the coalition that backed John F. Kerry was an alliance of religious minorities and the Unaffiliated (the Old Religion Gap) plus less observant white Christians. The strength of these partisan attachments varied, with some swing groups nearly evenly divided between the major party candidates.

The Meaning of the Religion Gaps: Issues and Coalitions. Issues are central to the political meaning of the Old and New Religion Gaps because they are a principal means by which religious groups are connected to voter coalitions. The "values voters" highlighted in the 2004 Election Night controversy were a good example of this phenomenon. President Bush used "moral values" appeals but also foreign and economic policy to exploit the Old and New Religion gaps, assembling a complex coalition. Senator Kerry relied largely on economic policy appeals to assemble his coalition. (Tables 4.3 and 4.4 encapsulate these findings.)

However, social issues are a recent addition to the political agenda and their appearance is closely associated with the development of the New Religion

Gap. Both religion gaps helped account for the social, foreign, and economic policy positions of religious communities. Moreover, they were also associated with ideology and partisanship, linkages that have changed dramatically since the mid-twentieth century. (Tables 4.8 and 4.9 encapsulate these findings.)

The Religion Gaps in Social Context: Gender, Age, and Income. The political impact of the Old and New Religion Gaps was not simply a reflection of other demographic factors, such as gender, age, or income. Indeed, the religion gaps were larger in 2004 than all other demographic factors except race and ethnicity (which are closely linked to religious affiliation). However, other aspects of demography mattered to the vote as well. Indeed, religious communities are closely intertwined with gender, age, and income, and their characteristic politics are influenced by these demographic factors.

Other "voter" gaps occurred within the context of religious communities, sometimes undermining the effects of religion and at other times reinforcing them. For example, there was a gender gap within most religious communities, with women voting more Democratic than men. There were also generation gaps in most of these communities, but the direction of the gap varied, so that sometimes younger voters were more Republican and sometimes more Democratic. The gender and generation gaps were often related to the New Religion Gap. Finally, there was also a persistent income gap within almost all of the religious communities, with higher income voters preferring the Republicans and lower income voters preferring the Democrats. The size of the income gap was related to the Old Religion Gap. (Tables 1.7, 5.3, 5.6, and 5.9 encapsulate these findings.)

The connection of each of these factors to the vote changed during the last half of the twentieth century. The gender gap paralleled the emergence of the New Religion Gap, reflecting the connection of gender to the cultural conflict of this era. The generation gap showed a similar pattern, declining over the period precisely when the New Religion Gap appeared. The income gap was more constant over time and not as closely linked to cultural conflict, although it did decline when the New Religion Gap made its biggest advances. It is worth noting that all three gaps increased in importance during the highly polarized 2004 election.

The Religion Gap in Regional Context. Because presidential elections are waged and won at the sub-national level, the regions reveal much about the impact of religion. There were important differences in the 2004 presidential election between the "red" regions won by Bush, the "blue" regions won by Kerry, and the highly competitive "purple" regions where the election was resolved. These regional patterns often differ starkly from 1944, revealing the effects of both demographic and political change. Indeed, the solidly "red" regions in 2004 were Democratic strongholds 60 years before, while solid "blue" New England was then Republican. And there was also evidence of political continuity: the Midwest was evenly divided in both eras.

Region matters politically in part because of enduring civic cultures, and these reflect in part the size and distribution of religious communities as well as long-standing ways that they interact with one another. The Old Religion Gap was in evidence in all of the regions. In fact, the dominant religious traditions helped explain the lack of competition in the solidly "red" and "blue" regions. And in many regions, the New Religion Gap was only modestly evident. However, both religion gaps were strongly evident in the highly competitive "purple" regions. Indeed, it was in the "purple" regions, especially the critical Midwestern states of Ohio and Michigan, that the Bush and Kerry campaigns sought to most fully exploit the Old and New Religion gaps. (Table 6.1 provides an overview and tables 6.4 through 6.11 cover each region.)

The Religion Gaps in Action: Campaign Contact and Activism. Commentary and news coverage in the 2004 campaign recorded extensive efforts to mobilize religious constituencies by the Bush and Kerry campaigns, their parties, and interest group allies. In addition, there was extensive activity by specialized political organizations of the Christian Right and the "religious left," plus considerable effort to activate votes at the congregational level.

Survey evidence reveals the magnitude of these activities. The campaign contacts were nearly equal between the rival presidential candidates, but Bush had a small but significant advantage in congregational contact. Both the incidence and partisan bias of political contacts appears to be associated with higher levels of turnout and support for particular candidates. A key factor here was the exploitation of the New Religion Gap, but also careful attention to the Old Religion Gap. The high level of contact among Weekly Attending Evangelical Protestants is a good example of all of these tendencies. (Tables 1.8, 7.3 and 7.4 encapsulate these findings.)

In 2004, religious constituencies were well represented among political activists, including campaign volunteers and delegates to the national party conventions. By and large, these activists were representative of each party's religious coalition among voters. Thus, the Old and New Religion Gaps are deeply embedded in the campaign process and partisan organizations. A look back over time suggests that congregational contacts are more common now than in the past, and that the religious character of political activists has changed as well, in keeping with the Old and New Religion Gaps. (Tables 7.7 and 7.9 encapsulate these findings.)

The Religion Gaps and the Future

What will the impact of religion on American politics be in the future? Here it is useful to divide the answer into the prospects for the immediate future (the next several years) and the more distant future (into the next generation). One can speculate on firmer ground with regard to the former, but the latter is much more uncertain.

The Immediate Future: More of the Same

The present situation is likely to prevail in the short run. That is to say, the Old and New Religion gaps are likely to continue to operate as in the 2004 election.

This pattern will certainly hold for the 2008 presidential campaign, which at this writing is already well under way, and it is very likely to persist well into the next decade. Put another way, religious divisions that caused such consternation in 2004 are likely to do so in the immediate future as well.

The reasons for this conclusion are straightforward. Each of the major parties has strong religious constituencies whose issue priorities and political identifications strongly bind them to the existing coalitions. Evangelical Protestants and especially the weekly attenders, other conservative Christians (of which the Latter Day Saints are a prime example), plus Weekly Attending Catholics and Mainline Protestants have become key constituencies for the Republicans. And for the Democrats, religious minorities, the Unaffiliated, and less observant white Christians are strong constituencies.

As was shown in chapters 2 and 3, these patterns have developed slowly over several decades, and it is very unlikely that such trends would be reversed in a few years. Short of a major catastrophe—always a real but remote possibility—the religious voters who care for these distinctions are unlikely to experience wholesale changes in their religious or political orientations.

The national political agenda is unlikely to change much in the near future either. For one thing, there is no indication that social issues will decline in importance. Conflict over abortion and marriage, not to mention other "moral values," shows no signs of diminishing. From the point of view of religious traditionalists, there is a steady stream of provocations, a good example of which is the continued pressure to recognize same-sex marriage. And from the perspective of less traditional religionists, there is also a constant series of confrontations, chief among them relentless attempts to limit abortion. Despite the desire of many Americans for compromise and resolution of these matters, some Americans are committed to continuing the conflict. As a consequence, the political agenda is likely to remain complex, with a mix of social, foreign policy, and economic concerns (as shown in chapter 4).

This reality is likely to be supported by the social context in which the religion gaps operate (see chapter 5). Other demographic factors that might compete with religion to create political distinctiveness are now closely entwined with it, and are likely to remain so in the near future. In this regard, the relationship of gender and age to religion serve to maintain cultural conflict by providing reinforcement for both sides. Income represents a somewhat different pattern, but even so, it largely serves to maintain the complexity of the issue agenda.

Along these lines, the regional context of the religion gaps is likely to support a continuation of the present situation in the near term (see chapter 6). The civic culture of the various regions is tenacious, with an extraordinary capacity to adapt to massive shifts in population over long periods of time. Thus, in the immediate future, the "red" and "blue" regions are likely to fly their colors proudly, and the "purple" regions will remain fiercely divided. No competent politician can ignore these regional realities.

Finally, the conduct of campaigns and characteristics of political activism strongly suggest continuity rather than change in the short run (see chapter 7). In terms of campaign contact, politicians and their allies have strong incentives to exploit the Old and New Religion Gaps. Advances in communications technology have made targeting of congenial religious voters into less of an art than a science. And in terms of campaign activism, the Old and New Religion gaps are so firmly embedded in the process of organizing and waging campaigns that seeking the votes of religious people is now second nature to many politicians. The Christian Right and other religious conservatives represent a potent force in this regard. And the potential revival of the "religious left" will only exacerbate this style of politics, by expanding the level of religious mobilization.

In sum, the burden of the evidence suggests that the Old and New Religion gaps will persist in the immediate future. It is important, however, not to overstate these prospects. For one thing, it is not clear that these trends will accelerate in the immediate future, so that the Old and New Religion gaps widen in the electorate. "Moral values" may not become more prominent, and the social, regional, and political contexts of the religion gaps may set limits on their growth. Indeed, the very factors that suggest no diminishment of religion's role in the next several years may prevent it from expanding further. The status quo cuts both ways.

Finally, the continued importance of the Old and New Religion gaps does not mean that the Republicans will always win elections. After all, the 2004 election was very close and could easily have produced another result with almost exactly the same religious patterns in the vote. Even if the present political era were one of Republican dominance (a fact that is far from clear at present), the Democrats could win some elections, much as Republican Dwight Eisenhower did during the Democratic era in the 1950s. The post-2004 foment in Democratic circles over how to cope with the "values voters" may well produce better candidates and more effective campaigns in 2008. Finally, short-term controversies, such as foreign policy crises, economic trouble, or personal scandals, can provide political opportunities. Of course, the post-Bush Republicans are concerned about these very same matters and will seek to adapt as well.

The results of the 2006 congressional elections add credence to these conclusions.[3] The Democrats won the mid-term elections and took over the control of both houses of Congress for the first time in twelve years. Overall, the congressional vote was close, with the Democrats winning some 53 percent of the two-party vote. Both the Old and New Religion gaps were strongly evident in the congressional vote, but unlike 2004 and 2002 (the previous mid-term election), the distribution of votes among these "gaps" favored the Democrats and not the Republicans. The small shifts in the vote across the Old and New Religion gaps in 2006 had many causes: more effective pursuit of religious voters by some Democratic candidates; opposition to the Iraq war; President Bush's low approval ratings; and scandals among GOP officeholders.

In sum, the Old and New Religion gaps are likely to be an integral part of the structure of American national elections in the immediate future, and within those parameters, a range of political outcomes are possible.

The More Distant Future: Three Scenarios

The evidence for the continuing impact of the religion gaps in the short run reflects the scale of change in religion and politics since the mid-twentieth century, as reported in the over time analysis in the previous chapters. However, this same analysis clearly reveals that quite dramatic changes can occur over a longer period. In fact, the 2004 election was the product of just such a transformation. With this history in mind, it is quite likely that the impact of religion will change in the next 30 to 60 years. While necessarily speculative, three scenarios suggest themselves.

Scenario One: The New Religion Gap Becomes Dominant. One possibility is that over the next generation the New Religion Gap based on religious traditionalism becomes dominant in politics, eclipsing the impact of religious tradition.

One way to visualize this scenario is to imagine that weekly worship attenders voted even more strongly for Republican candidates and the less observant voted even more strongly Democratic. Thus, the attendance gap in the two-party vote would continue to increase (in effect continuing the upward trend in figure 3.2). If all else remained equal, this would require that the affiliation gap decline. For example, Weekly Attending Black Protestants would vote Republican and Less Observant Evangelicals would support Democrats—rendering Black and Evangelical Protestants less distinctive overall.

The results of the 2006 congressional elections offer a good example of this possibility. One reason the Democrats did well was that the New Religion Gap expanded and did so in their favor: the largest percentage gains over the 2004 and 2002 congressional vote came among individuals who reported never attending worship. As a consequence, the religion gap between the most frequent and least frequent attenders increased.[4] This pattern reveals that the New Religion Gap had not reached its fullest development in 2004 and could become an even sharper division in the future.

If such a trend persisted for long enough, religious traditions would cease to matter in politics. This scenario has been suggested by James Davison Hunter, the chief advocate of the "culture wars" thesis.[5] Such a scenario would probably require that the subject of the "culture wars," social issues, become increasingly prominent: "moral values" priorities would increase and more people would take up opposite sides on such matters. In addition, many foreign policy and economic issues could be re-interpreted in terms of "moral values."

In all probability, such a development would require changes in American religion—in effect, an ongoing "restructuring" of religion. Traditionalist religious groups might grow in size, attracting an increasingly large following due to high birth rates and conversions. But by the same token, the secular population might grow as well. In this imagining, religious centrists would become rare, and theologically diverse bodies, such as the Catholic and Mainline Protestant churches, would decline. The manner and speed with which such religious changes occur could be crucial because it would determine the relative size of the rival religious groups. But such a world need not be bi-polar: different kinds of religious behavior and beliefs could generate different types of traditionalism—or for that matter, secularity.

Judging from the consternation provoked by the New Religion Gap in 2004, this scenario would not please many observers. After all, it conjures up the specter of the various theocracies around the world, not to mention the religious wars in history. But the results of this scenario need not be so severe. For instance, it might involve the institutionalizing of social issue divisions in political alignments, rather like the conflict over slavery after the Civil War or the debate over the welfare state after the Great Depression. And it is not clear which political party would be dominant in such an era. It could be the Republicans, now a party of "morality" and the voice of dominant religious traditionalists—or it could be the Democrats, now a party of "reason" and the voice of a non-religious majority.

Scenario Two: The Old Religion Gap Returns to Dominance. Another possibility is that over the next generation, the Old Religion Gap based on religious tradition becomes dominant in politics once again, and the impact of religious traditionalism diminishes.

This situation is easier to imagine because we have seen a good example: the party coalitions in 1944 (see chapter 2). Recall that religious behavior and belief had no apparent independent impact on the vote at that time, and that the New Deal Democrats and the rival Republicans were alliances of religious traditions. Of course, the religious traditions have changed a great deal since that time, so the building blocs of such coalitions would be quite different. For one thing, a new set of ethnic and religious minorities now characterize the religious landscape and there is every reason to believe such religious diversity will continue to grow. Evangelical Protestants have become much more numerous and so have the Unaffiliated.

Here, too, the results of the 2006 congressional election provide a good example of this possibility. For one thing, the non-Latino Catholics' vote swung back into the Democratic column, effectively erasing the Catholics' swing toward the Republicans in 2004.[6] And in some states, such as Pennsylvania and Ohio, the Democrats received large majorities of the Catholic vote. This development reflected a diminution of the influence of "moral values" and greater concern for foreign and economic policy in the 2006 campaign. If this trend were to continue, Catholics would be less divided by the New Religion Gap, and the Old Religion Gap would become more relevant (and the Catholic vote would look more like it did in the 1940s). Also in 2006, the Democrats increased their support from Hispanic Christians (in part due to the issue of immigration reform), Black Protestants, and the Unaffiliated (the Iraq war had a big impact on both groups). And despite predictions to the contrary, Evangelical Protestants voted strongly for Republican congressional candidates in 2006. This pattern reveals that the Old Religion Gap has not lost its potency and could be a source of sharper division in the future.

In all probability, this scenario would require the decline of social issues in the national political agenda. Such a change could happen in several ways. For example, a popular compromise could be struck on issues such as abortion or marriage so that they lose their power to mobilize voters. Or generational change could alter the opinions of Americans so that these matters no longer create much public controversy. At the same time, new issues would arise that would engage voters' affiliations rather than their practices and doctrines. For example, economic issues arising from the immigrant status or the consequences of globalization could differentiate the traditions. Perhaps foreign policy issues could function in this fashion, with some traditions adopting a strong internationalist perspective and others becoming strongly nationalistic.

Here, too, such a development would probably require changes in American religion. One possibility might be a reorganization of American denominations. The current tensions caused by traditionalism might be resolved by a series of denominational splits and mergers. Traditionalist Episcopalians might join with conservative Lutherans to form the "Confessional Anglican Church," while liberal Episcopalians attract liberal Catholics fed up with Rome to form the "Liberal Liturgical Communion," thus rendering the American Catholic church a more consistently orthodox body. And so on. Such an eventuality would resemble the fragmenting and reorganizing of American Protestantism in the early twentieth century. The end result would be religious traditions that were more homogeneous in terms of practice and doctrine, and thus distinctive politically.

No doubt many contemporary observers would appreciate this kind of development, if only for reasons of nostalgia. However, this scenario might not be any less conflictual than the present day. One needs only think back to bitter battles between Protestants and Catholics in the last century to see a negative example. Just to pick one possibility, the Republicans, now the party of "opportunity," could become an alliance of immigrant faiths, Other Non-Christians, and Catholics, while the Democrats, now the party of "security," could be an alliance of nativist Protestants, secular isolationists and eco-spiritualists. It is hard to say which coalition would normally prevail.

Scenario Three: An Alternative Religion Gap Appears. The final possibility is the most speculative: an alternative dimension of religion becomes important politically, cutting across religious traditions and traditionalism.

Such a possibility would be like the New Religion Gap, only with regard to another aspect of religion. It may be hard to imagine such a thing, but then the rise of the attendance gap and the "restructuring" of American religion might not have been easily imaginable in the 1940s. Another example is from the nineteenth century, when the major political division was being between the "pietist" (Methodists, Baptists, and Congregationalists) and the "liturgical" (Catholics,

Lutherans, and Episcopalians) Christians.[7] Something of this nature could certainly happen again.

The simplest version of this scenario requires an existing dimension of religion that is not politicized and an issue or issues that would do so. One candidate might be spirituality.[8] A part of many religious traditions, spirituality, including practices outside of organized religion, has been the subject of considerable interest in recent times. Thus, like worship attendance, spirituality extends across denominational boundaries, potentially uniting—and dividing—people of disparate religious backgrounds. And the degree of spirituality could be thought of with a reference point of material concerns, rendering it a continuum analogous to traditionalism.

What kind of issue might make spirituality relevant to politics? One possibility is the environment. Imagine that environmental disputes develop in such a way that individuals characterized by high levels of spirituality identify strongly with one side of the debate and individuals with low levels—or materialist perspectives—identify with the other side. Then the "spiritual" in the various religious traditions—and outside of them—would find themselves allied with one another in one of the major political parties, while their "material" co-religionists would coalesce together in the other party. Like the New Religion Gap, this alternative "spirituality gap" could initially complicate party coalitions by creating new religious constituencies on both sides of the partisan divide.

In fact, something like this scenario was suggested after the 2004 election by Michael Lerner in his book *The Left Hand of God;* the book was followed by a political conference in Washington, D.C., for the "spiritual Progressives," who offered a "Spiritual Covenant with America."[9] Clearly, Lerner believes that "spiritual politics" will benefit the Democrats. But of course, any new cleavage of this sort would affect the Republicans as well.

The likelihood that one or another of these scenarios will occur in the next generation is difficult to assess, and little credence should be placed in the particular examples offered. After all, religion and politics are among the most dynamic aspects of American society. However, these scenarios reinforce a critical point: religion is likely to have a significant role in American elections in the future, much as it does in the present and has in the past. Indeed, the political impact of religion will surely be a source of continuing consternation, with a great capacity to surprise.

Postscript
The Religion Gaps and the 2008 Election

What about the religion gaps and the 2008 presidential election? The initial evidence suggests that both the Old Religion Gap (based on religious affiliation) and the New Religion Gap (based on worship attendance) mattered in much the same way as in the 2004 election. Within this continuity there were, however, some important changes as well. The most important change by far was the increased Democratic vote by various kinds of religious minorities. In sum, the basic structure of American faith-based politics persisted in 2008, but unlike 2004, it worked on balance in the Democrats' favor.

As in 2004, religion played a prominent role in the 2008 campaign. In fact, the range and intensity of faith-based politics may have been greater.[1] For example, the Democrats made a greater effort to mobilize religious voters than in 2004, hoping to woo moderates and even some conservatives away from the Republicans, but without angering their liberal and secular followers. In this regard, Obama was particularly effective, speaking about his faith with a high degree of comfort (in a fashion reminiscent of George W. Bush). And, as in 2004, the Republicans also pursued religious votes, seeking to maintain the support of conservatives without alienating moderates and religious minorities. Here, McCain was less effective, being less comfortable speaking about his faith (much like John Kerry). The major party vice-presidential nominees highlighted these outreach efforts: Joe Biden to shore up the white Catholics for Obama and Sarah Palin to energize white Evangelicals for McCain.

New additions to faith-based politics included a surge of activism by religious progressives, false claims that Obama was a Muslim, and the prominence of Mormons. In fact, the campaign began and ended with the latter: Some Evangelicals opposed Mitt Romney in the presidential primaries because of his faith, and some gay activists demonstrated against the Latter Day Saints because of their support for banning same-sex marriage in California. At the same time, some standard themes in faith-based politics persisted, such as debates over social justice and sexuality. On this score, Catholics and Evangelical Protestants fought over the proper issue priorities.

An emblem of this expanded faith-based politics was a series of "pastor" controversies—left, right, and center. On the first count, Obama was troubled by Rev. Jeremiah Wright, his pastor for twenty years and an unapologetic proponent of black liberation theology. A combination of Wright's past sermons and contemporary public appearances ultimately led Obama to distance himself from him. Shortly thereafter, Obama chose to leave his Chicago congregation when a visiting Catholic priest, Rev. Michael Pfleger, mocked Hillary Clinton from the pulpit. On the second count, John McCain had pastor troubles as well: he eventually rejected the endorsements of conservative televangelists he had described as "spiritual advisers," Revs. John Hagee and Ron Parsely, when their past sermons that appeared to be critical of Jews and Muslims became public.

Such controversies extended to a centrist megachurch pastor and best-selling author, Rev. Rick Warren. In the summer of 2008, Warren invited both Obama and McCain to his California church for a televised interview—the first joint appearance by the major party nominees. Both the occasion and Warren's questions to the candidates drew criticism from many quarters. Then, after the election, Obama asked Warren to give the invocation at his inaugural, provoking ire across the ideological spectrum: some liberals were offended that an opponent of same-sex marriage would be accorded this honor, while some conservatives were offended that an Evangelical pastor would serve a pro-choice president in this capacity.

For these reasons, many observers expected substantial changes in the faith-based vote in 2008. Thus the continuity in faith-based voting is quite remarkable and worthy of discussion. A good place to begin is with a description of the two-party vote of key religious groups found in table 9.1. This table is modeled on table 1.3 in chapter 1, with two religious groups added to better illustrate the 2008 election results: "other minority" Protestants and Catholics (non-white voters that were neither African American nor Latino). Although the data presented in tables 9.1 and 1.3 are not strictly comparable, the basic patterns are strikingly similar.[2]

The Old Religion Gap is clearly evident in table 9.1. White Evangelical Protestants were the strongest Republican constituency in 2008, while Black Protestants were the strongest Democratic constituency. Note that weekly attending white Evangelicals voted more for McCain (84.2 percent) than weekly attending white Catholics (60.6 percent) or weekly attending white Mainline Protestants (54.4 percent). Similar differences appear among minority religious groups, with McCain doing better among Latino Protestants (50 percent) than other minority Protestants (40.6 percent), other minority Catholics (23.3 percent), and Latino Catholics (20.4 percent). Thus the "old politics of belonging" was strongly evident in the 2008 vote, especially among religious minorities.

Table 9.1 Religious Affiliation and Attendance, and the 2008 Two-Party Vote

| | Two-Party Vote | | | |
	McCain	Obama	Total	% Electorate
Weekly Attending White Evangelical Protestants	84.2	15.8	**100**	14.9
Less Observant White Evangelical Protestants	65.9	34.1	**100**	6.4
Weekly Attending White Mainline Protestants	54.4	45.6	**100**	5.8
Less Observant White Mainline Protestants	50.7	49.3	**100**	13.9
Latino Protestants	50.0	50.0	**100**	2.7
Other Minority Protestants	40.6	59.4	**100**	2.5
Weekly Attending Black Protestants	2.8	97.2	**100**	5.1
Less Observant Black Protestants	2.7	97.3	**100**	4.1
Weekly Attending White Catholics	60.6	39.4	**100**	7.4
Less Observant White Catholics	45.5	54.5	**100**	9.3
Latino Catholics	20.4	79.6	**100**	3.4
Other Minority Catholics	23.3	76.7	**100**	1.5
Other Christians	65.3	34.7	**100**	3.2
Jews	15.3	84.7	**100**	2.7
Other Faiths	29.7	70.3	**100**	3.1
Seculars	30.1	69.9	**100**	13.8
ALL	**47.0**	**53.0**	**100**	**100.0**

Source: Pooled 2008 Pew Research Center Surveys (Weekend and Post-election Surveys)

The New Religion Gap can also be seen clearly in table 9.1. Note that McCain received more votes from weekly worship attenders than the less observant among white Evangelicals (84.2 to 65.9 percent), white Catholics (60.6 to 45.5 percent), and white Mainline Protestants (54.4 to 50.7 percent). As reported in chapter 2, the New Religion Gap was much smaller among the religious minorities, such as Black Protestants. Thus the "new politics of behaving and believing" was also strongly evident in 2008, especially among white Christians.

What changes occurred between 2004 and 2008? Figure 9.1 compares the 2008 vote for Barack Obama among these religious groups (solid line) to the 2004 vote for John Kerry (dotted line) using comparable data in both years. For ease of presentation, the religious groups are arranged from Obama's strongest supporters to John McCain's strongest backers (in a fashion reminiscent of table 1.4).

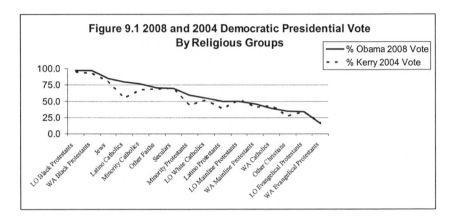

The difference between the solid and dotted lines in figure 9.1 show the change in the Democratic vote between 2004 and 2008. For the most part, Obama made gains across the religious groups. But note that the largest gains occurred among various kinds of religious minorities: Latino Catholics and Minority Catholics, Latino and Minority Protestants. Obama also made gains among Jews, and the composite categories of other faiths (such as Muslims and Buddhists) and other Christians (such as Eastern Orthodox and Mormons), and even among Black Protestants. Most of these groups voted heavily Democratic in 2004, but Obama received an often dramatic increase in support. Meanwhile, Obama made modest gains among the white Christian groups, making the least improvement among white Evangelicals.[3]

Looked at another way, the coalition that elected Barack Obama president in 2008 had the same basic structure as the one that nearly put John Kerry in the White House four years before. The key difference was much stronger support from religious minorities. In this regard, the affiliation gap became larger in 2008, with the difference in the Democratic vote between the most (Black Protestants) and least Democratic (white Evangelicals) groups expanding from 70 to 76 percentage points. At the same time, the attendance gap narrowed somewhat, with the difference in the Democratic vote between weekly and less than weekly worship attenders falling to 20 percentage points in 2008 from 22 percentage points in 2004. Here, too, the principal source of this decline was religious minorities, where Obama received more votes from regular worship attenders than Kerry did in 2004. These shifts in the religion gaps occurred in the context of other demographic and geographic changes, such as the strong support of younger voters for Obama and Obama's victories in southern, midwestern and western states won by Bush in 2004.

What happened to the "value voters" in 2008? The simple answer is that economic issues dominated the 2008 election, reducing the importance of social issues, such as same-sex marriage, to the electorate at large. This shift in the issue agenda may have helped intensify the support of religious minorities for the Democrats and at the same time may have undermined support of regular worship attenders for the Republicans (see chapter 4 on the issue agenda of religious groups in 2004). A more nuanced answer is that social issues still mattered to some religious groups in 2008. A glance back at figure 9.1 reveals that groups with conservative social issue positions, such as white Evangelicals and weekly attending white Christians, largely stayed in the Republican column in 2004 despite the bad economy. Meanwhile, religious groups with more liberal views on social issues, such as Jews and the unaffiliated, stayed with the Democrats.

Evidence of the continuing relevance of social issues was the victory of Proposition 8 in California. This ballot measure sought to amend the state constitution to ban same-sex marriage, in effect overturning a 2008 ruling of the California Supreme Court that legalized same-sex marriage in the Golden State. Proposition 8 won with 52 percent of the vote, an impressive figure given that Barack Obama carried California by 61 percent. The exit polls showed that Proposition 8 was strongly supported by weekly worship attenders (84 percent), white Evangelicals (81 percent), and Catholics (64 percent). But minority voters also backed Proposition 8, with 70 percent of African Americans and 53 percent of Latinos voting for the measure. Of course, many African Americans and Latinos were regular worship attenders with conservative views on same-sex marriage. Ironically, the minority religious groups that Obama helped mobilize on his way to the White House helped with the passage of Proposition 8.

What does the faith-based vote in 2008 suggest about the future and the three scenarios described in chapter 8? As in the 2006 election, there was evidence against the first scenario, the continued expansion of the New Religion Gap. After all, there was a modest decline in attendance gap in 2008. If this trend were to continue in the next several presidential elections, the attendance gap would become markedly less significant. But the fact that the dramatic 2008 campaign produced only a small reduction in the attendance gap suggests that such a change may occur slowly over several decades—about the same time period during which the New Religion Gap developed. Even under these circumstances, the "new politics of behaving and believing" is likely to remain important for some time.

In 2008, there was more evidence for the second scenario, a return of the Old Religion Gap. After all, there was a modest increase in the affiliation gap in 2008. The strong support Obama received from religious minorities suggests a strengthening of religious group identification. In some respects, the Obama coalition resembled the ethno-religious politics of the past. If this trend were to continue in the next several elections, abetted by the growing ethnic and religious diversity of the country, faith-based politics might slowly come to resemble the pattern of the 1940s, albeit with a new set of ethno-religious groups. In any event, the "old politics of belonging" is likely to remain important for some time.

Of course, the direction of faith-based politics will depend a great deal on the impact of President Obama. The Obama administration could help close the New Religion Gap and/or expand the Old Religion Gap—or return faith-based politics to the patterns of 2004. But most intriguing is the possibility that Obama could fundamentally change faith-based politics, creating an entirely new kind of connection between faith and the ballot box, perhaps of the sort suggested in the third scenario in chapter 8 (an alternative religion gap based on spirituality). Although there is little evidence of this sort of change in the 2008 vote, many observers earnestly hope it will come to pass.

Appendix A: Major Religious Traditions and Denominational Affiliation

The assignment of respondents to religious traditions in Chapter 2 (and table 2.1) is as follows (see text for further discussion of such assignments):

Evangelical Protestants:

Specific denominations: Advent Christian, Seventh-Day Adventist, World Wide Church of God; American Baptist Association, Baptist Bible Fellowship, Baptist General Conference, Baptist Missionary Association of America, Conservative Baptist Association of America, General Association of Regular Baptist Churches, National Association of Free Will Baptists, Independent Baptists, Primitive Baptists, Reformed Baptists, Southern Baptist Convention; Anglican Orthodox Church, Reformed Episcopal Church; Conservative Congregational Christian Conference, Congregational Christian Churches; Church of Christ, Churches of Christ and Christian Churches; Evangelical Covenant Church, Evangelical Church of North American, Evangelical Free Church; Evangelical Friends; Grace Brethren Church, Brethren in Christ, Mennonite Church, General Conference Mennonite Church, Mennonite Brethren, other Mennonite and Amish churches; Christian and Missionary Alliance, Church of God (Anderson, IN), Church of the Nazarene, Free Methodist Church, Salvation Army, Wesleyan Church, Church of God of Findlay, OH; Plymouth Brethren, Independent Fundamentalist Churches of America; Lutheran Church-Missouri Synod, Wisconsin Evangelical Lutheran Synod, Free Lutheran, Lutheran Brethren, Congregational Methodist Church, Assemblies of God, Church of God (Cleveland, TN), Church of God (Huntsville, AL), International Church of the Four Square Gospel, Pentecostal Church of God, Pentecostal

Holiness Church, Open Bible Standard Churches, Church of God of the Apostolic Faith, Church of God of Prophecy, the Vineyard; Associate Reformed Presbyterian, Cumberland Presbyterian Church, Presbyterian Church in America, Evangelical Presbyterian, Orthodox Presbyterian, Reformed Presbyterian Church; Christian Reformed Church.

Non-specific affiliations: Respondents with generic (i.e. "Just a Christian") or ambiguous affiliations ("Just a Baptist") or who reported being "non-denominational or independent" were assigned to the Evangelical Protestant tradition if they identified as "born again" or as "evangelical," "fundamentalist," "Pentecostal" or "charismatic," or if they reported a general affiliation associated with the Evangelical Protestant tradition, such as "Adventist," "bible believing," "Church of God," "Holiness," or "Pentecostal."

Mainline Protestants:

Specific denominations: American Baptist Churches U.S.A., Church of the Brethren, Episcopal Church in the U.S.A, United Church of Christ, Society of Friends, Evangelical Lutheran Church in America, United Methodist Church, Moravians, Presbyterian Church in the U.S.A., Reformed Church in America, Christian Church (Disciples of Christ).

Non-specific affiliations: Respondents with generic (i.e. "Just a Christian") or ambiguous affiliations ("Just a Baptist") or who reported being "non-denominational or independent" were assigned to the Mainline Protestant tradition if they identified as "liberal" or "progressive," or if they reported no other religious identification, but had a minimal level of religious commitment. Respondents who identified as inter-denominational and inter-faith were also included.

Black and Latino Protestants:

The largest historic black Protestant denominations are National Baptist Convention in the U.S.A., National Baptist Convention of America, Progressive National Baptist Convention, African Methodist Episcopal Church, African Methodist Episcopal Zion Church, Christian Methodist Episcopal Church, and Church of God in Christ. Due to ambiguity in religious affiliation data, many scholars define black Protestants by race. This procedure was followed in Chapter 2 for practical reasons. Similarly, Latino Protestants were defined by ethnicity.

Catholics:

The Roman Catholic Church and generic Catholic identifications. Latino Catholics were defined by ethnicity.

Other Christians:

Other important Christian churches include all Mormon Churches (of which the Church of Jesus Christ of the Latter Day Saints is the largest body); Orthodox (or Eastern Orthodox) Churches; Jehovah's Witnesses; Church of Christ, Scientist; the Metropolitan Community Church, and the Unitarian-Universalist Association. In this vein, scholars often put Unity, Divine Science, Humanist, Scientologists, New Age practitioners, Wiccans and pagans in this category, but these groups could also be placed in a separate category of "liberal faiths" and sometimes they are put in a non-Christian category.

Jews:

This category includes Reform, Conservative, and Orthodox Jews, and all other Jewish identifications.

Other Non-Christians:

This category includes all Muslims, Buddhists and Hindus, and also Bahias and other Asian religions as well as Native American and Afro-Caribbean faith.

Unaffiliated:

No religious preference, agnostics, and atheists. Respondents with generic affiliations and no evidence of religious commitment were assigned to the unaffiliated category.

Appendix B: Major Religious Traditions by State

The following table offers an estimate of the size of the major religious traditions as a percentage of the adult population in all fifty states in 2000 (each row adds to 100%). These figures are rough estimates based on a number of different sources, including the American Religious Landscape studies; pooled survey data from the Pew Research Center, the National Election Studies, and the General Social Survey; the 2000 Religious Congregations and Membership Survey; the published reports from the American Religious Identification Survey; and a number of state-level surveys. Each of these sources of information has its strengths and weakness, and these estimates sought to capitalize on the former and minimize the latter. While these estimates must be used with caution, they offer useful information for state-level religious affiliation in terms that are commonly employed by journalists and scholars.

State	Evangelical Protestant	Mainline Protestant	Latino Protestant	Black Protestant	Non-Latino Catholic	Latino Catholic	Other Christians	Mormons	Other Faiths	Muslims	Jews	No religion
Alabama	46.1	17.0	0.5	20.0	6.0	0.6	2.1	0.5	1.1	0.2	0.2	5.7
Alaska	24.0	20.0	0.0	1.0	15.0	3.0	1.9	3.0	2.3	0.2	0.6	29.0
Arizona	20.0	18.0	5.2	2.0	10.0	20.0	0.8	5.0	1.2	0.2	1.6	16.0
Arkansas	44.0	16.0	0.5	15.0	5.0	1.5	3.0	0.6	1.2	0.1	0.1	13.0
California	15.0	12.0	6.4	6.0	10.0	22.0	1.7	1.6	2.6	0.8	2.9	19.0
Colorado	25.0	18.1	3.0	2.3	12.0	11.0	2.1	2.1	1.3	0.3	1.7	21.0
Connecticut	7.3	15.0	2.0	7.7	39.9	5.6	1.7	0.3	1.4	0.9	3.2	15.0
Delaware	26.0	25.0	0.5	16.0	6.0	3.0	2.9	0.4	1.0	0.5	1.7	17.0
Florida	24.6	15.7	3.3	10.0	16.3	9.7	1.4	0.5	0.5	0.2	3.9	14.0
Georgia	32.7	16.3	1.8	23.4	5.9	3.0	2.5	0.5	1.3	0.5	1.1	11.0
Hawaii	15.0	15.0	0.0	0.5	15.0	5.0	1.7	3.5	25.0	0.1	0.2	19.0
Idaho	25.1	18.9	2.0	0.2	10.0	5.0	1.0	20.0	2.7	0.0	0.1	15.0
Illinois	22.5	16.0	2.3	10.4	21.5	7.5	0.8	0.3	1.0	1.0	2.2	14.5
Indiana	31.0	23.0	1.5	6.5	15.0	5.0	1.0	0.5	0.5	0.2	0.2	15.7
Iowa	25.4	33.8	1.4	2.0	21.0	2.0	0.5	0.5	0.1	0.2	0.2	12.9
Kansas	34.3	22.6	2.4	2.0	15.0	5.0	0.4	0.8	1.7	0.1	0.5	15.1
Kentucky	37.0	25.0	0.5	6.4	13.0	1.0	1.0	0.4	1.5	0.1	0.3	13.8
Louisiana	22.0	16.0	1.1	20.5	27.0	1.5	1.5	0.4	0.4	0.3	0.4	9.0
Maine	25.7	24.0	0.9	0.9	25.0	2.8	2.0	0.6	1.8	0.1	0.7	15.5
Maryland	16.2	18.4	2.4	19.1	19.4	1.6	1.3	0.5	1.2	1.0	4.1	14.9
Massachusetts	10.6	14.2	2.0	3.6	40.0	4.0	1.7	0.3	2.7	0.7	4.3	16.0
Michigan	25.0	19.0	1.4	12.5	20.5	2.5	0.9	0.3	1.0	0.8	1.1	15.0
Minnesota	25.2	29.6	0.3	2.0	22.0	3.0	0.7	0.4	1.6	0.3	0.9	14.0
Mississippi	35.6	15.0	0.8	30.6	4.0	0.7	2.0	0.5	1.2	0.1	0.0	10.0

Missouri	27.0	25.0	0.5	8.8	18.0	1.0	1.2	0.7	1.4	0.3	1.1	15.0
Montana	30.0	22.9	0.5	0.2	21.0	1.0	3.2	3.6	1.4	0.1	0.1	16.0
Nebraska	25.2	28.7	1.0	2.9	23.5	3.5	3.2	0.9	1.5	0.2	0.4	9.0
Nevada	20.0	14.7	4.5	4.0	11.0	13.0	1.4	5.9	1.5	0.1	3.9	20.0
N. Hampshire	22.3	20.6	0.5	0.5	34.0	1.0	1.0	0.2	1.8	0.3	0.8	17.0
New Jersey	9.7	16.2	2.6	10.3	28.6	8.4	0.9	0.2	1.1	1.4	5.6	15.0
New Mexico	18.0	12.0	4.8	0.5	10.2	30.0	1.0	2.3	2.5	0.1	0.6	18.0
New York	8.0	14.2	2.5	12.6	28.0	10.0	1.0	0.2	1.1	1.2	8.7	12.5
N. Carolina	40.0	16.0	1.6	17.8	9.4	1.6	1.1	0.5	1.4	0.3	0.3	10.0
North Dakota	16.2	30.2	0.5	0.4	29.5	0.5	3.5	0.6	2.4	0.1	0.1	16.0
Ohio	25.0	26.0	0.5	9.6	18.0	1.0	1.1	0.3	1.8	0.4	1.3	15.0
Oklahoma	46.3	18.9	1.5	6.5	4.0	3.0	2.0	0.7	3.0	0.2	0.1	13.8
Oregon	27.8	24.5	1.8	1.0	10.0	4.0	2.4	3.0	3.5	0.2	0.9	21.0
Pennsylvania	21.5	21.0	1.1	8.6	26.0	1.4	2.0	0.2	2.6	0.6	2.3	12.6
Rhode Island	6.7	12.9	2.5	3.5	46.5	4.5	2.9	0.2	2.4	0.2	1.5	16.0
S. Carolina	36.4	13.4	2.0	28.7	6.6	0.4	2.1	0.5	2.4	0.1	0.3	7.0
South Dakota	25.0	29.0	0.5	1.8	24.5	0.5	1.2	0.8	1.8	0.0	0.0	15.0
Tennessee	47.0	22.0	0.5	14.0	5.0	1.0	0.2	0.4	0.3	0.3	0.3	9.0
Texas	25.0	13.7	8.0	8.6	10.0	18.0	2.2	0.7	1.5	0.6	0.6	11.0
Utah	8.2	6.2	4.1	0.5	2.0	4.1	1.0	57.0	0.7	0.2	0.2	15.8
Vermont	16.0	20.0	0.0	0.1	38.0	0.0	0.4	0.5	2.0	0.0	1.0	22.0
Virginia	32.7	17.8	1.8	16.9	12.0	2.0	1.1	0.8	1.0	0.7	1.1	12.0
Washington	24.3	17.0	2.4	2.0	16.0	4.4	1.9	3.0	3.0	0.3	0.7	25.0
West Virginia	44.2	23.1	0.0	2.0	8.0	0.0	2.2	0.5	2.8	0.1	0.1	17.0
Wisconsin	22.5	25.1	0.5	4.5	29.0	2.0	0.5	0.3	0.5	0.1	0.5	14.5
Wyoming	26.0	23.0	1.0	0.0	14.0	4.0	1.0	9.5	1.3	0.1	0.1	20.0

Notes

Chapter 1

1. On the relationship between religion and politics see Andrew Kohut, John C. Green, Scott Keeter, and Robert Toth, *The Diminishing Divide: Religion's Changing Role in American Politics* (Washington, D.C.: Brookings Institution, 2000). Also see The Pew Center for The People and the Press, "The 2004 Political Landscape: Evenly Divided and Increasingly Polarized," November 5, 2003. http://people-press.org/reports/display.php3?ReportID=196 [Accessed August 2006].

2. Maureen Dowd, "The Red Zone," *New York Times,* November 4, 2004.

3. Thomas Friedman, "Two Nations Under God," *New York Times,* November 4, 2004.

4. Garry Wills, "The Day Enlightenment Went Out," *New York Times,* November 4, 2004.

5. Louis Bolce and Gerald De Maio, "The Anti-Christian Fundamentalist Factor in Contemporary Politics," *Public Opinion Quarterly,* 63 (1999): 508–42.

6. For a partial transcript of Falwell's remarks see "You Helped This Happen: Jerry Falwell and Pat Robertson react to the September 11 terrorist attacks on American soil." Beliefnet. http://www.beliefnet.com/story/87/story_8770_1.html. [Accessed August 2006].

7. Susan Jacoby, chapter 8 in *Freethinkers, A History of American Secularism* (New York: Henry Holt, 2004): 227–267.

8. Steven Thomma, "Americans' Religious Practices Serve As Gauge of Political Choice," *Philadelphia Inquirer*, December 2, 2003.

9. Felix Hoover, "Many Christians Vote by Ideology, Not Denomination," *Columbus Dispatch*, October 8, 2004.

10. Nicholas Kristof, "The God Gulf," *New York Times,* January 7, 2004.

11. The Revealer, "Ultimate Concerns," January 7, 2004. http://www.therevealer.org/archives/daily_000146.php [Accessed August 2006].

12. Susan Nielson, "Bush Won Millions of Swing Voters By Running as Their Moral All-American Guy," *Oregonian,* November 7, 2007.

13. Gayle White, "God's Country," *Atlanta Journal Constitution,* November 7, 2004.

14. Ellen Goodman, "Winning Back Values Voters," *Washington Post,* November 6, 2004.

15. See Peter Steinfelds, "Voters Say Values Matter," *New York Times,* November 6, 2004; and Charles Krauthammer, "The 'Moral Value' Myth," *Washington Post,* November 12, 2004.

16. David Brooks, "The Values-Vote Myth," *New York Times,* November 6, 2004.

17. E. J. Dionne, "Moderates, Not Moralists," *Washington Post*, November 9, 2004.

18. See James W. Ceaser and Andrew E. Busch, *Red Over Blue: The 2004 Elections and American Politics* (Lanham, MD: Rowman & Littlefield, 2005), especially Chapter 4.

19. C. Danielle Vinson and James L. Guth, "'Misunderestimating' Religion in the 2004 Presidential Campaign," in *Getting it Wrong: How the Media Missed the Story because it Missed Religion,* ed. Paul Marshall (Irvine CA: Fieldstead Institute, 2006), in press.

20. For a post-election analysis of the NEP's difficulties, see "Evaluation of Edison/Mitovsky Election System 2004" by Edison Media Research and Mitovsky International, available from The Roper Center for Public Opinion Research (www.RoperCenter.UConn.edu). The NEP reported a margin of error of plus or minus 3 percentage points for the entire national sample.

21. The ten groups used in Table 1.1 here were defined as follows: 1. Evangelical Protestants were "white born-again Protestants and Other Christians"; 2. Mainline Protestants were "white non-born again Protestants"; 3. Other Christians were "Mormons plus non-born again Other Christians"; 4. Other Faiths were "Muslims and regular worshiping Something Else"; 5. Black and Latino Protestants included "Protestants and Other Christians"; 6. the Unaffiliated were the "None and low attendance Something Else." A number of other very modest adjustments were made to these data based on experience with other surveys. The full coding is available from the author upon request.

22. See John C. Green, Corwin E. Smidt, James L. Guth, and Lyman A. Kellstedt, "The American Religious Landscape and the 2004 Presidential Vote: Increased Polarization," Pew Forum on Religion & Public Life. http://pewforum.org/docs/index.php?DocID=64 [Accessed August 2006].

23. The foreign policy category included the Iraq war (15.8%) and terrorism (20.4%). The economic policy category included economy/jobs (21.2%); taxes (5.7%); education (4.7%); and health care (8.6%). (Missing data were excluded in this analysis.)

24. See Laura R. Olson and John C. Green, "Introduction—'Gapology' and the Presidential Vote." *PS* 39 (2006): 443–446.

Chapter 2

1. For a good discussion of ethnicity in the nineteenth century, see Robert P. Swierenga, "Ethnoreligious Political Behavior in the Mid-Nineteenth Century: Voting, Values, Cultures," in *Religion & American Politics*, ed. Mark A. Noll (New York: Oxford University Press, 1990), 146–171; and for the twentieth century see Michael Barone, *Our Country,* (New York: Free Press, 1990).

2. Diana L. Eck, *A New Religious America,* (San Francisco: Harper San Francisco, 2001).

3. Andrew Greely, *The Denominational Society,* (Glenview, Ill., Scott, Foresman, 1972); Martin E. Marty, "Ethnicity: The Skeleton of Religion in America," in *Denominationalism,* ed. Russell E. Richey (Nashville: Abingdon Press, 1977).

4. On "American Exceptionalism," see Wayne Baker, *America's Crisis of Values,* (Princeton: Princeton University Press, 2005), 38–42.

5. See Richard L. McCormick, "Ethno-cultural Interpretations of American Voting Behavior," *Political Science Quarterly* 89 (1974): 351–77.

6. Lyman A. Kellsteadt and Mark A. Noll, "Religion, Voting for President, and Party Identification, 1948–1984," in *Religion & American Politics,* ed. Mark A. Noll (New York: Oxford University Press, 1990), 380–390.

7. Lyman A. Kellstedt, John C. Green, James L. Guth, and Corwin E. Smidt, "Grasping the Essentials: The Social Embodiment of Religion and Political Behavior," in *Religion and the Culture Wars,* eds. John C. Green, James L. Guth, Corwin E. Smidt, and Lyman A. Kellstedt (Landam, MD: Rowman & Littlefield, 1996), 174–192; Lyman A. Kellstedt and John C. Green, "Knowing God's Many People: Denominational Preference and Political Behavior," in *Rediscovering the Religious Factor in American Politics,* eds. David C. Leege and Lyman A. Kellstedt (Armonk, NY: M.E. Sharpe, 1993).

8. George M. Marsden, *Religion and American Culture.* (New York: Harcourt Brace, 1990).

9. Geoffrey C. Layman and John C. Green, "Wars and Rumors of Wars: The Contexts of Cultural Conflict in American Political Behavior," *British Journal of Political Science* 36 (2005):61–89.

10. Coding denominational affiliation in religious traditions, see: Kellstedt and Green, "Grasping the Essentials," 1996; Layman and Green, "Wars and Rumours of Wars," 2005; Kohut et al., *The Diminishing Divide,* 2000; and Brian Steensland, Jerry Z. Park, Mark D. Regnerus, Lynn D. Robinson, W. Bradford Wilcox, and Robert D. Woodberry, "The Measure of American Religion: Toward Improving the State of the Art," *Social Forces* 79 (2000):291–318. For a good overview of religious traditions, see Matthew Wilson, ed. *From Pews to Polling Places* (Washington, D.C.: Georgetown University Press, 2007).

11. The data in Table 2.1 come from pooling the National Surveys of Religion and Politics for 1992, 1996, 2000, and 2004 (total number of cases 17,043). These surveys were conducted at the University of Akron with support from the Pew Forum on Religion & Public Life. These surveys contain consistent and detailed measures of religious affiliation; the coding follows the citations in note 10. The exact coding is found in Appendix A.

12. These data also come from the pooled National Surveys of Religion and Politics. Weekly worship attendance was measured as the sum of greater than weekly and weekly attenders; scriptural authority was measured as a literal or inerrant view of the Bible; religious salience was measured as "important" and "provides a great deal or some guidance"; the religious relevance measure was the first two points on a five-point scale that asked how important the respondents' religion was to their politics.

13. Evangelical Protestants are defined in many ways. For example, Christian Smith employs "evangelical" self-identification, race, and worship attendance in *American Evangelicalism: Embattled and Thriving* (Chicago: University of Chicago Press). The Gallup Poll uses four criteria, including belief and behavior (Frank Newport and Joseph Carroll, "Another Look at Evangelicals in America Today" http://poll.gallup.com/content/

default.aspx?ci=20242 [Accessed August 2006]). And evangelical pollster George Barna uses an extensive battery of beliefs (see "Definitions" in "Evangelicals are ready to Re-Elect Bush, but other Americans are not so sure." http://www.barna.org/FlexPage.aspx? Page=BarnaUpdate&BarnaUpdateID=132 [Accessed November 2006]). None of these approaches is a strict measure of affiliation because they use other religious variables to define belonging. The Pew Research Center uses the combination of white, born-again Protestants to define evangelicals (see Kohut et. al. *The Diminishing Divide*, 2000), the approach available in the NEP in 2004. Some scholars lump evengelicals in with other "conservative Christians," such as Andrew Greeley and Michael Hout, *The Truth about Conservative Christians* (Chicago: University of Chicago, 2006).

14. David Bebbington, *Evangelicalism in Modern Britain* (London: Unwin Hyman, 1989); and Mark A. Noll, *American Evangelical Christianity* (Malden, MA; Blackwell Publishers, 2001). Also see Randall Balmer, *Mine Eyes Have Seen the Glory: A Journey into the Evangelical Subculture in America* (New York: Oxford, 1989).

15. Marsden, *Religion and American Culture*, 1990, 168–179.

16. The term "evangelical" was chosen by the founders of the NAE and their allies to be broad and inclusive. In this sense, "evangelical" (or originally "neo-evangelical") differed from "fundamentalist." But in terms of most religious behaviors and beliefs, the "evangelicals" and "fundamentalists" were quite similar and still are today.

17. Evangelicalism has had great influence on other American religious traditions in recent times. One example is the impact of Pentecostalism on Mainline Protestantism and Catholicism, largely by means of the charismatic movement. Another has been as a rallying point for traditionalists in other Christian denominations. Indeed, some highly traditional Mainline Protestants refer to themselves as "evangelical" to distinguish themselves from their less traditional co-religionists.

18. John C. Green, "Seeking a Place: Evangelical Protestants and Public Engagement in the Twentieth Century," in *Toward an Evangelical Public Policy*, ed. Ronald Sider and Diane Knipper, (Grand Rapids, MI: Baker Press, 2005).

19. George M. Marsden, *Understanding Fundamentalism and Evangelicalism* (Grand Rapids, MI: Eerdmans, 1991); and Joel Carpenter, *Revive Us Again: the Reawakening of American Fundamentalism* (New York: Oxford, 1997).

20. These data come from the Fourth National Survey on Religion and Politics, 2004.

21. A good example of this usage is the "Fundamentalism Project"; see Martin E. Marty and R. Scott Appleby, eds., *Fundamentalisms Comprehended,* vol. 5 (Chicago: University of Chicago Press, 1995). The General Social Survey recodes denominations into a "fundamentalist" category using this approach as well. Tom W. Smith, "Classifying Protestant Denominations," GSS Methodological Report, National Opinion Research Corporation, 1987.

22. Wade Clark Roof and William McKinney, *American Mainline Religion: Its Changing Shape and Future* (New Brunswick: Rutgers University Press, 1987); Martin E. Marty, *The Righteous Empire: The Protestant Experience in America* (New York: Dial Press, 1970).

23. Robert Wuthnow and John H. Evans, eds., *The Quiet Hand of God* (Berkley: University of California Press, 2002).

24. The classic statement of Mainline Protestant decline is Dean Kelley, *Why Conservative Churches are Growing* (San Francisco, CA: Harper and Row, 1972); also see Dean R. Hoge, Benton Johnson, and Donald A. Luidens, *Vanishing Boundaries* (Louisville, KY: Westminister/John Knox Press, 1994). For a comprehensive look at the

rise and decline of denominations in the U.S., see Roger Finke and Rodney Stark, *The Churching of America, 1776–1990: Winners and Losers in Our Religious Economy* (New Brunswick: N.J.: Rutgers University Press, 1993).

25. See Randall Balmer, *Grant Us Courage: Travels Along the Mainline of American Protestantism* (New York: Oxford University Press, 1996).

26. On Black Protestants, see Eric Lincoln and Lawrence H. Mamiya, *The Black Church in the African American Experience* (Durham, NC: Duke University Press, 1990). On Latin Protestants, see Tomas Rivera Policy Institute, "Religion in Latino Public Life: Findings from the HCAPL National Survey" (Claremont, CA: Tomas Rivera Policy Institute. December, 2000).

27. A good account of American Catholicism is Charles R. Morris, *American Catholic* (Random House: Times Books, 1997); also see James A. Davidson, Andrea S. Williams, Richard A. Lamanna, Jan Stenftenagel, Kathleen M. Weigert, William J, Whalen, and Patricia Wittenberg, *The Search for Common Ground: What Unites and Divides Catholic Americans* (Huntington, IN.: Our Daily Visitor Inc.).

28. The relative size of the Catholic population varies in survey, typically between 22 and 25 percent. The difference may be related to how the religious preference question is asked: if the term "Catholic" is included in the question, then the percentage of Catholics tends to be higher.

29. For a comprehensive look at the smaller religious groups in the U.S., see J. Gordon Melton, *The Encyclopedia of American Religions* (Detroit: Gale Research, 2004).

30. Jonathan D. Sarna, *American Judaism: A History* (New Haven: Yale University Press, 2004).

31. Karen Isaksen Leonard, *Muslims in the United States: The State of Research* (New York: Russell Sage Foundation, 2003).

32. Jacoby. *Freethinkers,* 2004.

33. A. James Reichley, *Religion in American Public Life,* (Washington, D.C.: Brookings Institute, 1985).

34. The 2004 data comes from the Fourth National Survey of Religion and Politics conducted at the University of Akron in 2004 with support from the Pew Forum on Religion and Public Life (4000 cases). The 1944 data come from a 1944 Gallup Poll (AIPO 335) conducted November 1944 (2529 cases). Both data surveys had detailed denominational affiliations and they were coded as comparably as possible using the approach used in Table 2.1 (see note 1). The 1944 Gallup and other data were used to estimate the religious traditions in the 1944 National Election Study (ICPSR 7210) (2564 cases), allowing this data set to be used on other variables. The 1944 data was weighted to reflect the 1944 election outcome and U.S. Census data. The margin of error in these surveys is roughly plus or minus 2 percent. More details are available from the author upon request.

35. See Green et al, "American Religious Landscape and the 2004 Election," 2004.

36. At the minimum, surveys should have a basic affiliation measure and the born again item. These items plus race and ethnicity can be used to create useful religious categories, such as those used in Table 1.1, based on the NEP survey. There are numerous versions of such questions.

Chapter 3

1. John R. Petrocik, "Party Coalitions in the American Public: Morality Politics, Issue Agendas, and the 2004 Election," in *The State of the Parties,* 5th ed., eds. John C. Green and Daniel Coffey (Lanham, MD: Rowman & Littlefield, 2006), 279–289. Also see Gerhardt Lenski, *The Religious Factor* (New York: Doubleday, 1961).

2. The term "restructuring" was introduced in Robert Wuthnow, *The Restructuring of American Religion* (Princeton, NJ: Princeton University Press, 1988); also see Robert Wuthnow, *The Struggle for America's Soul: Evangelicals, Liberals, and Secularism,* (Grand Rapids, MI: Eerdmans, 1989). The "culture wars" terminology was made prominent by James D. Hunter, *Culture Wars: The Struggle to Define America* (New York: Basic Books, 1991). On the internal struggles of the Mainline Protestant churches see Douglas E. Cowan, *The Remnant Spirit: Conservative Reform in Mainline Protestantism* (Westport, CT: Praeger Press).

3. Defenders of the "culture wars" thesis include James D. Hunter, *Before the Shooting Begins: Searching for Democracy in America's Culture War* (New York: Macmillan, 1994); and Gertrude Himmelfarb, *One Nation, Two Cultures.* New York: Vintage Books, 2001).

4. Morris Fiorina, with Samuel J. Abrams and Jeremy C. Pope, *Culture War? The Myth of a Polarized America* (New York: Pearson Longman, 2005); and Alan Wolfe, *One Nation, After All* (New York: Viking, 1998); also see James D. Hunter and Alan Wolfe, *Is There a Culture War?* (Washington, D.C.: Brookings Institute Press, 2006).

5. Rhys H. Williams, ed., *Cultural Wars in American Politics: Critical Reviews of a Popular Myth* (New York: De Gruyter, 1997).

6. The strongest proponent of this view is Hunter, *Culture Wars,* 1991.

7. Layman and Green, "Wars and Rumours of Wars," 2005.

8. Rodney Stark and Charles Glock, *American Piety: The Nature of Religious Commitment* (Berkeley, CA: University of California Press, 1968); and Rodney Stark and William S. Bainbridge, *The Future of Religion.* (Berkeley: University of California Press, 1985).

9. Kellstedt et al., "Grasping the Essentials," 1996; David C. Leege and Lyman A. Kellstedt, eds., *Rediscovering the Religious Factor in American Politics,* (Armonk, NY: M.E. Sharpe, 1993).

10. See James L. Guth, John C. Green, Corwin E. Smidt, Lyman A. Kellstedt, and Margaret Poloma, *The Bully Pulpit: The Politics of Protestant Clergy* (Lawrence, KS: University Press of Kansas, 1997), Chapter 3.

11. The survey used here is the Fourth National Survey of Religion and Politics, 2004.

12. The salience and religious relevance measure were the same as in Table 2.1.

13. The preservation of tradition item gave respondents three choices: (1) Strive to preserve its traditional beliefs and practices; (2) Be willing to adjust traditions in light of new ideas; or (3) Strive to adopt modern beliefs and practices.

14. Kohut et al., *The Diminishing Divide,* 2000.

15. C. Kirk Hadaway, Penny Long Marler, and Mark Chaves, "What the Polls Don't Show: A Closer Look at U.S. Church Attendance," *American Sociological Review* 58 (1993):741–752; C. Kirk Hadaway, Penny Marler, and Mark Chaves, "Over-reporting Church Attendance in America: Evidence that Demands the Same Verdict," *American Sociological Review* 63 (1998): 122–130.

16. Good examples are the attendance measures in the 2004 National Election Study and the General Social Survey. Voter turnout is also over reported in these and other surveys.

17. For a defense of survey-based estimates of worship attendance, see Frank Newport, "Estimating Americans' Worship Behavior," Part I http://poll.gallup.com/content/default.aspx?ci=20701&pg=1 [Accessed August 2006] and Part II http://poll.gallup.com/content/default.aspx?ci=20701&pg=1 [Accessed August 2006].

18. See Mark Chaves, *Congregations in America* (Boston: Harvard University Press, 2004).

19. Sidney Verba, Kay Lehman Schlozman, and Henry E. Brady, *Voice and Equality: Civic Voluntarism in American Politics* (Cambridge: Harvard University Press, 1995), 282–283.

20. This pattern may reflect the fact that a "tithe" has special significance among Evangelical Protestants and not in other traditions. On financial donations, see Mark Chaves and Sharon Miller, eds., *Financing American Religion* (Walnut Creek, CA: Altamira Press, 1997).

21. See Robert Wuthnow, *Sharing the Journey: Support Groups and America's New Quest for Community* (New York: Free Press, 1994).

22. On Catholic practices, see Davis et. al., *The Search for Common Ground*, 1995. These "Catholic" measures perform very much like the general measures.

23. See Guth et al., *The Bully Pulpit*, 1997, 164–168.

24. See Margaret M. Poloma and George Gallup. Jr., *Varieties of Prayer* (Philadelphia, PA: Trinity Press International, 1991).

25. Pippa Norris and Ronald Inglehart, *Sacred and Secular: Religion and Politics Worldwide* (New York: Cambridge University Press, 2004).

26. Lyman A. Kellstedt and Corwin E. Smidt, "Doctrinal Beliefs and Political Behavior: Views of the Bible," in *Rediscovering the Religious Factor in American Politics*, eds. David Leege and Lyman Kellstedt (Armonk, NY: M.E. Sharpe, 1993).

27. Edward J. Larson, *Trial and Error: The American Controversy Over Creation and Evolution* (New York: Oxford University Press, 2003).

28. Perhaps the best known use of the biblical for political purposes is by the Christian Right to justify conservative social issues, but the "religious left" regularly use the Bible to justify liberal economic positions.

29. The traditionalism score was calculated with a principal components factor analysis, which produced a single factor with an eigenvalue greater than 1.0.

30. See John C. Green, "The American Religious Landscape and Political Attitudes: A Baseline for 2004," The Pew Forum on Religion & Public Life, 2004, http://pewforum.org/docs/index.php?DocID=55 [Accessed August 2006] for a description of how these categories were calculated. In essence, the major religious traditions were divided into three parts on the basis of a traditionalism score very much like what was calculated here. The cut points were established by self-identification with traditionalist and modernist religious movements. The unaffiliated respondents were subdivided on the basis of belief. The Unaffiliated Believers were those with the same level of belief as the Centrists in the three largest traditions. Atheists and Agnostics were defined by self-identification, and the Seculars were the residual category. These categories are quite robust, with different means of calculation producing very similar results. For alternative versions of these categories, see James L. Guth, Lyman A. Kellstedt, Corwin E. Smidt, and John C. Green, "Religious Influences in the 2004 Presidential Election," *Presidential Studies Quarterly*

36 (June 2006): 223–242; David E. Campbell, ed. *A Matter of Faith: Religion in the 2004 Presidential Election* (Washington, D.C.: Brookings Institution Press, 2007); John C. Green and Steve Waldman, "Tribal Politics," *The Atlantic*, January/February 2006: 10–14. For a use of these data see Peitro S. Nivola and David W. Brady, eds. *Red and Blue Nation? Characteristics and Cause of America's Polarized Politics* (Washington, D.C.: Brookings Institution Press and the Hoover Institution, 2006).

31. The data used here are the same for the over time analysis in chapter 2, see note 34.

32. The 1944 question asked how many times the respondent had attended worship in the past four weeks. These data were recoded to match the marginal percentages in other surveys conducted in the 1940s, 1950s, and 1960s similar to the 2004 measure.

33. See Wuthnow, *The Restructuring of American Religion,* 1988, 15–16.

34. The data in Figure 3.2 come from the Gallup polls before 1952, the National Elections Study 1952 to 1996, and the National Surveys of Religion and Politics in 2000 and 2004. See John C. Green and Mark Silk, "The New Religion Gap," *Religion in the News* 6 (3), 2003.

Chapter 4

1. Gary Langer, "A Question of Values," *New York Times*, November 6, 2004.

2. Pew Research Center for the People and the Press, "Voters Liked Campaign 2004, But Too Much 'Mud-Slinging' Moral Values: How Important?" http://people-press.org/reports/display.php3?ReportID=233 [Accessed August 2006].

3. The replicated issue priorities question was worded as follows: "Which ONE issue mattered most to you in deciding how you voted for president? Taxes; Education; Iraq; Terrorism; Economy/jobs; Moral values; Health care."

4. The entry in table 4.2 is from the NEP; the next two are from the PRC post-election survey (see note 2); the final two items come from the American Religious Landscape post-election survey (see note 5).

5. These questions on social issues were worded as follows: "Were social issues, such as abortion or same-sex marriage, very important, somewhat important, or not very important to your vote for president?" Similar questions were asked about economic and foreign policy issues. Then the following question was asked: "Overall, what was MOST important to your vote: economic, foreign policy, or social issues?"

6. The 30 percent figure results from summing respondents who chose "moral/ethical values" and explicit mention of social issues for both responses, taken as a percent of all valid responses. If one looks only at the first response to the questions, "moral ethical values accounted for 39 percent of the respondents. (Los Angeles Times Poll # 2004–513).

7. The *Los Angeles Times* exit poll has asked the same question for a number of recent elections and the results suggest that "moral values" have become somewhat more important.

8. These open-ended data are from the 1944 National Elections studies, the 1952 Roper Commercial Poll (RCOM0059), the National Elections Study Cumulative File, and the 2004 Fourth National Survey of Religion and Politics. All economic and social welfare responses were coded as "economic issues" and all foreign policy and defense responses were coded as "foreign policy." The social issues included all mentions of moral or sexual matters, plus most public order problems, such as crime and substance abuse.

9. For an excellent examination of these trends, see Geoffrey Layman, *The Great Divide: Religious and Cultural Conflict in American Party Politics* (New York: Columbia University Press, 2001).

10. These data come from the same source as in Chapter 2 (see note 34), using the 1944 National Election Study.

Chapter 5

1. Ann Brande, "Women's History is American Religious History," in *Retelling U.S. Religious History*, edited by Thomas A. Tweed (Berkeley: University of California Press, 1997); Darren Sherkat, "Sexuality and Religious Commitment in the United States: An Empirical Examination," *Sociology of Religion* 41 (2002): 313–323.

2. On the gender gap, see Karen M. Kaufman, "The Gender Gap," *PS* 39 (2006): 447–455; John C. Green and Mark Silk, "Gendering the Religion Gap," *Religion in the News* 7 (2004): 11–13.

3. This data uses the 1944 Gallup data (see note 34 in Chapter 2).

4. On the marriage gap, see Anna Greenberg, "The Marriage Gap," *Blueprint Magazine*, July 12, 2001. http://www.ppionline.org/ndol/print.cfm?contentid=3559 [Accessed August 2006].

5. See Steve Sailer, "Baby Gap: How Birthrates Color the Electoral Map,"*The American Conservative,* December 20, 2004.

6. Wade Clark Roof, *A Generation of Seekers*, (San Francisco: Harper San Francisco, 1993), Chapters 2 and 6.

7. On generations and Catholics, see Davis et al., *The Search for Common Ground*, 1995, chapter 7.

8. There are many names given to these generations. Perhaps the most comprehensive of set of labels comes from Neil Howe and William Strauss. See, for example, *Millennials Rising* (New York: Random House, 2000).

9. There is a very strong relationship between voting and age, with older people voting at higher rates than younger people. Thus, the NEP tends to have more older people than the population as a whole.

10. Todd Gitlin, *The Whole World is Watching: Mass Media in the Making and Unmaking of the New Left* (Berkeley: University of California Press, 1980).

11. In the NEP data, the age cohorts are not uniform in their partisanship. This may reflect sampling error.

12. See Alejandro Portes and Rubén G. Rumbaut, *Immigrant America*, 3rd ed. (Berkeley, CA: University of California Press, 2006).

13. H. Richard Niebuhr, *The Social Sources of Denominationalism* (New York, Meridian Books, 1957).

14. Stephen Hart. *What Does the Lord Require? : How American Christians Think about Economic Justice* (New York: Oxford University Press, 1992).

15. Voting is also strongly associated with income, so the NEP data contain more upper income people than the population as a whole.

16. These measures are self-identification with terms such as "working" and "middle class." In these data, the class identification was dichotomized into working-class and middle/upper-class.

17. Scholars typically treat occupation and education along with income as measures of socio-economic class.

18. Highly educated "knowledge workers," such as lawyers, journalists, and college professors are more liberal politically than their income would suggest. On this issue see Steven G. Brint, "'New Class' and Cumulative Trend Explanations of the Liberal Attitudes of Professionals," *American Journal of Sociology* 90 (984): 30–71.

19. For a good summary of the income gap, see Jeffrey M. Stonecash, "The Income Gap," *PS* 39 (2006): 461–466.

20. See Kohut et al., *The Diminishing Divide*, 2000.

21. This index created nominal categories for all the combinations of gender, income, and age. Although only the income/gender combination was reported, age sometimes mattered as well. In most cases, the less affluent women and men were young. But in a handful of cases the less affluent women were old (Latino Protestants, Less Observant Black Protestants, Less Observant Catholics, and Latino Catholics). For these groups, plus Weekly Attending Black Protestants and the Other Faiths, the affluent men were older as well. This substitution was done to maximize the difference from the actual Bush vote.

Chapter 6

1. For a fuller description of the religion by regions project, see Mark Silk and Andrew Walsh, *One Nation Divisible: Religion and Region in the United States* (Walnut Creek, CA: AltaMira Press, 2006).

2. For another view on American regionalism and culture, see Daniel J. Elazar, *The American Mosaic* (Boulder, CO: Westview Press, 1994).

3. For a detailed look at region and voting in 2004, see Kevin J. McMahon, David M. Rankin, Donald W. Beachler, and John Kenneth White, *Winning the White House 2004: Region by Region, Vote by Vote* (New York: Palgrave Macmillan, 2005).

4. Potential population is measured by the U.S. Census Bureau's "voting age population": all adults over the age of 18. Many of these individuals cannot vote because they are not citizens or are incarcerated.

5. In 1944, the voting age population was all adults over the age of 21.

6. Virginia Gray and Russell L. Hanson, eds., *Politics in the American States: A Comparative Analysis* (Washington, D.C.: CQ Press, 2004), chapter 3.

7. Two sources of data were used in tables 6.3 to 6.10, each with their limitations. Even with the large sample size of the NEP, there were often relatively few cases for smaller religious groups in the regions. The NEP included state-level exit polls, but the religion measures were not always the same. In cases where the NEP data was inadequate by region, other survey data were used to make adjustments to the NEP data when the number of cases was very small. The national NEP data were also re-weighted to match the actual election outcome in the eight regions. The second source was a set of estimates for the size of the major religious groups in 2000 using pooled data from multiple surveys as well as standard information on religion by state. (See Appendix B and also beliefnet.com for a summary: *http://www.beliefnet.com/story/155/story_15528_1.html* [Accessed August 2006].) These state-level estimates were pooled by region and then regular church attenders were estimated from surveys that contained both worship attendance and denominational affiliation. The comparison of the adjusted NEP to the estimated religious affiliation by region is a critical part of the analysis.

8. William Lindsey and Mark Silk, eds., *Religion and Public Life in the Southern Crossroads: Showdown States* (Walnut Creek, CA: AltaMira Press, 2006).

9. Jan Shipps and Mark Silk, eds., *Religion and Public Life in the Mountain West: Sacred Landscapes in Transition* (Walnut Creek, CA: AltaMira Press, 2004).

10. Charles Reagan Wilson and Mark Silk, eds., *Religion and Public Life in the South: In the Evangelical Mode* (Walnut Creek, CA: AltaMira Press, 2005).

11. Andrew Walsh and Mark Silk, eds., *Religion and Public Life in New England: Steady Habits, Changing Slowly* (Walnut Creek, CA: AltaMira Press, 2005).

12. Randall Balmer and Mark Silk eds., *Religion and Public Life in the Middle Atlantic Region: The Fount Of Diversity* (Walnut Creek, CA: AltaMira Press, 2004).

13. Will Herberg, *Protestant, Catholic, Jew* (Garden City, N.Y., Anchor Books, 1960).

14. Wade Clark Roof and Mark Silk, eds., *Religion and Public Life in the Pacific Region: Fluid Identities* (Walnut Creek, CA: AltaMira Press, 2005).

15. Patricia O'Connell Killen and Mark Silk, eds., *Religion and Public Life in the Pacific Northwest Region: The None Zone* (Walnut Creek, CA: AltaMira Press, 2004).

16. Philip Barlow and Mark Silk eds., *Religion and Public Life in the Pacific Midwest: America's Common Denominator?* (Walnut Creek, CA: AltaMira Press, 2004).

17. John C. Green and Mark Silk, "Why Moral Values Did Count," *Religion in the News* 8 (2005): 5–8.

Chapter 7

1. Reichley, *Religion in American Public Life*, 1985.

2. Cited in Clyde Wilcox and Carin Larson, *Onward Christian Soldiers*, 3rd ed. (Boulder, CO: Westview Press), 110.

3. Russell Muirhead, Nancy L. Rosenblum, Daniel Schlozman, and Francis X. Shen, "Religion in the 2004 Presidential Election," in *Divided States of America: The Slash and Burn Politics of the 2004 Presidential Election*, ed. Larry Sabato (New York: Longman, 2005).

4. While speaking at the American Enterprise Institute in Washington D.C. on December 11, 2001, Rove said: "I will say this, I will say one of the ironies is, is that we probably failed to martial support among the base as well as we should have. If you look at the model of the electorate, and you look at the model of who voted, the big discrepancy is among self-identified white, evangelical Protestants, Pentecostals, and Fundamentalists. If they were a part of the voters of what they should have been if you had looked at the electoral model, there should have been 19 million of them, and instead there were 15 million of them. Just over four million of them failed to turn out and vote. And yet they are obviously part of our base. They voted for us, depending on who they were and where they were, by huge margins, 70 and 80 percent margins. And yet four million of them didn't turn out to vote that you would have anticipated voting in a normal presidential election year. I think we may have failed to mobilize them, but we may also be returning to a point in America where fundamentalists and Evangelicals and Pentecostals remain true to their beliefs, which are things of the—you know, politics is corrupt, and therefore we shouldn't participate. And I think we may be saying to some degree, or at least we did in 2000—and I hope it's temporary—some return to the sidelines of some of the previously politically involved religious conservatives." For the transcript, see http://www.aei.org/events/filter.all,eventID.14/transcript.asp [Accessed August 2006].

5. A good example of controversy was the request by the Bush campaign to its volunteers to submit their own church's membership directories for purposes of voter registration. Despite the controversy, the request was widely followed. David D. Kirkpatrick, "Churches See an Election Role and Spread the Word on Bush," *New York Times*, August 9, 2004.

6. For two good accounts of the religious aspects of the 2004 presidential campaign in Ohio, see John C. Green, "The Bible and the Buckeye State," in *The Values Campaign?* eds. John C. Green, Mark Rozell, and Clyde Wilcox (Washington D.C.: Georgetown University Press, 2006); and Stephen T. Mockabee, Michael Margolis, Stephen Brooks, Rick D. Farmer, and John C. Green, "The Battle for Ohio: The 2004 Presidential Campaign," in *Dancing without Partners*, eds. David B. Magleby, J. Quinn Monson, and Kelly D. Patterson (Landam, MD: Rowman & Littlefield, 2006).

7. The Bush campaign developed a manual for faith-based volunteers that specified 22 duties with regard to the campaign, along with a timeline. Examples of the duties included: "Identify another conservative church in your community who we can organize for Bush," "By Sunday, September 26th, all non-registered church members must be registered to vote," "Distribute voter guides in your church," "Get-out-the-vote program in your church—place reminder bulletin about all Christian citizens needing to vote in Sunday program or on a board near the church entrance." The Bush campaign reportedly sought to identify 1,600 conservative churches in Pennsylvania. Alan Cooperman, "Churchgoers Get Direction from Bush Campaign," *Washington Post*, July 1, 2004.

8. Dana Milbanks, "For the President, a Vote of Full Faith and Credit," *Washington Post*, November 7, 2004.

9. Muirhead et al., "Religion in the 2004 Presidential Election," 2004.

10. David D. Kirkpatrick and Laurie Goodstein, "Groups of Bishops Using Influence to Oppose Kerry," *New York Times*, October 12, 2004; and Kathleen D. Mylott, "Bishops and Campaign 2004," *National Catholic Register,* January 2–8, 2005.

11. Julia Duin, "Kerry Advisers Tell Hopeful to 'Keep Cool' on Religion," *Washington Times*, June 18, 2004; Matea Gold, "Democrats Are Trying to Make a Leap of Faith," *Los Angeles Times*, August 8, 2004; and David M. Halbfinger and David E. Sanger, "Kerry's Latest Attacks on Bush Borrow a Page from Scripture," *New York Times*, October 25, 2004.

12. David D. Kirkpatrick, "Black Pastors Backing Bush Are Rarities, but Not Alone," *New York Times*, October 5, 2004; and Jim Dwyer and Jodi Wilgoren, "Gore and Kerry Unite in Search for Black Votes," *New York Times,* October 25, 2004.

13. Bob Louis, "Falwell Answers Critics by Offering Political Seminar," *Associated Press*, August 6, 2004; and Alan Cooperman and Thomas Edsall, "Evangelicals Say They Led Charge For the GOP," *Washington Post*, November 8, 2004.

14. See Clyde Wilcox, Linda Merola, and David Beer, "The Gay Marriage issue and Christian Right Mobilization," in *The Values Campaign?* eds. John C. Green, Mark J. Rozell, and Clyde Wilcox (Washington D.C.: Georgetown University Press, 2006). Also see Avery Johnson, "Christian Coalition Working for a Revival," *Wall Street Journal*, June 21, 2004; and Eric Goski, "Focus is on Politics," *Denver Post*, June 3, 2005.

15. See Eyal Press, "Closing the Religion Gap," *The Nation*, August 12, 2004.

16. For election materials from The Interfaith Alliance, consult the TIA website, http://www.interfaithalliance.org/site/pp.asp?c=8dJIIWMCE&b=836427. For the Sojourners statement, see "God is Not a Republican," *New York Times*, August 30, 2004. Also see

Progressive Faith Media, "Highlights from 2004," November, 2004. http://therespublica.org/progressivefaithmedia.com/highlights.htm [Accessed August 2006].

17. See Rob Boston, "Church Service or Campaign Commercial?" *Church and State*, September 2004, 8–9, and Bill Broadway, "In Election Season, IRS Sits in Judgment," *Washington Post*, October 9, 2004.

18. Religion Link, "Local Stories Illuminate Religion-politics Tangle," August 23, 2004. http://www.religionlink.org/tip_040823a.php [Accessed August 2006].

19. For a good description of congregational mobilization, see John C. Green, "The Undetected Tide," *Religion in the News*. 6 (2003):4–6; and "Church Notes" nearby. For a good account of such activities in 2004, see Matthew Dolan and Frank Langfitt, "The Morality Factor," *Baltimore Sun*, November 7, 2004.

20. Good systematic investigations of church mobilization can be found in a series of articles: James L. Guth, Lyman A. Kellstedt, John C. Green, and Corwin E. Smidt, "Getting the Spirit? Religious and Partisan Mobilization in the 2004 Elections," in *Interest Group Politics*, 7th ed., eds. Allan J. Cigler and Burdett A. Loomis (Washington DC: CQ Press, 2007); James L. Guth, Lyman A. Kellstedt, John C. Green, and Corwin E. Smidt, "A Distant Thunder? Religious Mobilization in the 2000 Elections," in *Interest Group Politics*, 6th ed., eds. Allan J. Cigler and Burdett A. Loomis (Washington D.C.: CQ Press, 2002) 161–184; James L. Guth, Lyman A. Kellstedt, Corwin E. Smidt, and John C. Green, "Thunder on the Right? Religious Interest Group Mobilization in the 1996 Election," in *Interest Group Politics*, 5th ed., eds. Allan J. Cigler and Burdett A. Loomis (Washington, D.C.: CQ Press, 1998) 169–192.

21. See note 2 in Chapter 2 for information on this survey.

22. Direct mail was a potent tool for religious mobilization in 2004. See Green, "The Bible and the Buckeye State," 2006.

23. Religious appeals came via all these sources, see Mockabee et al., "The Battle for Ohio," 2006.

24. These data come from the Fourth National Survey of Religion and Politics in 2004. See Guth et al., "Getting into the Spirit?" 2007 for more details.

25. Clergy pulpit endorsements are rare, but clergy regularly endorse candidates by other means, see Guth et al., *The Bully Pulpit*, 1996, chapter 9.

26. These data came from the Fourth National Survey of Religion and Politics in 2004. See Guth et al., "Getting into the Spirit?" 2007 for more details.

27. As in most surveys, turnout was clearly over-reported in the Fourth National Survey of Religion and Politics in 2004. A statistical procedure was used to correct reported turnout to the official turnout rate.

28. The analysis returns to the NEP because of the larger number of cases.

29. See Guth et al., "Getting into the Spirit?" 2007.

30. Campaign volunteers were defined as voters who answered this question affirmatively: "Did you, yourself, volunteer any of your time to help one of the presidential election campaigns or not?" See note 2, Chapter 4 on the survey. On faith-based volunteers, see James L. Guth, John C. Green, Lyman Kellstedt, and Corwin E. Smidt. "Onward Christian Soldiers: Religious Interest Group Activists," in *Interest Group Politics,* 4th ed., eds. Allan Cigler and Burdett Loomis (Washington DC: CQ Press, 1994) 55–76.

31. See Mockabee et al., "The Battle for Ohio," for an estimate of the number of campaign volunteers in Ohio in 2004.

32. These data come from the 2004 portion of the Party Elite Study, directed by John S. Jackson. See John S. Jackson, Nathan S. Bigelow, and John C. Green, "The State of Party

Elites: National Convention Delegates, 1992–2004." In The State of the Parties, 5th ed., eds. John C. Green and Daniel M. Coffey (Landam, MD: Rowman & Littlefield, 2006). On religion and activists, see Layman, The Great Divide, 2001.

33. This judgment is based on comparing the 2004 campaign contact data to Gallup surveys in the mid-1950s.

34. The 1952 item came from a Roper Commercial Poll (RCom0059) and was worded: "Have you ever talked politics with any of the leaders in your church?"; the 1964 item came from the 1964 National Elections Study, and was worded: "Are election campaigns ever discussed at your church?" The 2004 item came from the Fourth National Survey on Religion and Politics, and was worded: "Did you discuss the 2004 election with friends at your place of worship?"

35. The 1952 volunteer data come from a Gallup Poll (AIPO 543); the delegate data for 1952 comes from the papers of Daniel W. Tuttle, University of Hawaii, and made available by the University Archives of the University of Hawaii.

Chapter 8

1. Recall the definition of religious tradition used here is "a set of religious denominations, movements, and congregations with similar doctrines, practices, and origins."

2. Recall the definition of religious traditionalism used here is "the extent to which individuals partake of the practices and doctrines that help define the religious tradition to which they belong."

3. John C. Green, "The Religious Vote in 2006," Christian Century, December 12, 2006.

4. Scott Keeter, "Election '06: Some Big Changes in Some Key Groups," Pew Research Center for the People and the Press, November 16, 2006. http://pewresearch.org/obdeck/?ObDeckID=93 [Accessed November 2006].

5. Hunter, Culture Wars, 1991, 43.

6. Joe Feuerherd, "God Gap Narrows as Democrats Take Majority of Catholic Vote," National Catholic Reporter, November 17, 2006. http://ncronline.org/NCR_Online/archives2/2006d/111706/111706h.php [Accessed November 2006].

7. Richard J. Jensen, The Winning of the Midwest: Social and Political Conflict, 1888–96 (Chicago: University of Chicago Press, 1971).

8. A common definition of spirituality is "a sense of connection to a much greater whole which includes a personal emotional experience of religious awe and reverence."

9. Michael Lerner, The Left Hand of God (New York: Harper Collins, 2006).

Postscript

1. For a good description of faith-based politics in 2008, see James L. Guth, "Religion in the 2008 Election," in Janet M. Box-Steffensmeier and Steven E. Schier, The American Elections of 2008 (Lanham, MD: Rowman & Littlefield, 2009), 117–136. This section depends on John C. Green, "What Happened to the Value Voters?" First Things (March 2009): 42–48.

2. The data used here comes from pooling two Pew Research Center surveys, one taken on the weekend before the 2008 election and the other taken after the election. The data were weighted to match the election outcome. For 2004, the comparable weekend and post-election surveys by the Pew Research Center were employed in a similar fashion. These

data are organized so as to be as comparable to the exit poll data used in table 1.3. However, exit polls and telephone surveys are not strictly comparable. A slightly different presentation of the data used here can be found at "A Post-Election Look at Religious Voters in the 2008 Election" (http://pewforum.org/events/?EventID=209 [Accessed June 2009]).

3.   The 2008 exit polls (the National Election Pool) found basically the same patterns in the faith-based vote as the data presented here, but with a larger shift toward Obama among white Evangelicals compared to the exit poll data in 2004 and 2000. See "How the Faithful Voted" (http://pewforum.org/docs/?DocID=367 [Accessed June 2009]).

Selected Bibliography on Religion and Politics

Alpert, Rebecca T., ed. *Voices of the Religious Left: A Contemporary Sourcebook.* Philadelphia, PA: Temple University Press, 2000.

Arrington, Leonard J. and Davis Bitton. *The Mormon Experience: A History of the Latter-day Saints.* New York, NY: Alfred A. Knopf, 1979.

Barker, David C., and Christopher Jan Carman. "The Spirit of Capitalism? Religious Doctrine, Values, and Economic Attitude Constructs." *Political Behavior* 22 (2000):1-27.

Bolce, Louis, and Gerald De Maio. "The Anti-Christian Fundamentalist Factor in Contemporary Politics." *Public Opinion Quarterly.* 63 (1999a): 508-42.

Brewer, Mark D. *Relevant No More? The Catholic/Protestant Divide in American Electoral Politics.* Lanham, MD: Lexington Books, 2003.

Byrnes, Timothy A. *Catholic Bishops in American Politics.* Princeton, NJ: Princeton University Press, 1991.

Calhoun-Brown, Allison. "African-American Churches and Political Mobilization: The Psychological Impact of Organizational Resources." *The Journal of Politics.* 58 (4, 1996): 935-953.

Campbell, David E., ed. *A Matter of Faith: Religion in the 2004 Presidential Election.* Washington, D.C.: Brookings Institution Press, 2007.

Campbell, David and Carin Larson. "Religious Coalitions For and Against Gay Marriage: The Culture War Rages On." In *The Politics of Same-Sex Marriage*, edited by Craig Rimmerman and Clyde Wilcox. Chicago: University of Chicago Press, 2005.

Chappell, David L. *A Stone of Hope: Prophetic Religion and the Death of Jim Crow.* University of North Carolina Press, 2004.

Cohen, Steven M. *The Dimensions of American Jewish Liberalism.* New York, NY: American Jewish Committee, 1989.

Craig, Robert H. *Religion and Radical Politics: An Alternative Christian Tradition in the United States.* Philadelphia, PA: Temple University Press, 1992.

Cromartie, Michael, ed. *The Religious New Right in American Politics*. Washington, DC: Ethics and Public Policy Center, 1993.

Cromartie, Michael. *Disciples & Democracy: Religious Conservatives and the Future of American Politics*. Grand Rapids, MI: Wm. B. Eerdmans Publishing Co., 1994.

D'Antonio, William V., James D. Davidson, Dean R. Hoge, and Katherine Meyer. *American Catholics: Gender, Generation, and Commitment*. Walnut Creek, CA: AltaMira Press, 2001.

Davidson, James D., Andrea S Williams, Richard A Lamanna, Jan Stenftenagel, Kathleen Weigert, William Whalen, and Patricia Wittberg. *The Search for Common Ground: What Unites and Divides Catholic Americans*. Huntington, IN: Our Sunday Visitor, 1997.

Davis, Nancy J., and Robert V. Robinson. "Are the Rumors of War Exaggerated? Religious Orthodoxy and Moral Progressivism in America." *American Journal of Sociology* 102 (1996a): 756-87.

Davis, Nancy J., and Robert V. Robinson. "Religious Orthodoxy in American Society: The Myth of a Monolithic Camp." *Journal for the Scientific Study of Religion* 35 (1996b): 229-45.

Davis, Nancy J., and Robert V. Robinson. "A War for America's Soul: The American Religious Landscape." In *Cultural Wars in American Politics: Critical Reviews of a Popular Myth*, ed. Rhys H. Williams. New York: De Gruyter, 1997.

De la Garza, Rodolfo; Louis DeSipio; F. Chris Garcia; John A Garcia; and Angelo Falcon. *Latino Voices: Mexican, Puerto Rican, and Cuban Perspectives on American Politics*. Boulder, CO: Westview Press, 1992.

DeSipio, Louis, with Harry Pachon; Rodolfo O. de la Garza; and Jongho Lee. *Immigrant Politics at Home and Abroad: How Latino Immigrants Engage the Politics of their Home Countries and the United States*. Claremont, CA: The Tomas Rivera Policy Institute, 2003.

Dionne, E.J., and Ming Hsu Chen, eds. *Sacred Places, Civic Purposes: Should Government Help Faith-based Charity?* Washington, DC: The Brookings Institution, 2001.

Dionne, E.J., and John J. DiIulio, eds. *What's God Got to Do with the American Experiment? Essays on Religion and Politics*. Washington, DC: The Brookings Institution, 2000.

Djupe, Paul A., and Christopher P. Gilbert. *The Prophetic Pulpit: Clergy, Churches, and Communities in American Politics*. Lanham, MD: Rowman & Littlefield, 2003.

Eck, Diana L. *A New Religious America*. San Francisco: Harper San Francisco, 2001.

Emerson, Michael O., and Christian Smith. *Divided by Faith: Evangelical Religion And the Problem of Race in America*. Oxford, UK: Oxford University Press, 2000.

Espinosa, Gaston; Virgilio Elizondo; and Jesse Miranda. "Hispanic Churches in American Public Life: Summary of Findings." Notre Dame, IN: Institute of Latino Studies. http://www.hcapl.org/HCAPL_Summary_of_Findings_English.pdf [Viewed May 6, 2003].

Findley, James F. *Church People in the Struggle: The National Council of Churches and the Black Freedom Movement, 1950-1970*. New York, NY: Oxford University Press, 1993.

Finke, Roger, and Rodney Stark. *The Churching of America, 1776-1990: Winners and Losers in our Religious Economy*. New Brunswick, NJ: Rutgers University Press, 1992.

Fiorina, Morris, with Samuel J. Abrams and Jeremy C. Pope. *Culture War? The Myth of a Polarized America*. New York: Pearson Longman, 2005.

Fowler, Robert Booth. *The Greening of Protestant Thought*. Chapel Hill, NC: University of North Carolina Press, 1995.

Fowler, Robert Booth, and Allen D. Hertzke. *Religion and Politics in America: Faith, Culture, and Strategic Choices*. Boulder, CO: Westview, 1995.

Freedman, Samuel G. *Jew v. Jew: The Struggle for the Soul of American Jewry*. New York, NY: Touchstone, 2000.

Friedland, Michael B. *Lift Up Your Voice Like a Trumpet: White Clergy and the Civil Rights and Antiwar Movements, 1954-1973*. Chapel Hill, NC: University Of North Carolina Press, 1998.

Gaines, Kevin K. *Uplifting the Race: Black Leadership, Politics, and Culture in the Twentieth Century*. Chapel Hill, NC: The University of North Carolina Press, 1996.

Gilbert, Christopher P. *The Impact of Churches on Political Behavior: An Empirical Study*. Westport, CT: Greenwood, 1993.

Goldscheider, Calvin, and Alan S. Zuckerman. *The Transformation of the Jews*. Chicago: University of Chicago Press, 1984.

Goldstein, Sidney. *Profile of American Jewry: Insights from the 1990 Jewish Population Study*. New York, NY: North American Jewish Data Bank, Council of Jewish Federations, 1993.

Greely, Andrew and Michael Hout. *The Truth about Conservative Christians*. Chicago: University of Chicago Press, 2006.

Green, John C. "Religion and Politics in the 1990s: Confrontations and Coalitions." In *Religion and American Politics: The 2000 Election in Context*, edited by Mark Silk 19-40. Hartford, CT: Center for the Study of Religion in Pubic Life, 2000.

Green, John C. "Evangelical Protestants and Civic Engagement: An Overview." In *A Public Faith: Evangelicals and Civic Engagement*, edited by Michael Cromartie, 11-30. Lanham, MD: Rowman & Littlefield, 2003.

Green, John C. "Two Faces of Pluralism in American Politics." In *One Electorate Under God? A Dialogue on Religion and American Politics,* edited by E.J. Dionne, Jean B. Elshtain, and Kayla M. Drogosz, 110-115. Washington D.C.: Brookings Institution, 2004.

Green, John C. "Seeking a Place: Evangelical Protestants and Public Engagement in the 20th Century." In *Toward an Evangelical Public Policy*, edited by Ronald Sider and Diane Knipper. Grand Rapids , MI: Baker Press, 2005.

Green, John C., and Nate Bigelow. "The Christian Right Goes to Washington: Social Movement Resources and the Legislative Process." In *The Interest Group Connection*, 2nd ed., edited by Ronald Shaiko, Paul Herrnson, and Clyde Wilcox, 189-211. Washington: D.C.: CQ Press, 2004.

Green, John C., James L. Guth, Corwin E. Smidt, and Lyman A. Kellstedt. *Religion and the Culture Wars: Dispatches from the Front*. Lanham, MD: Rowman & Littlefield, 1996.

Green, John C., Mark J. Rozell, and Clyde Wilcox, eds. *Prayers in the Precincts: The Christian Right in the 1998 Elections*. Washington, D.C.: Georgetown University Press, 2000.

Green, John C., Mark J. Rozell, and Clyde Wilcox. eds. *The Christian Right in American Politics: Marching to the Millennium.* Washington, D.C.: Georgetown University Press, 2003.

Green, John C., Mark J. Rozell, and Clyde Wilcox. eds. *The Values Campaign: The Christian Right in American Politics: Marching to the Millennium.* Washington, D.C.: Georgetown University Press, 2006.

Green, John C. and Steve Waldman. "Tribal Politics." *The Atlantic.* January/February 2006, 10-14.

Greenberg, Anna and Kenneth D. Wald. "Still Liberal After All These Years? The Contemporary Political Behavior of American Jews." In *Jews in American Politics*, edited by L. Sandy Maisel and Ira Forman.. Lanham, MD: Rowman and Littlefield, 2000.

Guth, James L., and John C. Green, eds. *The Bible and the Ballot Box: Religion and Politics in the 1988 Election.* Boulder, CO: Westview Press, 1991.

Guth, James L., and John C. Green. "Salience: The Core Concept?" In *Rediscovering the Religious Factor in American Politics*, edited by David C Leege and Lyman A Kellstedt, 157-174. Armonk, NY: M.E. Sharpe, 1993.

Guth, James L., John C. Green, Lyman Kellstedt, and Corwin E. Smidt. "Onward Christian Soldiers: Religious Interest Group Activists." In *Interest Group Politics,* 4th ed., edited by Allan Cigler and Burdett Loomis, 55-76. Washington DC: CQ Press, 1994.

Guth, James L., John C. Green, Corwin E. Smidt, Lyman A. Kellstedt, and Margaret Poloma. "Faith and the Environment: Religious Beliefs and Attitudes on Environmental Policy." *American Journal of Political Science* 39 (1995): 364-382.

Guth, James L., John C. Green, Corwin E. Smidt, Lyman A. Kellstedt, and Margaret Poloma. *The Bully Pulpit: The Politics of Protestant Clergy.* Lawrence, KS: University of Kansas Press, 1997.

Guth, James L., Lyman A. Kellstedt, John C. Green, and Corwin E. Smidt. "A Distant Thunder? Religious Mobilization in the 2000 Elections." In *Interest Group Politics*, 6th ed., edited by Allan J. Cigler and Burdett A. Loomis, 161-184. Washington D.C.: CQ Press, 2002.

Guth, James L., Lyman A. Kellstedt, John C. Green, and Corwin E. Smidt. "Getting the Spirit? Religious and Partisan Mobilization in the 2004 Elections." In *Interest Group Politics*, 7th ed., edited by Allan J. Cigler and Burdett A. Loomis. Washington DC: CQ Press, 2007.

Guth, James L., Lyman Kellstedt, Corwin Smidt, and John C. Green. "Thunder on the Right? Religious Interest Group Mobilization in the 1996 Election." In *Interest Group Politics*, 5th edition, edited by Alan Cigler and Burdett Loomis, 169-192. Washington, DC: Congressional Quarterly Press, 1998.

Guth, James L, Lyman A. Kellstedt, Corwin E. Smidt, and John C. Green. "Religious Influences in the 2004 Presidential Election." *Presidential Studies Quarterly* 36 (June 2006): 223-242.

Hadden, Jeffery K. *The Gathering Storm in the Churches.* Garden City, NY: Doubleday, 1969.

Hall, Mitchell K. *Because of Their Faith: CALCAV and Religious Opposition to The Vietnam War.* New York, NY: Columbia University Press, 1990.

Hanna, Mary T. *Catholics and American Politics.* Cambridge, MA: Harvard University Press, 1979.

Hart, Stephen. *What Does the Lord Require? How American Christians Think About Economic Justice*. New York, NY: Oxford University Press, 1992.

Hart, Stephen. *Cultural Dilemmas of Progressive Politics: Styles of Engagement Among Grassroots Activists*. Chicago, IL: University of Chicago Press, 2001.

Harris, Fredrick C. *Something Within: Religion in African-American Political Activism*. Oxford, UK: Oxford University Press, 1999.

Hofrenning, Daniel J.B. *In Washington but Not of It*. Philadelphia, PA: Temple University Press, 1995.

Harris, Fredrick C. *Something Within: Religion in African-American Political Activism*. Oxford, UK: Oxford University Press, 1999.

Hertzke, Allen. *Representing God in Washington: The Role of Religious Lobbies In the American Polity*. Nashville, TN: University of Tennessee Press, 1988.

Hertzke, Allen. *Echoes of Discontent: Jesse Jackson, Pat Robertson, and the Resurgence of Populism*. Washington, DC: CQ Press, 1993.

Hunter, James Davison. *Culture Wars: The Struggle to Define America*. New York, NY: Basic Books, 1991.

Hunter, James Davison. *Before the Shooting Begins: Searching for Democracy in America's Culture War*. New York: Macmillan, 1994.

Hunter, James Davison and Alan Wolfe. *Is There a Culture War?* Washington, D.C.: Brookings Institution Press and the Pew Forum on Religion and Public Life, 2006.

Inglehart, Ronald, and Pippa Norris. *Sacred and Secular: Religion and Politics Worldwide*. Cambridge, UK: Cambridge University Press, 2004.

Jelen, Ted G. *The Political Mobilization of Religious Belief*. New York, NY: Praeger, 1991.

Jelen, Ted G. "Research in Religion and Mass Political Behavior in the United States: Looking Both Ways After Two Decades of Scholarship." *American Politics Quarterly* 26 (1998): 110-134.

Jelen, Ted G., and Clyde Wilcox. *Public Attitudes Toward Church and State*. Armonk, NY: M.E. Sharpe, 1995.

Kelley, Dean. *Why Conservative Churches are Growing*. San Francisco, CA: Harper and Row, 1972.

Kellstedt, Lyman A. and Mark Noll. "Religion, Voting for President, and Party Identification, 1948-1984." In *Religion & American Politics: From the Colonial Period to the 1980s*, edited by Mark Noll, 355-379. New York, NY: Oxford University Press, 1990.

Kellstedt, Lyman A., John C. Green, James L. Guth, and Corwin E. Smidt. "Grasping the Essentials: The Social Embodiment of Religion and Political Behavior." In *Religion and the Culture Wars: Dispatches from the Front*, edited by John Green, James Guth, Corwin Smidt, and Lyman Kellstedt. Lanham, MD: Rowman & Littlefield, 1996.

Kellstedt, Lyman A., John C. Green, James L. Guth, and Corwin E. Smidt. "Religion Voting Blocs in the 1992 Election: The Year of the Evangelical?" *Sociology of Religion* 55 (1994): 307-25.

Layman, Geoffrey C. "Religion and Political Behavior in the United States: The Impact of Beliefs, Affiliations, and Commitment from 1980 to 1994." *Public Opinion Quarterly* 61 (1997):288-316.

Layman, Geoffrey C. *The Great Divide: Religious and Cultural Conflict in American Party Politics*. New York, NY: Columbia University Press, 2001.

Layman, Geoffrey C., and Edward G Carmines. "Cultural Conflict in American Politics: Religious Traditionalism, Postmaterialism, and U.S. Political Behavior." *Journal of Politics* 59 (1997): 751-777.

Layman, Geoffrey C., and John C. Green. "Wars and Rumors of Wars: The Contexts of Cultural Conflict in American Political Behavior." *British Journal of Political Science* 36 (1), 2005: 61-89.

Leege, David C., and Lyman A. Kellstedt. *Rediscovering the Religious Factor In American Politics.* Armonk, NY: M.E. Sharpe, 1993.

Leege, David C., Kenneth D. Wald, Brian S. Krueger, and Paul D. Mueller. *The Politics of Cultural Differences: Social Change and Voter Mobilization Strategies In the Post New Deal Period.* Princeton, NJ: Princeton University Press, 2002.

Liebman, Robert C., and Robert Wuthnow, eds. *The New Christian Right.* New York, NY: Aldine, 1984.

Lipset, Seymour Martin and Earl Raab. *Jews and the New American Scene.* Cambridge, MA: Harvard University Press, 1995.

Lincoln, C. Eric and Lawrence H. Mamiya. *The Black Church in the African American Experience.* Durham, NC: Duke University Press, 1990.

McCormick, Richard L. "Ethno-Cultural Interpretations of Nineteen-Century American Voting Behavior." *Political Science Quarterly* 89 (1974): 351-77.

McGreevy, John. *Catholicism and America: A History.* New York, NY: Norton, 2003.

McLoughlin, William G. *Revivals, Awakenings, and Reform.* Chicago, IL: University of Chicago Press, 1978.

Manza, Jeff, and Clem Brooks. *Social Cleavages and Political Change: Voter Alignments and U.S. Party Coalitions.* New York, NY: Oxford University Press, 1999.

Marsden, George M. *Fundamentalism and American Culture: The Shaping of Twentieth Century Evangelicalism 1870-1925.* New York, NY: Oxford University Press, 1980.

Martin, William. *With God on Our Side: The Rise of the Religious Right in America.* New York, NY: Broadway Books, 1996.

Marty, Martin. *Righteous Empire: The Protestant Experience in America.* New York, NY: Dial Press, 1970.

Moore, R. Laurence. *Religious Outsiders and the Making of Americans.* New York, NY: Oxford University Press, 1986.

Morris, Aldon D. *The Origins of the Civil Rights Movement: Black Communities Organizing for Change.* New York, NY: The Free Press, 1984.

Nivola, Peitro S. and David W. Brady, eds. *Red and Blue Nation? Characteristics and Causes of America's Polarized Politics.* Washington, D.C.: Brookings Institution Press and the Hoover Institution, 2006.

Paris, Peter J. *The Social Teaching of the Black Churches.* Philadelphia , PA: Fortress Press, 1985.

Pinn, Anthony B. *The Black Church in the Post-Civil Rights Era.* Maryknoll, NY: Orbis Books, 2002.

Quinley, Harold E. *The Prophetic Clergy: Social Activism among Protestant Ministers.* New York, NY: Wiley, 1974.

Roof, Clark Wade, and William McKinney. *American Mainline Religion: Its Changing Shape and Future.* New Brunswick, NJ: Rutgers University Press, 1987.

Rozell, Mark J., and Clyde Wilcox, eds. *God at the Grass Roots: The Christian Right in the 1994 Elections.* Lanham, MD: Rowman and Littlefield, 1995.

Rozell, Mark J., and Clyde Wilcox, eds. *God at the Grass Roots 1996*. Lanham, MD: Rowman and Littlefield, 1997.

Rozell, Mark J., Clyde Wilcox, and John C. Green. "Religious Constituencies and Support for the Christian Right in the 1990s." *Social Science Quarterly* 39 (1998): 815-821.

Shafer, Bryon E. *The State of American Politics*. Lanham, MD: Rowman & Littlfield, 2002.

Smidt, Corwin E., Lyman A. Kellstadt, John C. Green, and James L. Guth. "Religion and Politics in the United States." In *The Sacred and The Secular: Nation, Religion, and Politics*, edited by William Safran, 32-53. London, UK: Frank Cass, 2003.

Smidt, Corwin E., and James M. Penning, eds. *Sojourners in the Wilderness: The Christian Right in Comparative Perspective*. Lanham, MD: Rowman & Littlefield, 1997.

Smith, Christian. *Resisting Reagan: The U.S. Central America Peace Movement*. Chicago, IL: University of Chicago Press, 1996.

Smith, Christian, ed. *The Secular Revolution: Power, Interests, and Conflict in the Secularization of American Public Life*. Berkeley, CA: University of California Press, 2003.

Smith, Christian, with Michael Emerson, Sally Gallagher, Paul Kennedy, and David Sikkink. *American Evangelicalism: Embattled and Thriving*. Chicago, IL: University of Chicago Press, 1998.

Stark, Rodney, Bruce D. Foster, Charles Y. Glock, and Harold E. Quinley. *Wayward Shepherds: Prejudice and the Protestant Clergy*. New York, NY: Harper and Row, 1971.

Stark, Rodney, and Charles Glock. *American Piety: The Nature of Religious Commitment*. Berkeley, CA: University of California Press, 1968.

Steensland, Brian, Jerry Z. Park, Mark D. Regnerus, Lynn D. Robinson, W. Bradford Wilcox, and Robert D. Woodberry. "The Measure of American Religion: Toward Improving the State of the Art." *Social Forces* 79 (2000): 291-318.

Steinfels, Peter. *A People Adrift: The Crisis of the Roman Catholic Church in America*. New York: Simon and Schuster, 2003.

Stewart, Carlyle Fielding (III). *Black Spirituality and Black Consciousness: Soul Force, Culture and Freedom in the African-American Experience*. Trenton, NJ: African World Press, Inc, 1999.

Tate, Katherine. *From Protest to Politics: The New Black Voters in American Elections*. New York, NY: Russell Sage Foundation, 1994.

Thomas, Cal, and Ed Dobson. *Blinded by Might: Can the Religious Right Save America?*. Grand Rapids, MI: Zondervan, 1999.

Tomas Rivera Policy Institute. "Religion in Latino Public Life: Findings from the HCAPL National Survey." Claremont, CA: Tomas Rivera Policy Institute. December, 2000.

Verba, Sidney, Key Lehman Schlozman, and Henry E. Brady. *Voice and Equality: Civic Voluntarism in American Society*. Cambridge, MA: Harvard University Press, 1995.

Wald, Kenneth D. *Religion and Politics in the United States*, 4th edition. Lanham, MD: Rowman & Littlefield, 2003.

Wald, Kenneth D., Dennis E. Owen, and Samuel S. Hill, Jr. "Churches as Political Communities." *American Political Science Review* 82 (1988): 531-548.

Wald, Kenneth D., Dennis E. Owen, and Samuel S. Hill, Jr. "Political Cohesion in Churches." *Journal of Politics* 52 (1990): 197-215.

Warren, Mark R. *Dry Bones Rattling: Community Building to Revitalize American Democracy*. Princeton, NJ: Princeton University Press, 2001.

White, John Kenneth. *The Values Divide*. New York: Chatham, 2003.

Wilcox, Clyde. *God's Warriors: The Christian Right in Twentieth-century America*. Baltimore, MD: Johns Hopkins University Press, 1992.

Wilcox, Clyde. *Onward Christian Soldiers? The Religious Right in American Politics*. Boulder, CO: Westview, 1996.

Williams, Rhys H., ed. *Cultural Wars in American Politics: Critical Reviews of a Popular Myth*. New York: De Gruyter, 1997.

Wilson, J. Matthew, ed. *From Pews to Polling Places: Faith and Politics in the American Religious Mosaic*. Washington, D.C.: Georgetown University Press, 2007.

Wolfe, Alan. *One Nation, After All: What Middle-Class Americans Really Think About: God, Country, Family, Racism, Welfare, Immigration, Homosexuality, Work, the Right, the Left, and Each Other*. New York: Viking, 1998.

Wuthnow, Robert. *The Restructuring of American Religion: Society and Faith Since World War II*. Princeton, NJ: Princeton University Press, 1988.

Wuthnow, Robert. *The Struggle for America's Soul: Evangelicals, Liberals, and Secularism*. Grand Rapids, MI: Eerdmans, 1989.

Wuthnow, Robert. *God and Mammon in America*. New York. NY: Free Press, 1994.

Wuthnow, Robert. "Restructuring of American Religion: Further Evidence." *Sociological Inquiry* 66 (1996): 303-29.

Wuthnow, Robert. "Mobilizing Civic Engagement: The Changing Impact of Religious Involvement." In *Civic Engagement in American Democracy*, edited by T. Skocpol and M. Fiorina. Washington, DC: Brookings Institution Press/Russell Sage Foundation, 1999.

Wuthnow, Robert. "The Moral Minority." *The American Prospect*, May 22, 2000.

Wuthnow, Robert, and John H. Evans, eds. *The Quiet Hand of God: Faith-based Activism and the Public Role of Mainline Protestantism*. Berkeley, CA: University of California Press, 2002.

Index

About the Author

JOHN C. GREEN is Senior Fellow at the Pew Forum on Religion and Public Life and Distinguished Professor of Political Science at the University of Akron. He is also Director of the Ray C. Bliss Institute of Applied Politics at the University of Akron. He is the author or editor of *The Christian Right in American Politics: Marching to the Millennium, The Financiers of Congressional Elections, The Diminishing Divide: Religion's Changing Role in American Politics,* and *The Bully Pulpit: The Politics of Protestant Clergy.* He has published many other books and articles.